ExamWise
For
CFA 2006 Level I Certification:

The Candidates Question And Answer Workbook
For Chartered Financial Analyst

www.financialexams.com

Practice exam provided by
The Center For Financial Certification, Inc. Friendswood, Texas

Authors
Jane Vessey, CFA
M. Afdal Pamilih, CFA
David Stewart

Published by

TotalRecall Publications, Inc.
1103 Middlecreek
Friendswood, TX 77546
281-992-3131

TotalRecall Publications, Inc.

This Book Sponsored by The Center For Financial Certification, Inc.

Portions Copyright © 2001-2006 by TotalRecall Publications, Inc.. Portions Copyright © 2005-2006 by Pegasus, Inc.. All rights reserved. Printed in the United States of America. Except as permitted under the United States Copyright Act of 1976, No part of this publication may be reproduced, stored in a retrieval system, or transmitted in any form or by any means electronic or mechanical or by photocopying, recording, or otherwise without the prior permission of the publisher.

The views expressed in this book are solely those of the author, and do not represent the views of any other party or parties.

Printed in United States of America

Printed and bound by Lightning Source, Inc. in the USA and UK

Printed and bound by Booksurge, LLC around the world

Paper Back: ISBN: 1-59095-923-X

               UPC: 6-43977-93601-1

EBook: ISBN: 1-59095-927-2

               UPC: 6-43977-93661-5

The sponsoring editor for this book is Bruce Moran and the production supervisor is Corby R. Tate.

This book is dedicated to our fantastic children Adam and Julia who we love very much.

Jane Vessey & M. Afdal Pamilih

This Study Guide is dedicated to the widow(er)s and orphans of the "Silent Spring". Those who have sacrificed loved ones to the obscurity of quiet study and endured weekend sacrifice above and beyond the call of continuing education. On the alter of a profession's highest accreditation these unsung heroes have sacrificed time with their spouse, shopping with Mom, and pitch and catch with Dad. These patient supporters have endured tense attitudes, unfinished chores, extra duties, and received the respect and appreciation of all who have studied throughout the "Silent Spring".

In particular, never ending thanks to:

Carol Lee, Mary Elizabeth, Sophia Victoria, David Todd II

David Stewart

ExamWise®
For
CFA 2006 Level I Certification:

The Candidates Question And Answer Workbook For Chartered Financial Analyst

www.financialexams.com

BY

Authors
Jane Vessey, CFA
M. Afdal Pamilih, CFA
David Stewart

Jane Vessey

Jane Vessey manages a training company in the United Kingdom specializing in financial analysis and investment. She is a visiting lecturer at Cass Business School teaching classes in asset management and valuation. She also teaches a CFA® revision course at ISMA (the business school at Reading University) and is an associate at a leading London financial training company where she teaches courses covering investment management and related topics. She has developed online training programs for students taking the CFA examinations and teaches CFA courses for UKSIP (the UK Society of Investment Professionals).

Jane graduated in Mathematics from Oxford University, United Kingdom, and is a CFA charter holder. She has some eighteen years experience working in the investment industry, starting out as an equity analyst before becoming an investment manager. She was based in London and Tokyo and took responsibility for managing equity portfolios invested in the Japanese and other Asian markets. In 1990, Jane moved to Indonesia and established and ran an investment management operation on behalf of Mees Pierson. She took responsibility for all areas of the business, including investment, operations, marketing and administration. While in Asia, Jane was involved in providing training to capital market participants and state officials and teaching in courses provided by local universities.

M. Afdal Pamilih

Afdal has 18 years' experience working in the finance industry. He started his career with J.P. Morgan, and then with County NatWest Government Securities, in New York specializing in the development of quantitative products for foreign exchange and fixed income markets. After returning to Indonesia in 1989 he was responsible for the development of investment services and subsequently treasury management for leading banks in Jakarta.

Afdal has developed web-based training programs for the CFA examinations and has wide teaching experience, including instructing at the School of Management, University of Surrey, United Kingdom.

He obtained a MSc in Mathematics from the University of Texas at Arlington and holds the Chartered Financial Analyst ("CFA") qualification.

David Stewart:

David Stewart has extensive experience in venture capital and business structural reorganizations. As president of a private client broker dealer firm, he has business valuation and project valuation experience on the venture capital side and portfolio management on the asset management side. His analysis, commentary, books, and study guides have appeared in the financial management, securities, and exam prep industries.

David has collaborated with experts in the field to produce the 2001 through 2006 editions of this study guide. His extensive research into the CFA exam program and past exam histories, field work, and consistent review of CFA Institute information allows him and his co-authors to deliver high quality and up to date information.

About the Book:

ExamWise For CFA Level I Concept Check Q&A Workbook With Preliminary Reading Assignments is designed to give you plenty of practice questions to test your readiness for the CFA exam. It offers 480+ concept check questions based 18 exam study sessions that cover the Learning Outcome Statements and their associated CFA Assigned Readings. For additional practice, there is an accompanying free download test engine that generates multiple mock exams similar in design and difficulty to the real CFA exam. The questions and explanations have references to the page number in the related Reading and to the related LOS.

Use this workbook to test your understanding of the basic concepts covered in the CFA Readings and identify your strengths and weaknesses. Then you can move on to more advanced study materials to sharpen your weakest knowledge areas.

This book is divided into Study Sessions (1 – 18) that cover the 79 Learning Outcome Statements and the associated Assigned Readings. Appendix A (Exhibits 1 – 4), is a collection of exhibits and flow charts for condensed reference and review, including examples of accounting statements, puts and calls, PE breakdown, and financial ratios.

The 18 2006 CFA Level I Study Sessions breakout is as follows:

Ethical and Professional Standards

Study Session 1: Ethical and Professional Standards

Investment Tools

Study Session 2. Quantitative Methods: Basic Concepts

Study Session 3. Quantitative Methods: Application

Study Session 4. Economics: Macroeconomic Analysis

Study Session 5. Economics: Microeconomic Analysis

Study Session 6. Economics: Global Economic Analysis

Study Session 7. Financial Statement Analysis: Basic Concepts

Study Session 8. Financial Statement Analysis: Financial Ratios and Earnings Per Share

Study Session 9. Financial Statement Analysis: Assets

Study Session 10. Financial Statement Analysis: Liabilities

Study Session 11. Corporate Finance: Corporate Investing & Financing Decisions

Asset Valuation

Study Session 12. Equity Investments: Securities Markets

Study Session 13. Equity Investments: Industry and Company Analysis

Study Session 14. Fixed Income Investments: Basic Concepts

Study Session 15. Fixed Income Investments: Analysis and Valuation

Study Session 16. Derivative Investments

Study Session 17. Alternative Investments

Portfolio Management

Study Session 18. Portfolio Management

Online Information:

1. CFA Program:

   http://www.cfainstitute.org/cfaprogram/

2. The Code of Ethics (Full Text)

   http://www.cfainstitute.org/standards/ethics/code/

3. International Code Of Ethics And Standards Of Professional Conduct

   http://www.cfainstitute.org/cfacentre/ethics/codeandstandards.html

4. Interpretations of CFA Institute's Code of Ethics and Standards of Professional Conduct

   http://www.cfainstitute.org/standards/pps/gips_library.html

5. The Standards of Professional Conduct

   Standard I: Fundamental Responsibilities

   Standard II: Relationships with and Responsibilities to the Profession

   Standard III: Relationships with and Responsibilities to the Employer

   Standard IV: Relationships with and Responsibilities to Clients and Prospects

   Standard V: Relationships with and Responsibilities to the Public

   http://www.cfainstitute.org/standards/ethics/conduct/index.html

   http://www.cfapubs.org/ap/issues/v2003n4/toc.html

   http://www.cfainstitute.org/cfacentre/ips/

   http://www.cfainstitute.org/cfacentre/pdf/English2006CodeandStandards.pdf

6. CFA Institute-PPSTM AIMR Performance Presentation Standards

   http://www.cfainstitute.org/standards/pps/ppsstand.html

7. Global Investment Performance Standards

   http://www.cfainstitute.org/standards/pps/gips_standards.html

8. Soft Dollar Learning Module

   http://www.cfainstitute.org/standards/ethics/soft_dollar/index.html

List of Chapters

Table of Contents

2006 CFA Level I Study and Examination Program Textbooks:

2006 Level I Program Curriculum, $395.00

Self-contained volumes that offer everything you need for your study program. Includes all required materials, learning outcome statements, and solutions. (CFA Institute)

Preliminary Readings (Not Required) $152.00

Economics: Private and Public Choice, 10th ed., $80.00

Financial Accounting, 8th ed. , $72.00

Dates Regarding the June 2006 CFA Examination

15 July 2005   Study Guides available

15 July 2005   Textbooks available for purchase from book distributor

15 September 2005   Initial deadline for new registrations and enrolments to be received by CFA Institute

November 2005   Past years' constructed response essay examination questions and guideline answers for Level III available from book distributor

February 2006   Online sample examinations available for a fee from the CFA Institute website

15 February 2006   Second deadline for new registrations and enrolments to be received by CFA Institute

15 March 2006   Final deadline for new registrations and enrolments to be received by CFA Institute

20 March 2006   Final deadline for special test center requests, disability accommodation requests and requests for religious alternative dates to be received by CFA Institute

3 April 2006   All test center change requests must be received by CFA Institute

Late April 2006 Examination Admission tickets available online

3 June 2006   Examination Day

4 June 2006   Examination Day in Eastern Asia and Oceania

June - July 2006 Examination papers graded

Late July 2006   Examination results available online for Level I and II candidates

Mid-August   Examination results available online for Level III candidates

September 2006CFA Charter Holders announced for year 2006

Note: Fee schedules including registration deadlines can be found on the CFA Institute website at **www.cfainstitute.org/cfaprogram/feeschedule.html**

Preface

The purpose of The Candidate's guide is to supply you the information and practice required to pass the CFA Level I exam. It is the first in a series of three exams, in addition to industry experience, needed to obtain the CFA designation. Once you have passed the CFA Level I exam, you are considered to have mastered the basics and the general breadth, but not the depth, of the information necessary to function as an analyst in today's global economy.

The Candidate's Guide Tutorials provides two main sections for each Study Session:

1. Book / eBook CFA Workbook includes, a series of 480+ Concept Check questions.
2. The 2006 Introductory Readings:
    Study Session 4 Economics:
    Study Session 7 Financial Statement Analysis.
3. The FinancialExam's Self Help and Interactive Exam Study Aids.

This workbook is designed to give you the basic concepts and exam practice to identify your strongest and weakest CFA Level 1 knowledge areas. Once you know your weakest topics, you can focus your limited study time on sharpening them to a passing level.

The 18 Study Sessions cover all 79 Learning Outcome Statements (LOS) and their associated CFA Assigned Readings. It is suggested that you read each Study Session and then test your understanding with the Concept Check Questions that follow. There are a total of 480+ questions with this workbook, and for additional exam practice, you may download the FinancialExams Quizzer test engine (see information below).

Your comments are welcome at anytime at support@financialexams.com :

Publishing high-quality learning tools is our business, but errors can slip through. If you think you have found one, please use the Error Reporting Form at www.financialexams.com or www.cfaexams.com. Errors with their corrections will be posted on our website. We will send an e-mail message to you whenever new corrections are posted.

ExamSavers™ Communication
Communicate with your Author/Instructor throughout your Certification Process.
asktheauthor@financialexams.com   **Only $449.99**

Now that you have purchased this product you have access to the Instructors/Authors that authored this book. Send you questions to us and we will answer them for you.

Practice Questions and Answers

After reviewing the Learning Outcome Statements, CFA Assigned Readings, and the Concept Questions, use the FinancialExams Quizzer testing engine to solidify what you have learned and to prepare you for rigors of taking and passing the exam.

In the early 1990's we pioneered computer certification test engines for the IT industry, which were later incorporated into the exam prep manuals of major computer book publishers such as McGraw-Hill and Wiley. We also developed the adaptive testing software now used in preparing for the GMAT, LSAT and other exams. We have taken that same proven, user-friendly software and applied it to helping you practice, practice, practice to pass the CFA exam your first time.

Our **Practice Exams** are designed to save you precious time by quickly identifying your weakest knowledge areas so you can allocate your available study time to getting those areas up to a passing level.

Our **Simulated Exams**—lasting the same number of hours and including the same number of questions as the real CFA exam—are designed to give you the confidence and endurance for the real thing.

The FinancialExams Quizzer generates randomized practice exams and simulated exams drawn from a large database of questions. It **offers you four helpful testing formats:**

1) Adaptive Exams generates 44-55 questions in 1-hour sessions to help you identify your strengths and weaknesses in each exam category. You save hours by then focusing your available study time on bringing your weakest knowledge areas up to a passing level.

We recommend that you start by taking three adaptive exams, which include questions from all exam categories and different levels of difficulty. Our software keeps track of how you perform and develops a Historical Analysis, which visually shows you exactly how you are scoring in each exam category. When you reach a passing level in a particular topic or LOS, then you can allocate your study time to those areas you need to strengthen. The Historical Analysis keeps track of all of your practice tests and lets you see your progress on a day-by-day basis. It offers visual proof throughout your study process that you are retaining what you are learning.

2) Study Sessions help strengthen your weakest knowledge areas by generating up to 250 questions per exam category until you can answer each correctly. We go beyond simple answers by giving you thorough explanations that are linked to a page number reference to the relevant CFA Institute assigned reading and to specific chapters in an accompanying eBook study manual. We help you develop a complete understanding of *why* an answer is correct. We also help you solve all of the questions pertaining to mathematical formulas by walking you through them step by step. By focusing primarily on your rough spots, we guarantee to get you certified fast—*guaranteed* or get money back on your purchase.

3) Simulated Exams are timed 6-hour exams with a 1.5-hour break and comprised of 240 questions about all of the exam categories—just like the real CFA exam. As you finish each automatically ending exam, the software displays for comparison your score in each category and the passing score required by CFA. You may review each question that you answered incorrectly, display the correct answer, identify a learning resource, link to a specific chapter in an accompanying eBook for further explanation. Note: You can limit your time to 3 hours if you wish and get a Mock Exam of 120 questions.

Our simulated exams are designed to look and feel just like the real CFA exam. You have the same number of questions from the same exam categories that you will cover on the real exam. Each question is timed, with a clock ticking in the corner of your monitor, putting pressure on you just like the real exam. After each exam, you can monitor your performance by comparing your score to the required CFA exam passing score. You can then check your Historical Analysis to see exactly where you might need to go back and spend more time on a specific exam category.

The software continuously randomizes all questions so you will never take the same exam twice. Our software also automatically tosses out questions that you have answered correctly, and continues to feed you the types of questions your have missed until you get them right. Again, we help you focus on what you need to learn rather than what you already know.

4) Flash Card Drills present questions to answer mentally and then allow you to click F4 to display the correct answer. You can also create your own portable flash card questions by printing directly from the test engine software.

This is a free Feature of Http://www.financialexams.com

✳ Home

0-9 A B C D E F G H I J K L M N O P Q R S T U V W X Y Z

Records Per Page: 250

Welcome to Campbell R. Harvey's Hypertextual Finance Glossary

The worlds largest financial glossary on the Internet with Over 8,000 Entries and 18,000 Hyperlinks

This current version is coauthored with the 2002 Pulitzer Prize winner for financial writing, Gretchen Morgenson of the New York Times.

Dr. Campbell R. Harvey
Fuqua School of Business, Duke University
Durham, NC 27708-0120, USA
cam.harvey@duke.edu
Phone: +1 919.660.7768
Fax: +1 919.660.8030

For our complete study manual that covers all 18 Learning Outcome Statements, which references by page number each of the CFA Institute's assigned readings and explains them in detail, you need our companion book:

ExamInsight For CFA 2006 Level I: **The Candidates Guide to Chartered Financial Analyst Learning Outcome Statements. ISBN 1-59095-922-1 I**

CFA Program

The CFA Program is an exhaustive self-study curriculum for developing the fundamentals of financial analysis and portfolio management. It is designed to broaden and deepen your knowledge of the entire field of investment valuation and portfolio management. The program assumes the candidate has mastered undergraduate finance and accounting and seeks to build a platform for individual and sector analysis, equity and fixed income valuation, and asset management emphasizing competence and integrity within the profession of investment management.

Requirements

There are no prerequisites to begin this area of study. This can, however, be considered a fairly comprehensive study if these concepts are totally new to you. CFA Institute assumes you have mastered undergraduate finance and accounting. Although every effort is made to cover all the material you may encounter at exam time, this book does not go into detail in areas that most financial professionals should already know.

http://www.cfainstitute.org/cfaprogram/exam/exam_details.html

Before the Exam

1. Read the CFA Institute Study Guide, since the rules are very strict on what you can or cannot take into the exam room. Don't forget your exam admission ticket and passport, or other form of permitted identification.
2. Remember that the only calculators you can use are the TI BAII plus and HP 12C 11. We strongly recommend you take two calculators or at the very least a spare battery.
3. Ensure you know the location of the exam and how to get there. It is the CFA Institute's policy to close the doors 30 minutes before the exam starts.
4. Read CFA Institute Candidate Bulletins to check for changes to the exam procedures.

Study Program

It is critical that you design a study program. There are no short cuts to passing the CFA exam, and pass rates have been falling. It is a tough exam and you will need to both learn the underlying material as well as do plenty of practice questions to test your knowledge and to get used to the CFA style of questions. Although the Candidate's Guide Tutorials are designed to cover the entire CFA curriculum and give a concise summary of the material you need to know for the exam, we encourage candidates to also refer to the source text books, particularly for subjects with which they are not so familiar.

The CFA Institute recommends approximately 10 to 15 hours study per study session plus extra time for final revision. That means if you plan to cover one study session per week you will need to start studying in January for the June exam or July for the December exam. The CFA curriculum sets out very clearly what you need to know to pass the exam. Focus on the Learning Outcome Statements (LOS) and the command words. Questions on the exam will relate to the LOS not to other parts of the text.

In addition to doing all the questions in The Candidate's guide Tutorials we recommend you try the sample exam provided by the CFA Institute.

CFA Institute Exam Rules

IMPORTANT:

Use no. 2 or hb pencils for multiple choice answer sheet! Do not use mechanical pencils with synthetic non-graphite (non electrical conducting) compounds which will not be compatible with the electronic scan grading.

CALCULATORS Allowed:

Hewlett Packard 12c

Texas Instruments Baii Plus

TESTING REGULATIONS:

No beepers or cell phones allowed in test area

No removing exam materials from the test room

No writing after the proctor says "stop."

This is very much part of your test:

CFA Institute is quite serious about their exam rules, follow them.

Taking the Exam

Many people do not test well on exams. Often, the student knows the material, but does not know how to take exams. The CFA Level I exam is based upon the multiple-choice format. You receive points for each question answered correctly. No points are subtracted for a wrong or unanswered question. Since the wrong answer is no worse than an unanswered question, never leave an exam with an unanswered question. Any guess is better than a blank. Example: Answering letter "B" throughout the exam will give you approximately a grade of 25. In the last minute finish the exam by selecting a single letter and marking it as the correct answer on all unanswered questions.

The exams have time limits that provide adequate time for you to read and think about the question. You should be able to reach the end of the exam before the time runs out. You should also have time to return to the unanswered questions to provide an answer. You will not have time for to continuously search the answered questions trying to find the ones you later felt you marked wrong. With this thought in mind, be careful to make sure that when you answer a question it is the last time you will read that question. The answer you give is the one you will keep. The following is a blueprint for taking an exam to insure you have answered to the maximum of your knowledge and capability:

Note: Keep in mind that this is a timed test!

A. Starting with the first question, begin to answer the multiple choice questions that you know to be correct.

B. Remember there may not be enough time to go back. If you do not know the exact answer or if it is a choice between two or more answers, skip it. Often later questions will trigger the correct answer to this question for you.

C. Skip all the long scenario questions; they are time consuming, and often you will be better prepared to answer them later in the test session.

D. You should answer at least 50% of the questions with certainty.

E. Return to the beginning and start again on the unanswered questions. Do not take time with the questions you have already answered. If you can narrow a question to two possible answers, pick the best one.

F. You must always finish your test before time runs out! In the last minute quickly answer all remaining questions with your favorite letter!

On the Exam Day

The CFA Level I exam is 100% multiple choice questions, the morning and afternoon paper will each contain 120 questions.

You will be under time pressure in the exam and need to answer on average one question every 1½ minutes so you must keep moving through the questions. We recommend the following strategies:

1. There is a strong argument for working methodically through the questions in the order they are set but you might wish to start with a subject where you feel confident and which you can work through fairly quickly. But avoid hopping from one subject to another, this will waste time and you may end up missing one section of questions out.
2. Don't panic if you hit some difficult questions, you can probably get as many as 30 or 40 questions incorrect on each paper and still pass the exam.
3. Ethics in study session 1 is an important topic, if you are a marginal candidate your ethics score could be the deciding factor whether you pass the exam.
4. There is no penalty for getting an answer incorrect, so if you don't know the answer eliminate any obviously wrong answers and guess which one is correct.
5. Mark questions in the exam booklet when you are not sure of the answer or where the calculation needs checking and come back to them when you have finished all the other questions.
6. Do not get distracted by a question that does not make sense, if the question turns out to be ambiguous then it will be excluded when it comes to grading the paper.
7. Read the questions carefully, particularly when there is a negative statement in the question.
8. Leave time to check your answers on the answer sheet, be careful you don't miss answering a question and mark subsequent answers against the wrong question number on the answer sheet.

*** Make sure that ALL Questions contain an answer ***

2006 CFA Level I Study Guide Outline

2006 Examination Guideline Topic Area Weights				
Topic	**Survey Results**	**Level I**	**Level II**	**Level III**
Ethical and Professional Standards	10%	15%	10%	10%
Investment Tools: • Economics* • Quantitative Analysis • Financial Statement Analysis**	10 10 20	10 12 28	0–10 0–10 25–35	0 0–10 0
Asset Valuation***	35	30	35–45	30–40
Portfolio Management***	15	5	5–15	40–60
TOTAL	100%	100%	100%	100%

*Economics is part of Portfolio Management at Level III.

**Corporate Finance is part of Financial Statement Analysis at Level I and Level II.

***Derivatives is a part of Asset Valuation at Level I and Level II and Portfolio Management at Level III.

Terminology you must know to take the exam.

Analyze	To study or determine the nature and relationship of the parts of by analysis.
Appraise	To judge and analyze the worth, significance, or status of.
Appraisal	For real estate, the process of estimating the current market value of a property.
Arrange	To put into a proper order or into a correct or suitable sequence, relationship, or adjustment.
Calculate	To ascertain or determine by mathematical processes.
Characterize	To describe the essential character or quality of.
Cite	To quote by way of evidence, authority, or proof.
Classify	To arrange in classes; to assign to a category.
Closed-end investment company	An investment company that issues a fixed number of shares, the shares are then traded in the secondary market.
Combine	To bring into such close relationship as to obscure individual characteristics.
Comment	To observe, remark, or express an opinion or attitude concerning what has been seen or heard about the subject at hand.
Comparative sales approach	The value of a real estate is , at the most, the cost of the land and constructing the building at current prices.
Compare	To examine the character or qualities of, for the primary purpose of discovering resemblances.
Compose	To form by putting together; to form the substance of.
Compute	To determine, especially by mathematical means.
Conclude	To make a decision about; to reach a logically necessary end by reasoning.
Construct	To create by organizing ideas or concepts logically and coherently.
Contrast	To compare in respect to differences.
Convert	To change from one form or function to another.
Create	To produce or bring about by a course of action or imaginative skill.
Criticize	To consider the merits and demerits of and judge accordingly; to find fault with.
Critique	To offer a critical review or commentary.

Define	To set forth the meaning of; specifically, to formulate a definition of.
Demonstrate	To prove or make clear by reasoning or evidence; to illustrate and explain, especially with examples.
Describe	To transmit a mental image, an impression, or an understanding of the nature and characteristics of.
Design	To conceive or plan out in the mind.
Determine	To come to a decision as the result of investigation or reasoning; to settle or decide by choice among alternatives or possibilities.
Diagram	To represent by or put into the form of a diagram.
Differentiate	To mark or show a difference in; to develop different characteristics in.
Discriminate	To mark or perceive the distinguishing or peculiar features of; to distinguish by discerning or exposing differences.
Discuss	To discourse about through reasoning or argument; to present in detail.
Distinguish	To perceive a difference in; to separate into kinds, classes, or categories.
Draft	To draw up, compose, prepare, frame.
Draw	To express graphically in words; to delineate.
Estimate	To judge the value, worth, or significance of.
Evaluate	To determine or fix the value of; to determine the significance or worth of, usually by careful appraisal and study.
Explain	To give the meaning or significance of; to provide an understanding of; to give the reason for or cause of.
First-stage financing	Venture capital provided for initial commercial manufacture and sales.
Formulate	To put into a systematized statement or expression; to prepare according to a formula.
Give	To yield or furnish as a product, consequence, or effect; to offer for the consideration, acceptance, or use of another.
Identify	To establish the identity of; to show or prove the sameness of.
Illustrate	To make clear, especially by giving examples or instances.
Income approach	The value of real estate is the present value of it future income.

$V_r = PV(FI)$

以溢前价值 衡量将来收入 = value of real estate

Indicate	To point out or point to with more or less exactness; to show or make known with a fair degree of certainty.	
Infer	To derive as a conclusion from factors or premises.	
Interpret	To explain or tell the meaning of; to present in understandable terms.	
Judge	To form an opinion about through careful weighing of evidence and testing of premises.	
Justify	To prove or show to be valid, sound, or conforming to fact or reason; to furnish grounds or evidence for.	
Leveraged buyouts (LBOs) ✓	Capital to fund a management group (a management buyout) or other investors who wish to purchase a business or company.	
List	To enumerate.	
Investment company ✓	A company that sell its own shares and uses the proceeds to buy stocks, bonds or other financial instruments. 投資公司利用自己shar	
Load fund ✓ 收費	A fund that makes an initial sales charge, so the offering price is the net asset value plus a load. Offering Price = NAV + Load.	
Market capitalization rate ✓	Divide a property's net operating income by the appropriate market capitalization rate to arrive at an estimate for its current market value. It reflects the rate of return required by investors in such a property. Rᵣ determined by MC rate. NOT	
Match	To pair up or put in a set as possessing equal or harmonizing attributes.	
Mezzanine (or bridge) financing ←	Venture capital provided for a company that expects to go public in the near future.	
Modify	To make minor changes to give a new orientation to or to serve a new end.	
Mutual fund 類	An open-end investment company.	
Name	To mention or identify by name.	
No-load fund ✓	Shares are sold at net asset value, with no sales charge added.	
Open-end investment company	A company that offers new shares to investors and redeems shares continuously. (Mutual fund).	
Order	To put in order; to arrange.	

Outline	To indicate the principal features or different parts of.
Real Estate Investment Trust (REIT)	A closed-end investment company that invests in real estate and mortgages on real estate.
Real Estate Limited Partnership (RELP)	A real estate syndicate that invests in different types of real estate.
Positive leverage	The return from a real estate investment is higher than the cost of debt, an investor will achieve a higher rate of return if he/she uses leverage to purchase the property.
Predict	To declare in advance; to foretell on the basis of observation, experience, or reason.
Prepare	To put into written form; to draw up.
Present	To offer or convey by way of message; to furnish or provide.
Rearrange	To put back into proper order or into a correct or suitable sequence, relationship, or adjustment.
Recommend	To bring forward as being fit or worthy; to indicate as being one's choice for something or as otherwise having one's approval or support.
Record	To set down in writing; to make an answer.
Relate	To show or establish logical or causal connection between.
Respond	To say or write something in return; to make an answer.

Restate	To state again in a new form.
Review	To make a formal or official examination of the state of; to go over or examine critically or deliberately.
Revise	To make a new, amended, improved, or up-to-date version of.
Seed financing	Venture capital provided for product development and market research, the product is still at the 'idea' stage.
Select	To choose from a number or group — usually, by fitness, excellence, or other distinguishing feature.
Separate	To set or keep apart; to make a distinction between; to sort.
Show	To set forth in a statement, account, or description; to make evident or clear.
Solve	To find a solution for a problem.
Start-up financing	Venture capital provided for early stage product development and initial marketing.
State	To express in words.
Subdivide	To divide the parts into more parts.
Summarize	To tell in or reduce to a summary.
Support	To provide with verification, corroboration, or substantiation.
Turnarounds	Capital provided to restructure a company that has problems.
Write	To put on paper; to record, state, or explain.

STUDY SESSION 1

Ethical and Professional Standards

Overview

Questions on Ethical and Professional Standards have a guideline weighting of 15 percent of the total Level I exam questions, and the score for this section will probably be the deciding factor in marginal pass/fail papers. This is a very important Study Session to master and much of the material will be covered again at Levels II and III. The material is straightforward, but it needs to be memorized. Don't underestimate the amount of time you need to spend on this Session. Care needs to be taken in answering the exam questions – they are not always as easy as you might expect and you will often need to focus on identifying the best answer.

Our study notes summarize the Standards of Professional Conduct, and we recommend that you also read the required pages of the Standards of Practice Handbook (SOPH). Ensure that you have the new ninth edition, not the old eighth edition of SOPH. Given the high number of questions on the Standards, you will need to know each Standard and how it is applied in a variety of situations. The third and fourth Reading Assignments cover standards for reporting investment performance, or GIPS®, and you will need to master the main requirements and recommendation of the GIPS standards. The final Reading considers corporate governance issues for companies and how investors can identify companies which practice high standards of corporate governance. This is a new Reading to Level I for 2006.

The June 2006 examinations for all three Levels will be the first time that the new SOPH will be tested. Even if you excelled at Ethics in prior study years, ensure that you study the latest SOPH and take note of the changes to the previous edition, for example CFA Institute has dropped the requirement that members and candidates need to provide a copy of the Code and Standards to their direct supervisor.

Reading Assignments

1.   "Code of Ethics and Standards of Professional Conduct ," Standards of Practice Handbook, 9th edition (CFA Institute, 2005)

2.   "Guidance," for Standards I – VII, Standards of Practice Handbook, 9th edition (CFA Institute, 2005)

3.   Introduction to the Global Investment Performance Standards (GIPS®)

4.   Global Investment Performance Standards (GIPS®), pp. i-iii and 1-9, (CFA Institute, 2005)

      A.   Preface: Background of the GIPS Standards

      B.   I. Introduction

      C.   II.0. Provisions of the Global Investment Performance Standards – Fundamentals of Compliance

5.   The Corporate Governance of Listed Companies: A Manual for Investors (CFA Institute, 2005)

1   Code of Ethics and Standards of Professional Conduct

Learning Outcome Statements (LOS)

1	The Code of Ethics establishes the framework for ethical decision-making in the investment profession. The candidate should be able to **state** the six components of the Code of Ethics.
	The Standards of Professional Conduct are organized into seven standards:
	I. Professionalism.
	II. Integrity of Capital Markets.
	III. Duties to Clients and Prospective Clients.
	IV. Duties to Employers.
	V. Investment Analysis, Recommendations and Action.
	VI. Conflicts of Interest.
	VII. Responsibilities as a CFA Institute Member or CFA Candidate.
	Each standard contains multiple provisions for which the candidate is responsible.
	The candidate should be able to **identify** the ethical responsibilities required by the Code and Standards.

Introduction

The CFA Institute sees one of its main roles as promoting high standards of ethical conduct which involves educating its members on ethical standards and bringing disciplinary action against members who violate the Code and Standards. It also sees its role as providing leadership in the development of global standards and promoting the increasing awareness of ethics and use of the Code and Standards within the investment profession.

The Code of Ethics sets out the ethical standards that all CFA Institute Members ('members') and CFA Candidates ('candidates') must follow.

1   Concept Check Questions

1.   Which of the following is *not* included in the main components of the Code of Ethics?
    A.   Maintain and improve efficiency.

    B.   Exercise independent professional judgment.

    C.   Maintain and improve professional competence.

    D.   Place clients' interests above a member's own interests

---

2.   The Code of Ethics requires members to act with integrity, competence, diligence, respect and in an ethical manner when dealing with:
    A.   The public only.

    B.   Clients and prospective clients only

    C.   The public, clients and prospective clients only.

    D.   The public, clients and prospective clients, and employers, employees, and colleagues in the investment profession.

3.   Which of the following is part of Standard IV: Duties to Employers?
   A.   Responsibilities of supervisors.
   B.   Maintaining knowledge of the law.
   C.   Not compromising the integrity of the CFA designation.
   D.   Maintaining independence when making recommendations.

4.   Which of the following is *not* part of Standard V: Investment Analysis, Recommendations, and Actions? Members and candidates must:
   A.   distinguish between facts and opinions.
   B.   use diligence and thoroughness in making recommendations.
   C.   use reasonable judgment in the inclusion or exclusion of relevant factors.
   D.   ensure a recommendation is in line with a client's risk and return objectives.

1   Concept Check Answers

1.   Which of the following is *not* included in the main components of the Code of Ethics?

    A.   Maintain and improve efficiency.

    B.   Exercise independent professional judgment.

    C.   Maintain and improve professional competence.

    D.   Place clients' interests above a member's own interests

Correct Answer: 1   A

The Code guides good ethical behavior, and does not promote business efficiency (or profitability).

---

2.   The Code of Ethics requires members to act with integrity, competence, diligence, respect and in an ethical manner when dealing with:

    A.   The public only.

    B.   Clients and prospective clients only

    C.   The public, clients and prospective clients only.

    D.   The public, clients and prospective clients, and employers, employees, and colleagues in the investment profession.

Correct Answer: 2   D

The first component of the Code of Ethics is:

'Act with integrity, competence, dignity, and in an ethical manner when dealing with the public, clients, prospects, employers, employees, and fellow members'.

3.   Which of the following is part of Standard IV: Duties to Employers?

   A.   Responsibilities of supervisors.

   B.   Maintaining knowledge of the law.

   C.   Not compromising the integrity of the CFA designation.

   D.   Maintaining independence when making recommendations.

Correct Answer: 3   A
B is part of Standard I 'Professionalism'.
C is part of Standard VII 'Responsibilities as a CFA Institute Member or CFA Candidate'.
D is part of Standard V 'Investment Analysis, Recommendations, and Actions '.

---

4.   Which of the following is *not* part of Standard V: Investment Analysis, Recommendations, and Actions? Members and candidates must:

   A.   distinguish between facts and opinions.

   B.   use diligence and thoroughness in making recommendations.

   C.   use reasonable judgment in the inclusion or exclusion of relevant factors.

   D.   ensure a recommendation is in line with a client's risk and return objectives.

Correct Answer: 4   D
Ensuring a recommendation is in line with a client's risk and return objectives is part of Standard
   III Duties to Clients.

2   Guidance for Standards I - VII

Learning Outcome Statements (LOS)

2	The guidance in the Standards of Practice Handbook addresses the application of the Standards of Professional Conduct. For each standard, the Handbook offers guidance for the standard, presents recommended procedures for compliance, and provides examples of the standard in practice. The candidate should be able to:
2-a	**demonstrate** a thorough knowledge of the Standards of Professional Conduct by recognizing and applying the standards to specific situations;
2-b	**distinguish** between conduct that conforms to the Code and Standards and conduct that violates the Code and the Standards.

Introduction

Candidates need to understand (1) the purpose and scope of each Standard, (2) the application of each Standard and (3) procedures for compliance with each Standard. Candidates can expect to be given a number of situations in which members of the CFA Institute or candidates are faced with making a decision on the best course of action to take to comply with the Standards. We re-emphasize that candidates should purchase their own copy of the Standards of Practice Handbook and work through the numerous examples of applications of each Standard that are provided in the handbook, and study the sample exam questions at the end. The sample exam is essential because the questions most likely conform to the style and level of difficulty used by CFA Institute Council of Examiners (COE).

2   Concept Check Questions

1.   Peter Seller, CFA, works for an investment bank that is acting as the principal underwriter for an issue of stock of a large tire manufacturer. Seller found out that the prospectus has concealed an impending product recall due to a quality control error. Since the number of items affected is relatively small, the product recall is planned to be a quiet affair. However Seller is aware that recently a competitor's product recall received a large amount of adverse publicity. The preliminary prospectus has been distributed. According to the Code and Standards:

A.   Seller should do nothing as it may jeopardize the success of the issue.

B.   Seller should inform CFA Institute of the violation of the Code and Standards so he can clear himself of the possible misrepresentation.

C.   Seller should revise the preliminary prospectus to include the omitted information to avoid any possible misrepresentation.

D.   Seller should inform his supervisor and let him/her deal with the situation since Seller himself should not jeopardize the success of the issue.

2.   Which of the following is a statement of a member's duty under the Code and Standards?

A.   In the absence of a specific applicable law and other rules and regulations, the Code and Standards govern the member's actions.

B.   When the applicable local law, rules and regulations do not adequately cover the use of material nonpublic information; a member is free to take advantage of the loophole.

C.   When there is a conflict between the Code and Standards and local law, rules and regulations a member can use their discretion when deciding which rules or Standards to comply with.

D.   A member is required to comply only with the Code and Standards even when the applicable local law, rules and regulations impose a higher degree of responsibility and duty on the member.

3.　　As an expression of gratitude, Tracy Blanc, CFA, a portfolio manager, is invited to spend a three-week vacation valued at $10,000 with her spouse in a luxurious resort owned by a wealthy private client after she skillfully protected the value of the client's capital during a severe market downturn. The private client is a fee-paying client of Blanc's firm. According to Standard IV(B) – Disclosure of Additional Compensation Arrangements:

A.　　Blanc must refuse the invitation as it may jeopardize her investment judgment.

B.　　Blanc is recommended to donate the monetary value of the vacation to a charity of her choice.

C.　　Blanc may accept such an invitation as long as she reports it in writing to her employer and gains their approval.

D.　　Blanc may accept the invitation if she reports it in writing to CFA Institute citing the full monetary value of the vacation.

4.　　Rachael Jocund, CFA, is an equity analyst following cigarette companies and a rising star in her firm. Her supervisor has been recommending D. Morass as a 'buy' and asks Jocund to take over the coverage of the company. He tells Jocund that she can only change the recommendation upon his approval. Standard I(B) suggests that:

A.　　Jocund must be independent and objective in her analysis.

B.　　Jocund should follow her supervisor's direction as she reports to him.

C.　　Jocund should discuss the situation with the legal officer of the firm.

D.　　Jocund should report the situation to CFA Institute and try to seek legal protection.

2   Concept Check Answers

1.   Peter Seller, CFA, works for an investment bank that is acting as the principal underwriter for an issue of stock of a large tire manufacturer. Seller found out that the prospectus has concealed an impending product recall due to a quality control error. Since the number of items affected is relatively small, the product recall is planned to be a quiet affair. However Seller is aware that recently a competitor's product recall received a large amount of adverse publicity. The preliminary prospectus has been distributed. According to the Code and Standards:

A.   Seller should do nothing as it may jeopardize the success of the issue.

B.   Seller should inform CFA Institute of the violation of the Code and Standards so he can clear himself of the possible misrepresentation.

C.   Seller should revise the preliminary prospectus to include the omitted information to avoid any possible misrepresentation.

D.   Seller should inform his supervisor and let him/her deal with the situation since Seller himself should not jeopardize the success of the issue.

Correct Answer: 1   C
Standard VI(C) requires that members shall make reasonable and diligent efforts to avoid any material misrepresentation in any research report or investment recommendation. C is the best answer.

---

2.   Which of the following is a statement of a member's duty under the Code and Standards?

A.   In the absence of a specific applicable law and other rules and regulations, the Code and Standards govern the member's actions.

B.   When the applicable local law, rules and regulations do not adequately cover the use of material nonpublic information; a member is free to take advantage of the loophole.

C.   When there is a conflict between the Code and Standards and local law, rules and regulations a member can use their discretion when deciding which rules or Standards to comply with.

D.   A member is required to comply only with the Code and Standards even when the applicable local law, rules and regulations impose a higher degree of responsibility and duty on the member.

Correct Answer: 2   A
The rule of thumb: If an applicable law is stricter than the requirements of the Code and Standards, members must adhere to the law; otherwise they must adhere to the Code and Standards. This relates to Standard I(A) Knowledge of the Law.

3.   As an expression of gratitude, Tracy Blanc, CFA, a portfolio manager, is invited to spend a three-week vacation valued at $10,000 with her spouse in a luxurious resort owned by a wealthy private client after she skillfully protected the value of the client's capital during a severe market downturn. The private client is a fee-paying client of Blanc's firm. According to Standard IV(B) – Disclosure of Additional Compensation Arrangements:

   A.   Blanc must refuse the invitation as it may jeopardize her investment judgment.

   B.   Blanc is recommended to donate the monetary value of the vacation to a charity of her choice.

   C.   Blanc may accept such an invitation as long as she reports it in writing to her employer and gains their approval.

   D.   Blanc may accept the invitation if she reports it in writing to CFA Institute citing the full monetary value of the vacation.

Correct Answer: 3   C
Blanc needs to report in writing the additional compensation so her supervisor and the firm can assess whether it is potentially a conflict of interest.

---

4.   Rachael Jocund, CFA, is an equity analyst following cigarette companies and a rising star in her firm. Her supervisor has been recommending D. Morass as a 'buy' and asks Jocund to take over the coverage of the company. He tells Jocund that she can only change the recommendation upon his approval. Standard I(B) suggests that:

   A.   Jocund must be independent and objective in her analysis.

   B.   Jocund should follow her supervisor's direction as she reports to him.

   C.   Jocund should discuss the situation with the legal officer of the firm.

   D.   Jocund should report the situation to CFA Institute and try to seek legal protection.

Correct Answer: 4   A
As part of responsibilities to clients and prospects, members must maintain independence and objectivity so their clients will have the benefit of their work and opinions unaffected by any potential conflict of interest or other circumstance adversely affecting their judgment.

3   Introduction to the Global Investment Performance Standards (GIPS®)
and

4   Global Investment Performance Standards

Learning Outcome Statements (LOS)

4-a	**Explain** why the GIPS standards were created.
4-b	**Explain** what parties the GIPS standards apply to and whom the standards serve.
4-c	**Characterize** "composites".
4-d	**Explain** the purpose of verification.
4-e	**Explain** why a global standard is needed and how it is being implemented.
4-f	**State** the "vision" of the GIPS standards.
4-g	**State** the objectives and key characteristics of the GIPS standards.
4-h	**State** the appropriate disclosure when the GIPS standards and local regulations are in conflict.
4-i	**Explain** the scope of the GIPS standards with respect to definition of the firm, historical performance record, and compliance.
4-j	**Name** and **characterize** the eight major sections of the GIPS standards.
4-k	**Explain** the fundamentals of compliance with the GIPS standards.

Introduction

These Reading Assignments look at Global Investment Performance Standards or GIPS® which cover the professional and ethical standards that should be followed for the calculation and presentation of investment performance. Candidates are expected to know the objectives of GIPS as well as the key characteristics of GIPS and the compliance procedures.

Note: Reading Assignment 3 does not contain any LOS; however, sections from "Introduction to the Global Investment Performance Standards" have been incorporated into the LOS for Reading Assignment 4.

3 and 4 Concept Check Questions

1.   Which of the following is *not* one of the eight main sections of GIPS?

A.   Input data.

B.   Verification.

C.   Composite construction.

D.   Calculation methodology.

---

2.   Which of the following is *most appropriate*? A firm can claim compliance:

A.   if its consulting actuary is compliant.

B.   if its track record is less than 5 years.

C.   with a "moving window" of 5-year compliant results.

D.   without all of their composites meeting the GIPS requirements.

3.   Which one of the following is *least likely* to be a reason why the Global Investment
Presentation Standards (GIPS) were created?

   A.   Clients and prospective clients reside in different countries.

   B.   Investment management firms have operations in multiple countries.

   C.   Many countries have not established comprehensive investment performance
   standards.

   D.   GIPS were established to compete with the European-based mandatory global
   investment performance standards.

---

4.   Which one of the following statements about GIPS verification is *least accurate*?

   A.   Verification is a pre-requisite for conducting a global investment management
   business.

   B.   Verification performed by an independent third party brings credibility to a claim of
   compliance.

   C.   Verification reviews whether the firm's process and procedures of calculation follows
   GIPS requirements.

   D.   Verification reviews whether the firm is compliant on a firm-wide basis and the
   construction of all the composites follows GIPS requirements.

3 and 4 Concept Check Answers

1.   Which of the following is *not* one of the eight main sections of GIPS?

   A.   Input data.

   B.   Verification.

   C.   Composite construction.

   D.   Calculation methodology.

Correct Answer: 1   B
Verification is not part of the eight sections, although strongly recommended.

___

2.   Which of the following is *most appropriate*? A firm can claim compliance:

   A.   if its consulting actuary is compliant.

   B.   if its track record is less than 5 years.

   C.   with a "moving window" of 5-year compliant results.

   D.   without all of their composites meeting the GIPS requirements.

Correct Answer: 2   B
If the firm is in existence for less than five years, it can claim compliance since its inception, but
   disclosure of the fact is required.

3.   Which one of the following is *least likely* to be a reason why the Global Investment Presentation Standards (GIPS) were created?

A.   Clients and prospective clients reside in different countries.

B.   Investment management firms have operations in multiple countries.

C.   Many countries have not established comprehensive investment performance standards.

D.   GIPS were established to compete with the European-based mandatory global investment performance standards.

Correct Answer: 3   D
GIPS were created to fill the void of a globally recognized investment performance standard, not to compete with European standards. There are no mandatory global standards.

---

4.   Which one of the following statements about GIPS verification is *least accurate*?

A.   Verification is a pre-requisite for conducting a global investment management business.

B.   Verification performed by an independent third party brings credibility to a claim of compliance.

C.   Verification reviews whether the firm's process and procedures of calculation follows GIPS requirements.

D.   Verification reviews whether the firm is compliant on a firm-wide basis and the construction of all the composites follows GIPS requirements.

Correct Answer: 4   A
Verification is not required but strongly recommended, and is not a requirement to conduct investment business.

5   The Corporate Governance of Listed Companies: A Manual for Investors

Learning Outcome Statements (LOS)

5-a	Identify the factors in evaluating the quality of corporate governance and the relative strength of shareowner rights.
5-b	Define corporate governance and identify practices that constitute good corporate governance.
5-c	Define independence as used to describe corporate board members, and explain the role of independent board members in corporate governance.
5-d	List and explain the major factors that enable a board to exercise its duty to act in the best long-term interests of shareowners.
5-e	Identify characteristics of a board that contribute to the board's independence, and state why each characteristic is important for shareowners' interests.
5-f	Identify factors that indicate a board and its members possess the experience required to govern the company for the benefit of its shareowners.
5-g	Explain the importance to shareowners of a board's ability to hire external consultants.
5-h	Identify advantages and disadvantages of annual board elections compared to less frequent elections.
5-i	Explain the implications of a weak corporate code of ethics with regard to related party transactions and personal use of company assets.
5-j	Critique characteristics and practices of board committees, and determine whether they are supportive of shareowner protection.
5-k	Identify the information needed for evaluating the alignment of a company's executive compensation structure and practices with shareowner interests.
5-l	State the provisions that should be included in a strong corporate code of ethics.

5-m	Identify components of a company's executive compensation program that positively or negatively affect shareowners' interests.
5-n	Explain the implications for shareowners of a company's proxy voting rules and practices.
5-o	State whether a company's rules governing shareowner-sponsored board nominations, resolutions, and proposals are supportive of shareowner rights
5-p	Explain the implications of different classes of common equity for shareowner rights.
5-q	Determine the probable effects of takeover defenses on share value

Introduction

This Reading moves on to a new topic which has been introduced in the 2006 curriculum.

Research finding states there is a strong correlation between good corporate governance and better valuation results of listed companies; one of the reasons it is important to alert investors to the importance of corporate governance. The manual considers how investors can evaluate the quality of corporate governance.

Corporate governance is topical, and the full document can be downloaded free of charge at

- http://www.cfainstitute.org/cfacentre/cmp/pdf/cfa_corp_governance.pdf

The first part deals with the role of the Board, its independence, qualifications, and the resources that should be available for the Board to exercise its independence.

The second part deals with the ethical issues that are the responsibility of management and reflect good governance.

The last part discusses the rights of shareowners, particularly in terms of their involvement in the governance of a company, such as voting, sponsoring resolutions and other shareowners' issues.

5   Concept Check Questions

1.   The case that the board chair also holds the title of chief executive, from the corporate governance point of view, is:

A.   unacceptable because it is universally prohibited in all jurisdictions.

B.   acceptable, because combining the two positions will save costs and hence enhance shareholder value.

C.   acceptable, because the effectiveness of the chief executive would be enhanced by his or her position as the chairperson of the board.

D.   unacceptable because combining the two positions may reduce the ability and willingness of independent board members to exercise their independent judgment.

2.   Which one of the following is *least likely* to be an ethical action by a board member?

A.   Avoid conflicts of interest with their position as a board member.

B.   Use their experience to make the right decisions about the company's future.

C.   Align their interests to those of the shareowners, for example by being investors themselves.

D.   Have strong connections with the governments in the countries the company operates in.

3.   A company prohibits itself from offering shares at discounted prices to management, board members and other insiders prior to a public offering of its securities. This practice is,

A.   preferred by the tax office because it avoids imputation of income taxes for the executives.

B.   preferred by investors because it demonstrates that the company aligns itself with the investors' interests.

C.   not preferred by the capital markets regulatory body because it might encourage an opportunity for insiders' trading.

D.   not preferred from a corporate governance point of view because it might encourage the executives to compensate themselves from short-term share transactions.

5   Concept Check Answers

1.   The case that the board chair also holds the title of chief executive, from the corporate governance point of view, is:

    A.   unacceptable because it is universally prohibited in all jurisdictions.

    B.   acceptable, because combining the two positions will save costs and hence enhance shareholder value.

    C.   acceptable, because the effectiveness of the chief executive would be enhanced by his or her position as the chairperson of the board.

    D.   unacceptable because combining the two positions may reduce the ability and willingness of independent board members to exercise their independent judgment.

Correct Answer: 1   D
Choice A is incorrect because there are some jurisdictions that allow the combining of the two positions.
Choice B is incorrect, because the saving in cost is not the main issue from the corporate governance point of view.
Choice C is incorrect because it is not the effectiveness of the chief executive that is being questioned.
The main issue is whether the board's independence would be compromised.

---

2.   Which one of the following is *least likely* to be an ethical action by a board member?

    A.   Avoid conflicts of interest with their position as a board member.

    B.   Use their experience to make the right decisions about the company's future.

    C.   Align their interests to those of the shareowners, for example by being investors themselves.

    D.   Have strong connections with the governments in the countries the company operates in.

Correct Answer: 2   D
Choice D is questionable from a corporate governance point of view. It might involve some kind of political favor that would not necessarily benefit the long-term interests of the shareowners.

3.   A company prohibits itself from offering shares at discounted prices to management, board members and other insiders prior to a public offering of its securities. This practice is,

   A.   preferred by the tax office because it avoids imputation of income taxes for the executives.

   B.   preferred by investors because it demonstrates that the company aligns itself with the investors' interests.

   C.   not preferred by the capital markets regulatory body because it might encourage an opportunity for insiders' trading.

   D.   not preferred from a corporate governance point of view because it might encourage the executives to compensate themselves from short-term share transactions.

Correct Answer: 3   B
This is a preferred practice from a corporate governance point of view, which indicates it is beneficial for the long-term interests of the investors.

STUDY SESSION 2
Quantitative Methods: Basic Concepts
Overview

Quantitative Methods, covered in Study Sessions 2 and 3, have a guideline weighting of 12% of the questions in the 2006 exams. For candidates without a strong maths background, parts of these two study sessions can be tough and time consuming but it is vital that you make the necessary effort to master the key principles. They will reoccur in several other study sessions in the Level I syllabus and again when you move on to Levels II and III. Remember that the focus is not just on learning the equations and quantitative methods but being able to apply them to decision-making in an investment context.

Study Session 2 starts out with the Reading Assignment on time value of money, which establishes the link between present and future values of sums of money, whether they are a single cash flow or multiple cash flows such as annuities and perpetuities. In the second Reading Assignment we move on to the application of time value of money techniques to calculating internal rates of return and net present values of investments to enable us to value securities. The third Reading Assignment provides an introduction to statistical concepts and provides the tools to describe and analyze data. The Study Session concludes with an introduction to probability which will help us to make investment decisions when outcomes are uncertain.

Reading Assignments

Quantitative Methods for Investment Analysis, 2nd edition, Richard A Defusco, Dennis W. McLeavey, Jerald E. Pinto, and David E. Runkle (CFA Institute, 2004)

6.   "The Time Value of Money," Ch. 1

7.   "Discounted Cash Flow Applications," Ch. 2

8.   "Statistical Concepts and Market Returns," Ch. 3

9.   "Probability Concepts," Ch. 4

6   The Time Value Of Money

Learning Outcome Statements (LOS)

6-a	**Explain** an interest rate as the sum of a real risk-free rate, expected inflation, and premiums that compensate investors for distinct types of risk.
6-b	**Calculate** and **interpret** the effective annual rate, given the stated annual interest rate and the frequency of compounding.
6-c	**Solve** time value of money problems when compounding periods are other than annual.
6-d	**Calculate** the PV of a perpetuity.
6-e	**Calculate** and **interpret** the FV and PV of a single sum of money, ordinary annuity, annuity due, or a series of uneven cash flows.
6-f	**Draw** a time line, **specify** a time index, and **solve** problems involving the time value of money as applied, for example, to mortgages and savings for college tuition or retirement.
6-g	**Show** and **explain** the connection between present values, future values, and series of cash flows.

Introduction

This is one of the most important Reading Assignments at Level I, and you must excel at calculating the present value and future value of cash flows. The time value of money is not only important at Level I but also at Levels II and III. Your investment now will pay off in your future studies.

When possible answer questions with your CFA Institute-approved financial calculator: Hewlett-Packard HP-12C or Texas Instruments BA II Plus. Practicing questions on the HP-12C or BA II Plus from the outset will help bolster your confidence for examination day, and you need not worry about learning new keystrokes at the last minute before the exam.

Note for BA II Plus users: before you attempt any of the examples, change the default number of annual compounding periods from 12 to 1. Do this by following these keystrokes:

$$\boxed{\text{2nd}}\ [\text{P/Y}]\ 1\ \boxed{\text{ENTER}}\ \boxed{\text{2nd}}\ [\text{QUIT}]$$

6   Concept Check Questions

1.   Money is deposited into an account paying interest annually at the rate of 6 percent; and $300 is deposited at the end of the first year, $500 at the end of the second year and $500 at the end of the third year. If no money is withdrawn the amount of money in the account at the end of the three years will be *closest* to:

    A. $1,367.08.

    B. $1,449.10.

    C. $1,460.68.

    D. $1,548.32.

2.   An annuity will make annual payments of $300 at the end of each of the next 20 years. If interest rates are 5 percent the present value of the annuity is *closest* to:

    A. $3,738.

    B. $6,000.

    C. $6,139.

    D. $11,562.

3.   A perpetuity is selling for $1,000 and interest rates are 8 percent. What is the implied annual payment?

    A. $80.

    B. $125.

    C. $800.

    D. $1,250.

---

4.   A mortgage has an annual quoted interest rate of 12 percent. If mortgage payments are made monthly, then the effective annual interest rate is *closest* to:

    A.   11.40%.

    B.   12.36%.

    C.   12.55%.

    D.   12.68%.

---

5.   A deposit of $1,000,000 earns a return of 5% compounded continuously for 8 years. The future value is *closest* to:

    A. $1,400,000.

    B. $1,477,000.

    C. $1,492,000.

    D. $1,500,000.

6   Concept Check Answers

1.   Money is deposited into an account paying interest annually at the rate of 6 percent; and $300 is deposited at the end of the first year, $500 at the end of the second year and $500 at the end of the third year. If no money is withdrawn the amount of money in the account at the end of the three years will be *closest* to:

    A. $1,367.08.

    B. $1,449.10.

    C. $1,460.68.

    D. $1,548.32.

Correct Answer: 1.   **A**

$FV = \$300(1.06)^2 + \$500(1.06)^1 + \$500 = \$1{,}367.08$

---

2.   An annuity will make annual payments of $300 at the end of each of the next 20 years. If interest rates are 5 percent the present value of the annuity is *closest* to:

    A. $3,738.

    B. $6,000.

    C. $6,139.

    D. $11,562.

Correct Answer: 2.   **A**

$$PV = A \frac{\left[1 - \dfrac{1}{(1+r)^N}\right]}{r}$$

$= \$300\,(20 - 7.537)$

$= \$3{,}738$

3.   A perpetuity is selling for $1,000 and interest rates are 8 percent. What is the implied annual payment?

    A. $80.

    B. $125.

    C. $800.

    D. $1,250.

Correct Answer: 3.   A
Value of perpetuity = PMT/i.
$1000 = PMT/0.08
PMT = $80

---

4.   A mortgage has an annual quoted interest rate of 12 percent. If mortgage payments are made monthly, then the effective annual interest rate is *closest* to:

    A.   11.40%.

    B.   12.36%.

    C.   12.55%.

    D.   12.68%.

Correct Answer: 4.   D

$$EAR = \left(1 + \frac{r_S}{m}\right)^m - 1$$

= (1.01)^{12} - 1
= 12.68%

---

5.   A deposit of $1,000,000 earns a return of 5% compounded continuously for 8 years. The future value is *closest* to:

    A. $1,400,000.

    B. $1,477,000.

    C. $1,492,000.

    D. $1,500,000.

Correct Answer: 5.   C

$$FV_N = PVe^{r_S \times N}$$

$$= \$1,000,000e^{0.05 \times 8}$$

$$= \$1,491,825$$

7   Discounted Cash Flow Applications

Learning Outcome Statements (LOS)

7-a	**Calculate** and **interpret** the net present value (NPV) and the internal rate of return (IRR) of an investment.
7-b	**Contrast** the NPV rule to the IRR rule.
7-c	**Discuss** problems associated with the IRR method.
7-d	**Calculate, interpret** and **distinguish** between the money-weighted and time-weighted rates of return of a portfolio and appraise the performance of portfolios based on these measures.
7-e	**Calculate** and **interpret** the bank discount yield, holding period yield, effective annual yield, and money market yield for a U.S. Treasury bill.
7-f	**Convert** and **interpret** among holding period yields, money market yields, and effective annual yields.
7-g	**Calculate** and **interpret** the bond equivalent yield.

Introduction

In the section we apply time value of money analysis to valuing financial instruments. First of all we consider internal rates of return and net present value calculations; these provide a critical input to the decision whether any investment (bond, equity, real estate etc.) is attractive or not. We also consider alternative measures for calculating portfolio returns and the impact of the choice of method on the calculation results. Finally we analyze cash flows from short-term money market instruments and look at the different methods for calculating yields.

7   Concept Check Questions

1.   A company is considering two projects X and Y. The projects will run for one year and two years respectively after which they will have zero value, the cost of capital is 10%. The cash flows are shown below:

Project	Investment t = 0	Cash Flow, t=1	Cash Flow t=2
X	$1,000,000	$1,200,000	0
Y	$2,000,000	0	$2,600,000

If the company has sufficient funds should they, based on NPV analysis,

A.   accept both projects.

B.   accept only project X.

C.   accept only project Y.

D.   accept neither project.

---

2.   Using the above data, using IRR analysis which project looks the most attractive?

A.   Project X.

B.   Project Y.

3.   The following data is provided on the quarterly performance of a fund.

	1st Quarter	2nd Quarter	3rd Quarter	4th Quarter
Beginning value	$1,000,000	$1,200,000	$1,500,000	$1,500,000
Cash inflow at beginning of quarter	$100,000	$100,000	($200,000)	$300,000
Ending value	$1,200,000	$1,500,000	$1,500,000	$1,600,000

The time-weighted return for the year is *closest* to:

    A.   6.6%.

    B.   28.7%.

    C.   29.1%.

    D.   61.4%.

4.   A T-bill has a face value of $1,000,000 and 180 days until maturity. The bank discount yield, if it is selling at $976,000 is *closest* to:

    A.   2.40%.

    B.   4.80%.

    C.   4.86%.

    D.   9.76%.

7   Concept Check Answers

1.   A company is considering two projects X and Y. The projects will run for one year and two years respectively after which they will have zero value, the cost of capital is 10%. The cash flows are shown below:

Project	Investment t = 0	Cash Flow, t=1	Cash Flow t=2
X	$1,000,000	$1,200,000	0
Y	$2,000,000	0	$2,600,000

If the company has sufficient funds should they, based on NPV analysis,

    A.   accept both projects.

    B.   accept only project X.

    C.   accept only project Y.

    D.   accept neither project.

Correct Answer: 1.   **A**
The NPV of project X is (-$1,000,000 + $1,090,909) = $90,909
The NPV of project Y is (-$2,000,000 + $2,148,760) = $148,760
Both projects are expected to add to stockholders' wealth.

---

2.   Using the above data, using IRR analysis which project looks the most attractive?

    A.   Project X.

    B.   Project Y.

Correct Answer: 2.   **A**
The IRR for X is given by:

$$\$1,000,000 = \frac{\$1,200,000}{(1 + IRR_X)}$$

$IRR_X = 20\%$
The IRR for Y is given by:

$$\$2,000,000 = \frac{\$2,600,000}{(1 + IRR_Y)^2}$$

$IRR_Y = 14.02\%$
So project X offers the highest IRR.

3.   The following data is provided on the quarterly performance of a fund.

	1st Quarter	2nd Quarter	3rd Quarter	4th Quarter
Beginning value	$1,000,000	$1,200,000	$1,500,000	$1,500,000
Cash inflow at beginning of quarter	$100,000	$100,000	($200,000)	$300,000
Ending value	$1,200,000	$1,500,000	$1,500,000	$1,600,000

The time-weighted return for the year is *closest* to:

    A.   6.6%.

    B.   28.7%.

    C.   29.1%.

    D.   61.4%.

Correct Answer: 3.   **C**
Q1, HPR = ($1,200,000 - $1,100,000)/$1,100,000 = 9.09%
Q2, HPR = ($1,500,000 - $1,300,000)/$1,300,000 = 15.38%
Q3, HPR = ($1,500,000 - $1,300,000)/$1,300,000 = 15.38%
Q4, HPR = ($1,600,000 - $1,800,000)/$1,800,000 = -11.11%

(1.0909) x (1.1538) x (1.1538) x (0.8889) –1 = 0.2909

---

4.   A T-bill has a face value of $1,000,000 and 180 days until maturity. The bank discount yield, if it is selling at $976,000 is *closest* to:

    A.   2.40%.

    B.   4.80%.

    C.   4.86%.

    D.   9.76%.

Correct Answer: 4.   **B**

$$r_{BD} = \frac{D}{F} \times \frac{360}{t} = \frac{\$24,000}{\$1,000,000} \times \frac{360}{180} = 4.80\%$$

8   Statistical Concepts and Market Returns

Learning Outcome Statements (LOS)

8-a	**Describe** the nature of statistics and **differentiate** between descriptive statistics and inferential statistics and between a population and a sample.
8-b	**Explain** the concepts of a parameter and a sample statistic.
8-c	**Explain** the differences among the types of measurement scales.
8-d	**Define** and **interpret** a frequency distribution.
8-e	**Define, calculate** and **interpret** a holding period return (total return).
8-f	**Calculate** and **interpret** relative frequencies and cumulative relative frequencies, given a frequency distribution.
8-g	**Describe** the properties of data presented as a histogram or a frequency polygon.
8-h	**Define, calculate** and **interpret** measures of central tendency, including the population mean, sample mean, arithmetic mean, weighted average or mean (including a portfolio return viewed as a weighted mean), geometric mean, and harmonic mean, median and mode.
8-i	**Describe** and **interpret** quartiles, quintiles, deciles, and percentiles.
8-j	**Define, calculate** and **interpret** 1) a range and mean absolute deviation, and 2) a sample and a population variance and standard deviation.
8-k	**Contrast** variance with semivariance and target semivariance.
8-l	**Calculate** and **interpret** the proportion of observations falling within a specified number of standard deviations of the mean, using Chebyshev's inequality.
8-m	**Define, calculate** and **interpret** the coefficient of variation and the Sharpe ratio.
8-n	**Define** and **interpret** skew, **explain** the meaning of a positively or negatively skewed return distribution, and **describe** the relative locations of the mean, median, and mode for a nonsymmetrical distribution.
8-o	**Define** and **interpret** kurtosis, and measures of population and sample skew and kurtosis.

Introduction

This section provides the tools for describing and analyzing data, and then for drawing conclusions from the analysis. The focus is on return distributions and defining firstly the average or central tendency and secondly the dispersion around this average. We also consider the different types of distributions of returns including normal and skewed distributions. The candidate will be expected to apply these concepts to returns from different investments or portfolios and interpret the implications of different return distributions.

8   Concept Check Questions

1.   The following data is provided:

35   65   82   24   55   42   66   28   45   48   27   39
75   50   56   63   67   71   29   33   51   85   76   67

A frequency distribution is constructed with 7 classes. The first class is '20 up to 30'. The class frequency of the *third* class is:

A.   3.

B.   4.

C.   9.

D.   10.

---

2.   Using the data shown in question 1, the relative frequency of the third class is *closest* to:

A.   12.5%.

B.   16.7%.

C.   42.9%.

D.   45.0%.

3. The following information was collected on the average numbers of hours worked per day by the 15 employees of a shop over the last month:

| 5 | 5 | 8 | 4 | 4 | 6 | 7 | 6 |
| 6 | 5 | 4 | 2 | 7 | 7 | 5 | |

The mean, median and mode are *closest* to:

	Mean	Median	Mode
A.	5.4	5.0	6.0
B.	5.0	6.0	5.4
C.	5.4	5.0	5.0
D.	5.0	6.0	5.0

---

4. In a negatively skewed distribution, which of the following is generally **TRUE**?
    A. The median is less than both the mode and mean.
    B. The mean is less than both the mode and median.
    C. The mean is greater than both the mode and median.
    D. The median is greater than both the mode and mean.

5.   A sample of rainfalls across the country is taken and the readings are 3 cm, 3 cm, 4 cm, 5 cm, 7 cm, and 8 cm. The sample standard deviation is *closest* to:

    A.   2.1.

    B.   2.3.

    C.   4.4.

    D.   5.5.

---

6.   Stock A has a coefficient of variation of 30% and stock B has a coefficient of variation of 60%. Which of the following statements is **CORRECT**?

    A.   The dispersion of returns relative to the mean is lower for stock A than stock B.

    B.   The dispersion of returns relative to the mean is higher for stock A than stock B.

    C.   The standard deviation of stock A is double that of stock B, if the mean returns of both stocks are the same.

    D.   The variance of stock A is double that of stock B, if the mean returns of both stocks are the same.

7.   If the mean of a distribution is 6 and the standard deviation is 3 then Chebyshev's inequality states that the percentage of the observations that lie between 0 and 12 is:

A.   25%.

B.   40%.

C.   75%.

D.   94%.

---

8.   The value of a portfolio starts at $100 million, at the end of the first year it has fallen to $80 million, at the end of the second year it has risen to $105 million, and at the end of the third year it has risen to $115 million. The geometric mean rate of return is *closest* to:

A.   3.2%.

B.   4.1%.

C.   4.8%.

D.   6.7%.

8   Concept Check Answers

1.   The following data is provided:

    35   65   82   24   55   42   66   28   45   48   27   39
    75   50   56   63   67   71   29   33   51   85   76   67

A frequency distribution is constructed with 7 classes. The first class is '20 up to 30'. The class frequency of the *third* class is:

    A.   3.

    B.   4.

    C.   9.

    D.   10.

Correct Answer: 1.   A
The third class is '40 up to 50' and there are 3 observations in this class.

---

2.   Using the data shown in question 1, the relative frequency of the third class is *closest* to:
    A.   12.5%.

    B.   16.7%.

    C.   42.9%.

    D.   45.0%.

Correct Answer: 2.   A
This is the percentage of observations falling in the third class, which is given by 3/24 = 12.5%

3.   The following information was collected on the average numbers of hours worked per day by the 15 employees of a shop over the last month:

5	5	8	4	4	6	7	6
6	5	4	2	7	7	5	

The mean, median and mode are *closest* to:

	Mean	Median	Mode
A.	5.4	5.0	6.0
B.	5.0	6.0	5.4
C.	5.4	5.0	5.0
D.	5.0	6.0	5.0

Correct Answer: 3.   C

$$\text{Mean} = X = \frac{\sum w_i X_i}{\sum w_i} = [1(2) + 3(4) + 4(5) + 3(6) + 3(7) + 1(8)]/15 = 5.4$$

The median is the middle observation, which is 5.
The mode is the most frequently occurring observation, which is 5.

---

4.   In a negatively skewed distribution, which of the following is generally **TRUE**?
   A.   The median is less than both the mode and mean.
   B.   The mean is less than both the mode and median.
   C.   The mean is greater than both the mode and median.
   D.   The median is greater than both the mode and mean.

Correct Answer: 4.   B
In a negatively skewed distribution the mean will be lowest, and the median will generally be less than the mode.

5.   A sample of rainfalls across the country is taken and the readings are 3 cm, 3 cm, 4 cm, 5 cm, 7 cm, and 8 cm. The sample standard deviation is *closest* to:

    A.   2.1.

    B.   2.3.

    C.   4.4.

    D.   5.5.

Correct Answer: 5.   A

The mean is $(3 + 3 + 4 + 5 + 7 + 8)/6 = 5$

$$s^2 = \frac{\sum_{i=1}^{n}(X_i - \overline{X})^2}{n-1}$$

$= (4 + 4 + 1 + 4 + 9)/5 = 4.4$

$s = 2.1$

---

6.   Stock A has a coefficient of variation of 30% and stock B has a coefficient of variation of 60%. Which of the following statements is **CORRECT?**

    A.   The dispersion of returns relative to the mean is lower for stock A than stock B.

    B.   The dispersion of returns relative to the mean is higher for stock A than stock B.

    C.   The standard deviation of stock A is double that of stock B, if the mean returns of both stocks are the same.

    D.   The variance of stock A is double that of stock B, if the mean returns of both stocks are the same.

Correct Answer: 6.   A

$$CV = \frac{S}{\overline{X}} \times 100$$

Answers C and D are incorrect since, if the mean return is the same the standard deviation of stock A is half that of B.

7.   If the mean of a distribution is 6 and the standard deviation is 3 then Chebyshev's inequality states that the percentage of the observations that lie between 0 and 12 is:

    A.   25%.

    B.   40%.

    C.   75%.

    D.   94%.

Correct Answer: 7.   C

0 and 12 are 2 standard deviations away from the mean so if k = 2, 1 – 1/k2 or 75% of observations will lie within this range.

---

8.   The value of a portfolio starts at $100 million, at the end of the first year it has fallen to $80 million, at the end of the second year it has risen to $105 million, and at the end of the third year it has risen to $115 million. The geometric mean rate of return is *closest* to:

    A.   3.2%.

    B.   4.1%.

    C.   4.8%.

    D.   6.7%.

Correct Answer: 8.   C

$$R_G = \sqrt[n]{(1+R_1)(1+R_2).....(1+R_n)} - 1$$
$$= (0.80 \times 1.313 \times 1.095)^{1/3} - 1$$
$$= 0.0476$$

9 Probability Concepts

Learning Outcome Statements (LOS)

9-a	**Define** a random variable, an outcome, an event, mutually exclusive events, and exhaustive events.
9-b	**Explain** the two defining properties of probability.
9-c	**Distinguish** among empirical, subjective, and a priori probabilities.
9-d	**State** the probability of an event in terms of odds for or against the event.
9-e	**Describe** the investment consequences of probabilities that are mutually inconsistent.
9-f	**Distinguish** between unconditional and conditional probabilities.
9-g	**Define** a joint probability and **calculate** and **interpret** the joint probability of two events.
9-h	**Calculate** the probability that at least one of two events will occur, given the probability of each and the joint probability of the two events.
9-i	**Distinguish** between dependent and independent events.
9-j	**Calculate** a joint probability of any number of independent events.
9-k	**Calculate,** using the total probability rule, an unconditional probability.
9-l	**Explain** the use of conditional expectation in investment applications.
9-m	**Calculate** an expected value using the total probability rule for expected value.
9-n	**Diagram** an investment problem, using a tree diagram.
9-o	**Define, calculate** and **interpret** covariance and correlation.
9-p	**Calculate** and **interpret** the expected value, variance, and standard deviation particularly for return on a portfolio.
9-q	**Calculate** covariance given a joint probability function.
9-r	**Calculate** and **interpret** an updated probability, using Bayes' formula.
9-s	**Calculate** and **interpret** the number of ways a specified number of tasks can be performed using the multiplication rule of counting.

9-t	**Solve** counting problems using the factorial, combination, and permutation notations.
9-u	**Calculate** the number of ways to choose r objects from a total of n objects, when the order in which the r objects is listed matters, and **calculate** the number of ways to do so when the order does not matter.
9-v	**Identify** which counting method is appropriate to solve a particular counting problem.

Introduction

This section starts with a definition of the terms and the rules used in probability. It then considers the application to the key concepts used in investment including expected return and variability of returns for both single securities and portfolios. At the end of the Reading there is a summary of shortcuts used for counting possible outcomes. Candidates will be expected to do both the necessary calculations and also to be able to interpret the results of calculations.

9   Concept Check Questions

1.   If 4 out of 15 apples are red, what is the probability that the first two apples, selected one by one from a bag of 15 apples, will be red?

    A.   1.6%.

    B.   5.7%.

    C.   7.1%.

    D.   13.3%.

---

2.   A driving test has two sections, 40% of candidates fail the first section and 20% fail the second section. 15% of candidates fail both sections. What is the probability that a candidate has failed at least one section?

    A.   35%.

    B.   45%.

    C.   60%.

    D.   75%.

3.   A shop buys pens from two manufacturers, 55% from Mountain Pens and 45% from Valley Pens. The shop knows that 3% of the pens supplied by Mountain Pens are defective and 5% of the pens supplied by Valley Pens are defective. The pens in the shops are mixed together. If a pen is chosen at random and found to be defective what is the probability that it was supplied by Mountain Pens?

    A.   33.3%.

    B.   42.3%.

    C.   55.0%.

    D.   60.0%.

---

4.   There is a competition in which there are six contestants and you need to pick winners for 1st, 2nd and 3rd places, how many ways can they be selected?

    A.   20.

    B.   36.

    C.   120.

    D.   720.

---

5.   An analyst states "…. the odds against the company increasing its dividend are twelve to one". This means that the analyst believes that the probability of it increasing the dividend is closest to:

    A.   0.0769.

    B.   0.0833.

    C.   0.9166.

    D.   0.9230.

9   Concept Check Answers

1.   If 4 out of 15 apples are red, what is the probability that the first two apples, selected one by one from a bag of 15 apples, will be red?

    A.   1.6%.

    B.   5.7%.

    C.   7.1%.

    D.   13.3%.

Correct Answer: 1.   **B**
Use the general rule of multiplication:
$P(AB) = P(A)\,P(B|A) = 4/15 \times 3/14 = 0.057$

---

2.   A driving test has two sections, 40% of candidates fail the first section and 20% fail the second section. 15% of candidates fail both sections. What is the probability that a candidate has failed at least one section?

    A.   35%.

    B.   45%.

    C.   60%.

    D.   75%.

Correct Answer: 2.   **B**
Use the general rule of addition:
$P(A \text{ or } B) = P(A) + P(B) - P(A \text{ and } B)$
$$= 40\% + 20\% - 15\%$$
$$= 45\%$$

3.   A shop buys pens from two manufacturers, 55% from Mountain Pens and 45% from Valley Pens. The shop knows that 3% of the pens supplied by Mountain Pens are defective and 5% of the pens supplied by Valley Pens are defective. The pens in the shops are mixed together. If a pen is chosen at random and found to be defective what is the probability that it was supplied by Mountain Pens?

    A.   33.3%.

    B.   42.3%.

    C.   55.0%.

    D.   60.0%.

Correct Answer: 3.   **B**

Apply Bayes' formula: $P(A_1 \mid B) = \dfrac{P(A_1)P(B \mid A_1)}{P(A_1)P(B \mid A_1) + P(A_2)P(B \mid A_2)}$

define A_1 - Mountain Pens supply the pen
A_2 - Valley Pens supply the pen
    B - the information that the pen is defective

$$P(A_1 \mid B) = \dfrac{0.55 \times 0.03}{(0.55 \times 0.03) + (0.45 \times 0.05)}$$
$$= 0.423$$

---

4.   There is a competition in which there are six contestants and you need to pick winners for 1st, 2nd and 3rd places, how many ways can they be selected?

    A.   20.

    B.   36.

    C.   120.

    D.   720.

Correct Answer: 4.   **C**

Apply $\dfrac{n!}{(n-r)!}$ = $6!/(6-3)! = 120$

5.   An analyst states "…. the odds against the company increasing its dividend are twelve to one". This means that the analyst believes that the probability of it increasing the dividend is closest to:

    A.   0.0769.

    B.   0.0833.

    C.   0.9166.

    D.   0.9230.

Correct Answer: 5.   A

Odds against of twelve to one, means the probability is $1/(12 + 1) = 0.0769$, there is a one in thirteen chance it will happen.

STUDY SESSION 3

Quantitative Methods: Applications

Overview

You will probably find Study Session 3 is more demanding than Study Session 2. We are moving on to focus on the application of the concepts and tools covered in the previous Session, and in particular their use in financial analysis and decision making.

In the first Reading Assignment we look at different discrete and continuous probability distributions, and how probability distributions can help us estimate the probability of achieving a specific outcome. In the next two Reading Assignments we study sampling, estimation and hypothesis testing. The objective is to examine the tools which will enable us to test whether a statement or hypothesis is to be 'accepted' or rejected. More specifically we are looking for evidence from a sample that the hypothesis is not correct, a statement that we can make with a certain level of confidence. Hypothesis testing involves understanding the different ways of selecting a sample, confidence intervals and how to select the appropriate test statistic and decision rule, before doing the number crunching to arrive at a decision to reject or not reject the hypothesis being tested.

In the final Reading Assignment we cover correlation and regression. Calculating and interpreting correlation, or the way two variables move together is relatively simple whereas regression analysis is more complex. Here we are looking at the relationship between a dependent variable (e.g. a stock return) and independent variable or variables (e.g. the market index return). We need to know how to calculate a regression equation and also how to apply the equation and test its significance.

Reading Assignments

Quantitative Methods for Investment Analysis, 2nd edition, Richard A Defusco, Dennis W. McLeavey, Jerald E. Pinto and David E. Runkle (CFA Institute, 2004)

10.   "Common Probability Distributions" Ch. 5

11.   "Sampling and Estimation" Ch. 6

12.   "Hypothesis Testing" Ch. 7

13.   "Correlation and Regression" Ch. 8

10   Common Probability Distributions

Learning Outcome Statements (LOS)

10-a	**Define** and **explain** a probability distribution.
10-b	**Distinguish** between and **give** examples of discrete and continuous random variables.
10-c	**Describe** the set of possible outcomes of a specified random variable.
10-d	**Define** a probability function, **state** its two key properties, and determine whether a given function satisfies those properties.
10-e	**Define** a probability density function.
10-f	**Define** a cumulative distribution function and **calculate** and **interpret** probabilities for a random variable, given its cumulative distribution function.
10-g	**Define** a discrete uniform random variable and **calculate** and **interpret** probabilities, given a discrete uniform distribution.
10-h	**Define** a binomial random variable and **calculate** and **interpret** probabilities, given a binomial probability distribution, and **calculate** the expected value and variance of a binomial random variable.
10-i	**Construct** a binomial tree to **describe** stock price movement.
10-j	**Describe** the continuous uniform distribution and **calculate** and **interpret** probabilities, given a continuous uniform probability distribution.
10-k	**Explain** the key properties of the normal distribution.
10-l	**Distinguish** between a univariate and a multivariate distribution.
10-m	**Explain** the role of correlation in the multivariate normal distribution.
10-n	**Construct** and **explain** confidence intervals for a normally distributed random variable.
10-o	**Define** the standard normal distribution, **explain** how to standardize a random variable, and **calculate** and **interpret** probabilities using the standard normal distribution.
10-p	**Define** shortfall risk, **calculate** the safety first ratio and **select** an optimal portfolio using Roy's safety-first criterion.

10-q	**Explain** the relationship between the lognormal and normal distributions and **explain** and **interpret** the use of the lognormal distribution in modeling asset prices.
10-r	**Distinguish** between discretely and continuously compounded rates of return; and **calculate** and **interpret** the continuously compounded rate of return, given a specific holding period return.
10-s	**Explain** Monte Carlo simulation and historical simulation and **describe** their major applications and limitations.

Introduction

This Reading focuses on probability distributions that will enable us to make clearer statements about a random variable, for example the return on a stock or earnings per share. Four distributions are considered: uniform, binomial, normal and lognormal distributions. These are used widely in finance, for example to estimate the probability of achieving a certain return and to control risk. Probability distributions will form the basis for understanding hypothesis testing and regression analysis, which are covered later in the Study Session. At the end of the section we touch on Monte Carlo simulations; these are analytical procedures which involve identifying risk factors and their probability distributions.

10   Concept Check Questions

1.   If the mean of a distribution is 50 and the standard deviation is 4, the standard normal random variable z for an observation of 44 is *closest* to:

    A.   -1.5.

    B.   0.7.

    C.   1.5.

    D.   6.0.

2.   A stock market rises by an average of 10% a year and the standard deviation of returns is 6%. The probability of the stock market falling by more than 2% in a year is *closest* to:

    A.   2.3%.

    B.   4.6%.

    C.   15.9%.

    D.   31.7%.

3.   A client wishes to protect the value of his capital. Which of the following portfolios will be optimal from a safety-first analysis?

Asset	Expected Return	Standard Deviation
A	25	12
B	15	8
C	10	6

A.   Portfolio A.

B.   Portfolio B.

C.   Portfolio C.

---

4.   Which of the following statements regarding lognormal distributions is **CORRECT**?

A.   The distribution is bell shaped.

B.   The mean of the distribution is zero.

C.   Y is a lognormal distribution if LnY is normally distributed.

D.   Lognormal distributions are frequently used to reflect the distribution of stock returns.

10 Concept Check Answers

1. If the mean of a distribution is 50 and the standard deviation is 4, the standard normal random variable z for an observation of 44 is *closest* to:

    A.   -1.5.

    B.   0.7.

    C.   1.5.

    D.   6.0.

Correct Answer: 1.   A

$Z = (X - \mu)/\sigma = (44 - 50)/4 = -1.5$

---

2. A stock market rises by an average of 10% a year and the standard deviation of returns is 6%. The probability of the stock market falling by more than 2% in a year is *closest* to:

    A.   2.3%.

    B.   4.6%.

    C.   15.9%.

    D.   31.7%.

Correct Answer: 2.   A

A fall of 2% is two standard deviations from the mean. 95.4% of observations fall between the mean plus or minus two standard deviations so 4.6% lie outside this range. Therefore 2.3% will be below -2% and 2.3% will be above 22%.

3.   A client wishes to protect the value of his capital. Which of the following portfolios will be optimal from a safety-first analysis?

Asset	Expected Return	Standard Deviation
A	25	12
B	15	8
C	10	6

    A.   Portfolio A.

    B.   Portfolio B.

    C.   Portfolio C.

Correct Answer: 3.   **A**
Calculate the S F Ratio for each portfolio:
S F Ratio(A) = 25/12 = 2.08
S F Ratio(B) = 15/8 = 1.875
S F Ratio(C) = 10/6 = 1.667
A has the highest S F Ratio and is the correct answer.

---

4.   Which of the following statements regarding lognormal distributions is **CORRECT**?
    A.   The distribution is bell shaped.

    B.   The mean of the distribution is zero.

    C.   Y is a lognormal distribution if LnY is normally distributed.

    D.   Lognormal distributions are frequently used to reflect the distribution of stock returns.

Correct Answer: 4.   **C**
A. is not correct, they are positively skewed distributions.
B. is not correct, the lower bound is zero.
D. is not correct, they are frequently used to show the distribution of stock prices.

11   Sampling and Estimation

Learning Outcome Statements (LOS)

11-a	**Define** simple random sampling, **define** and **interpret** sampling error, and **define** a sampling distribution and **interpret** sampling error.
11-b	**Distinguish** between simple random and stratified random sampling.
11-c	**Distinguish** between time-series and cross-sectional data.
11-d	**State** the central limit theorem and **describe** its importance.
11-e	**Calculate** and **interpret** the standard error of the sample mean.
11-f	**Distinguish** between a point estimate and a confidence interval estimate of a population parameter.
11-g	**Identify** and **describe** the desirable properties of an estimator.
11-h	**Explain** the construction of confidence intervals.
11-i	**Describe** the properties of Student's t-distribution.
11-j	**Calculate, explain** and **interpret** degrees of freedom.
11-k	**Calculate** and **interpret** a confidence interval for a population mean when sampling from a normal distribution with 1) a known population variance, 2) an unknown population variance, or 3) when sampling from a population with an unknown variance when the sample size is large.
11-l	**Discuss** the issues regarding selection of the appropriate sample size.
11-m	**Define** and **discuss** data-mining bias, sample selection bias, survivorship bias, look-ahead bias, and time-period bias.

Introduction

This Reading Assignment examines how data in a sample can be collected and then used to provide information on the wider population. Many of the examples are concerned with the mean of the sample being used to estimate the population mean, this is a practice often used in finance. The Central Limit Theorem allows us to make probability statements about a population mean based on sample data. It is imperative that you understand the concept and calculation of confidence intervals for the population mean and when to use the z-statistic or t-statistic before moving on to hypothesis testing in the next section.

11   Concept Check Questions

1.   A higher degree of confidence leads to:
    A.   wider confidence intervals.

    B.   narrower confidence intervals.

2.   The following are all ways to select a probability sample EXCEPT:
    A.   vertical sampling.

    B.   simple random sampling.

    C.   stratified random sampling.

    D.   systematic random sampling.

3.   The standard deviation of a population is 25 and a sample of 50 observations is taken from the population. The standard error of the sample mean is *closest* to:
    A.   0.10.

    B.   0.28.

    C.   3.54.

    D.   10.00.

4.   A sample of 100 observations is taken from a normally distributed population with a standard deviation of 2. The sample mean is 6. The 99% confidence level is *closest* to:

    A.   between 4.45 and 7.55.

    B.   between 5.48 and 6.52.

    C.   between 5.61 and 6.39.

    D.   between 5.95 and 6.05.

---

5.   Historic analysis suggests that stocks trading on a low price/book value have tended to outperform the market. If the analysis has not included companies that have gone bankrupt then the analysis could be biased due to:

    A.   look-ahead bias.

    B.   data-mining bias.

    C.   survivorship bias.

    D.   data-snooping bias.

11   Answers

1.   A higher degree of confidence leads to:
    A.   wider confidence intervals.

    B.   narrower confidence intervals.

Correct Answer: 1.   A

2.   The following are all ways to select a probability sample **EXCEPT:**
    A.   vertical sampling.

    B.   simple random sampling.

    C.   stratified random sampling.

    D.   systematic random sampling.

Correct Answer: 2.   A

3.   The standard deviation of a population is 25 and a sample of 50 observations is taken from the population. The standard error of the sample mean is *closest* to:
    A.   0.10.

    B.   0.28.

    C.   3.54.

    D.   10.00.

Correct Answer: 3.   C
The standard error of the sample mean is $25/7.07 = 3.54$.

4.   A sample of 100 observations is taken from a normally distributed population with a standard deviation of 2. The sample mean is 6. The 99% confidence level is *closest* to:

    A.   between 4.45 and 7.55.

    B.   between 5.48 and 6.52.

    C.   between 5.61 and 6.39.

    D.   between 5.95 and 6.05.

Correct Answer: 4.   B

The 99% confidence level is $6 \pm (2.58 \times 2)/10$ which is between 5.48 and 6.52.

---

5.   Historic analysis suggests that stocks trading on a low price/book value have tended to outperform the market. If the analysis has not included companies that have gone bankrupt then the analysis could be biased due to:

    A.   look-ahead bias.

    B.   data-mining bias.

    C.   survivorship bias.

    D.   data-snooping bias.

Correct Answer: 5.   C

It has been argued that if all companies had been included, the companies that went bankrupt would have been trading on low price/book multiples, and this would have lowered the average performance of the low price/book value stocks.

12 Hypothesis Testing

Learning Outcome Statements (LOS)

12-a	**Define** a hypothesis, **describe** the steps of hypothesis testing; **define** and **interpret** the null hypothesis and alternative hypothesis, and **distinguish** between one-tailed and two-tailed tests of hypotheses.
12-b	**Discuss** the choice of the null and alternative hypotheses.
12-c	**Define** and **interpret** a test statistic, a Type I and a Type II error, and a significance level, and **explain** how significance levels are used in hypothesis testing.
12-d	**Define** and **interpret** a decision rule and the power of a test.
12-e	**Explain** the relation between confidence intervals and hypothesis tests.
12-f	**Distinguish** between a statistical decision and an economic decision.
12-g	**Identify** the appropriate test statistic and **interpret** the results for a hypothesis test concerning the population mean of a normally distributed population with 1) known or 2) unknown variance.
12-h	**Identify** the appropriate test statistic and **interpret** the results for a hypothesis test concerning the equality of the population means of two normally distributed populations, based on independent random samples with 1) equal or 2) unequal assumed variances.
12-i	**Identify** the appropriate test statistic and **interpret** the results for a hypothesis test concerning the mean difference of two normally distributed populations (paired comparisons test).
12-j	**Identify** the appropriate test statistic and **interpret** the results for a hypothesis test concerning the variance of a normally distributed population.
12-k	**Identify** the appropriate test statistic and **interpret** the results for a hypothesis test concerning the equality of the variance of two normally distributed populations, based on two independent random samples.
12-l	**Distinguish** between parametric and nonparametric tests and **describe** the situations in which the use of nonparametric tests may be appropriate.

Introduction

In order to test statements in finance such as 'have the fund's returns been statistically different to the benchmark's returns?' or 'is the beta of a stock statistically different to 1?' we need to understand the procedure behind hypothesis testing. Essentially we need to state a null hypothesis and then collect data from a sample which will decide whether we have a basis for rejecting the null hypothesis. We will not be certain whether the null hypothesis can be rejected but will be able to state with a certain probability, or confidence level, whether we have evidence to reject it.

The focus of hypothesis testing is on testing a hypothesis concerning the population mean, although you need to be familiar with the tests that are used for population variances, difference between means and differences between variances.

12   Concept Check Questions

1.   Hypothesis testing is used to determine the mean of a population and the null hypothesis is defined as the mean is equal to 100. This is an example of:

   A.   a one-tailed test.

   B.   a two-tailed test.

---

2.   An analyst is studying the monthly income of workers at a factory. He is told that the mean income is $5,000 per month and he decided to look at a sample 100 workers to see if this is correct. The sample mean is $5,018 with a standard deviation of 80. If he sets the null hypothesis as the population mean is $5,000 he should:

   A.   reject the null hypothesis at both the 1% and 5% significance level.

   B.   accept the null hypothesis at both the 1% and 5% significance level.

   C.   accept the null hypothesis at the 1% significance level and reject it at the 5% significance level.

   D.   accept the null hypothesis at the 5% significance level and reject it at the 1% significance level.

3.   A p-value of 0.1 indicates that:

A.   there is extremely strong evidence that H0 should be rejected.

B.   there is extremely strong evidence that H0 should not be rejected.

C.   there is a probability of 0.1 of observing a sample value at least as extreme as the value observed, assuming H0 is correct.

D.   there is a probability of 0.1 of observing a sample value at least as extreme as the value observed, assuming H0 is rejected.

4.   You are analyzing the monthly returns from a fund over the last year and calculate that the mean return was 1.25% with a sample standard deviation of 1.0%. You expected the fund to have achieved a return of 1.4% in line with the risk taken on by the fund and wish to decide at the 10% significance level whether the results are consistent with a population mean return of 1.4%. Given that t0.05,11= 1.796 you can conclude that:

A.   the results are consistent with a mean of 1.4%.

B.   the results are not consistent with a mean of 1.4%.

5.   A chi-square test statistic (χ^2)could be used for hypothesis tests for:

A.   the mean for a single normally distributed population.

B.   the variance for a single normally distributed population.

C.   the mean for a single non-normally distributed population.

D.   the variance for a single non-normally distributed population.

12   Concept Check Answers

1.   Hypothesis testing is used to determine the mean of a population and the null hypothesis is defined as the mean is equal to 100. This is an example of:

   A.   a one-tailed test.

   B.   a two-tailed test.

Correct Answer: 1.   B
If there is no direction (greater or less than) in the null hypothesis it is two-tailed.

---

2.   An analyst is studying the monthly income of workers at a factory. He is told that the mean income is $5,000 per month and he decided to look at a sample 100 workers to see if this is correct. The sample mean is $5,018 with a standard deviation of 80. If he sets the null hypothesis as the population mean is $5,000 he should:

   A.   reject the null hypothesis at both the 1% and 5% significance level.

   B.   accept the null hypothesis at both the 1% and 5% significance level.

   C.   accept the null hypothesis at the 1% significance level and reject it at the 5% significance level.

   D.   accept the null hypothesis at the 5% significance level and reject it at the 1% significance level.

Correct Answer: 2.   C
$Z = (5018-5000)/8 = 2.25$. This is less than 2.58 (the critical value for the 1% significance level and more than 1.96 (the critical value for the 5% significance level).

3.   A p-value of 0.1 indicates that:

A.   there is extremely strong evidence that H0 should be rejected.

B.   there is extremely strong evidence that H0 should not be rejected.

C.   there is a probability of 0.1 of observing a sample value at least as extreme as the value observed, assuming H0 is correct.

D.   there is a probability of 0.1 of observing a sample value at least as extreme as the value observed, assuming H0 is rejected.

Correct Answer: 3.   C
The p-value is the probability of observing a value as extreme or more extreme than the value observed, for it to be extremely strong evidence it would need to be 0.001 or less.

---

4.   You are analyzing the monthly returns from a fund over the last year and calculate that the mean return was 1.25% with a sample standard deviation of 1.0%. You expected the fund to have achieved a return of 1.4% in line with the risk taken on by the fund and wish to decide at the 10% significance level whether the results are consistent with a population mean return of 1.4%. Given that $t0.05,11 = 1.796$ you can conclude that:

A.   the results are consistent with a mean of 1.4%.

B.   the results are not consistent with a mean of 1.4%.

Correct Answer: 4.   A
Set the null hypothesis as H_0: $\mu = 1.4\%$. We need to apply the t-test because it is a small sample.

$$t_{n-1} = \frac{\overline{x} - \mu}{s/\sqrt{n}} = \frac{1.25 - 1.4}{1.0/\sqrt{12}} = -\frac{0.15}{0.29} = -0.52$$

This is within the confidence interval so the null hypothesis is not rejected.

5. A chi-square test statistic (χ^2)could be used for hypothesis tests for:

A. the mean for a single normally distributed population.

B. the variance for a single normally distributed population.

C. the mean for a single non-normally distributed population.

D. the variance for a single non-normally distributed population.

Correct Answer: 5. B

13   Correlation and Regression

Learning Outcome Statements (LOS)

13-a	**Define** and **interpret** a scatter plot.
13-b	**Calculate** and **interpret** a sample covariance and a sample correlation coefficient.
13-c	**Formulate** a test of the hypothesis that the population correlation coefficient equals zero and **determine** whether the hypothesis is rejected at a given level of significance.
13-d	**Differentiate** between the dependent and independent variables in a linear regression and **explain** the assumptions underlying linear regression.
13-e	**Define, calculate** and **interpret** the standard error of estimate and the coefficient of determination.
13-f	**Calculate** a confidence interval for a regression coefficient.
13-g	**Formulate** a null and an alternative hypothesis about a population value of a regression coefficient, **select** the appropriate test statistic, and **determine** whether the null hypothesis is rejected at a given level of significance.
13-h	**Interpret** a regression coefficient.
13-i	**Describe** the use of analysis of variance (ANOVA) in regression analysis and **interpret** ANOVA results.
13-j	**Calculate** and **interpret** a predicted value and a confidence interval for the predicted value for the dependent variable given an estimated regression model and a value for the independent variable.
13-k	**Discuss** the limitations of regression analysis and **identify** problems with a particular regression analysis or its associated results and any conclusions drawn from them.

Introduction

The last part of this Study Session looks at correlation and regression, tools that are used to examine the relationship between two or more financial variables. Whereas correlation measures the linear relationship between two variables, regression looks at the relationship between a dependent variable and independent variables. In addition to calculating correlation and regression coefficients you will need to be able to interpret the numbers, test their significance and discuss their limitations.

13   Concept Check Questions

1.   If the correlation coefficient between two variables is 0.3, then the percentage of the dependent variable's movement that can be explained by the independent variable's movement is *closest* to:

    A.   9%.

    B.   30%.

    C.   33%.

    D.   90%.

---

2.   The regression line, when X is the independent variable and Y the dependent variable:

    A.   minimizes the sum of the distances between the estimated Y values and the actual Y values.

    B.   minimizes the sum of the distances between the estimated X values and the actual X values.

    C.   minimizes the sum of the squares of the distance between the estimated Y values and the actual Y values.

    D.   minimizes the sum of the squares of the distance between the estimated X values and the actual X values.

3.   It is found that the growth in sales of food items is dependent on the growth in total consumer spending in a country. The slope of the regression line is 0.8 and the Y-axis intercept is 2%. If consumer spending grows at 3% then the estimated growth in the sales of food items is *closest* to:

    A.   0.4%.

    B.   2.4%.

    C.   4.0%.

    D.   4.4%.

---

4.   Which of the following does **NOT** reflect the limitations of regression analysis?

    A.   Regression relations change over time.

    B.   The expected value of the error term is zero.

    C.   The tests and predictions of the regression analysis are only valid if the independent variable is random.

    D.   Any violations of the classical normal linear regression model assumptions will make the tests and predictions invalid.

13   Concept Check Answers

1.   If the correlation coefficient between two variables is 0.3, then the percentage of the dependent variable's movement that can be explained by the independent variable's movement is *closest* to:

    A.   9%.

    B.   30%.

    C.   33%.

    D.   90%.

Correct Answer: 1.   A

The coefficient of determination, which is the proportion of the variation in the dependent variable that is explained by the variation independent variable, is equal to r^2.

---

2.   The regression line, when X is the independent variable and Y the dependent variable:

    A.   minimizes the sum of the distances between the estimated Y values and the actual Y values.

    B.   minimizes the sum of the distances between the estimated X values and the actual X values.

    C.   minimizes the sum of the squares of the distance between the estimated Y values and the actual Y values.

    D.   minimizes the sum of the squares of the distance between the estimated X values and the actual X values.

Correct Answer: 2.   C

This is the least squares principle. If Y is the dependent variable it is the one being estimated.

3.   It is found that the growth in sales of food items is dependent on the growth in total consumer spending in a country. The slope of the regression line is 0.8 and the Y-axis intercept is 2%. If consumer spending grows at 3% then the estimated growth in the sales of food items is *closest* to:

    A.   0.4%.

    B.   2.4%.

    C.   4.0%.

    D.   4.4%.

Correct Answer: 3.   **D**
$Y = a + bX = 2\% + (0.8 \times 3\%) = 4.4\%$.

---

4.   Which of the following does **NOT** reflect the limitations of regression analysis?

    A.   Regression relations change over time.

    B.   The expected value of the error term is zero.

    C.   The tests and predictions of the regression analysis are only valid if the independent variable is random.

    D.   Any violations of the classical normal linear regression model assumptions will make the tests and predictions invalid.

Correct Answer: 4.   **C**
On the contrary, one of the classical normal linear regression model assumptions states that the independent variable should not be random.

STUDY SESSION 4 Introduction

Introductory Readings

Economics: Private and Public Choice, 10th edition, James D. Gwartney, Richard L. Stroup, Russell S. Sobel, and David A. Macpherson (South-Western, 2003)

"Supply, Demand, and the Market Process," Ch. 3

"Supply and Demand: Applications and Extensions" Ch. 4

"Taking the Nation's Economic Pulse," Ch. 7

"Working with Our Basic Aggregate Demand/Aggregate Supply Model," Ch. 10

"Keynesian Foundations of Modern Macroeconomics," Ch. 11

Supply, Demand, and the Market Process CH 5

Introduction

This chapter is centered on the laws of supply and demand. The law of supply says that a higher price means producers produce more of the product, and the law of demand says that consumers buy less of a good if the price rises, and vice versa. Candidates should know what type of factors cause shifts in the supply and demand curves and movements along the curves and understand the concept of market equilibrium.

Consumer choice and the Law of Demand

Consumers are forced to make choices regarding how they spend their income in order to get the most value for their money. **The Law of Demand** states that there is an inverse relationship between the price of a product and the amount or quantity of it that consumers are willing to purchase.

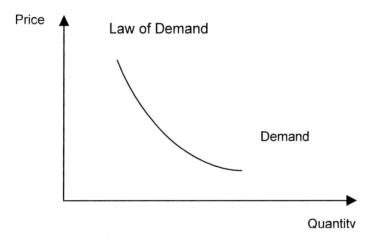

A **consumer surplus** is the difference between the maximum price that consumers are willing to pay and the price that they actually pay; this is a net gain to the buyers of the good.

Producer choice and the Law of Supply

All economic participants in an economy are aiming to generate profit, which is the excess of sales revenue over the production costs. The Law of Supply states that there is a direct relationship between the price of a product and the amount of it that is offered for sale.

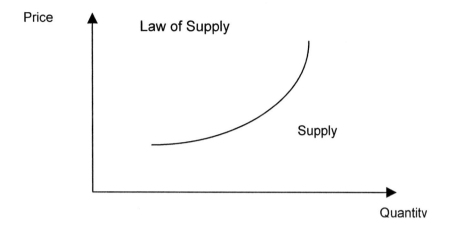

Price changes and demand and supply

Consumers buy less of a product as the price increases because of the availability of substitutes. The availability of substitutes is a major factor in deciding the sensitivity to the quantity demanded to a change in price. If the demand for a product is elastic it means a small price change will lead to a large change in demand. In the diagram below when the price moves from P1 to P2, the quantity demanded falls sharply from Q1 to Q2. If demand is inelastic it means that a change in price only has a small impact on the quantity demanded, so prices move from Q1 to Q2. Unitary elastic means that a percent change in quantity demanded leads to a percent change in price.

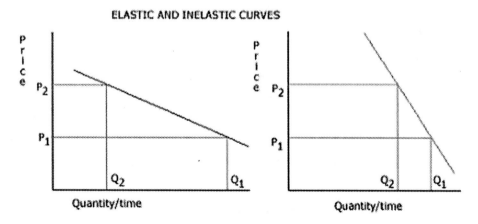

Similarly a supply curve is elastic when the quantity supplied is very responsive to a change in price (a flat curve) and inelastic when quantity supplied is not very responsive to a change in price (a steep curve).

Shifts in demand

A **shift** in the demand curve will be a result of a change in demand due to factors other than price. Factors that lead to a shift include increases in consumer income, changes in taxes on the product, changes in price or availability of competing products, and changes in expectations of future prices. It is important to differentiate between **changes in demand** (a shift of the demand curve) and **changes in quantity demanded** (a movement along the same demand curve).

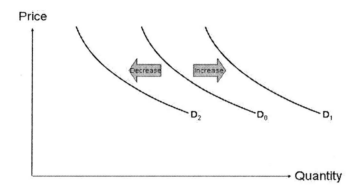

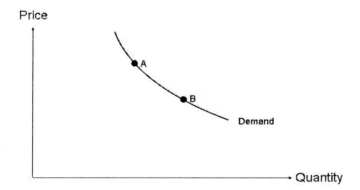

Shifts in supply

A change in supply indicates a shift in the supply curve. The following are examples of factors that could lead to a change in supply – changes in resource costs, technology improvements, natural disasters which limit supply of a product, changes in taxes on the producers of the product.

Equilibrium is defined as a state of balance between forces such as supply and demand. It is important to differentiate between **short run** (an insufficient time period for decision makers to fully adjust to changes in market conditions) and **long run** (a sufficient time for decision makers to make adjustments).

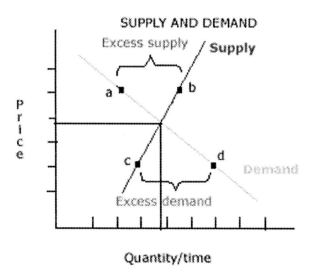

High prices will tend to lead to an excess supply illustrated by the points a and b, producers will tend to lower prices until supply and demand are in balance. On the other hand if prices are too low, demand will exceed supply, illustrated by points c and d, and producers will increase prices until equilibrium is reached.

Impact of changes in demand and supply

Increase in demand – the demand curve shifts to the right, which will increase both the equilibrium price and quantity.

Decrease in demand – the demand curve shifts to the left, which will decrease both the equilibrium price and quantity.

Increase in supply – the supply curve shifts to the right, which will decrease the equilibrium price and increase the equilibrium quantity.

Decrease in supply – the supply curve shifts to the left, which will increase the equilibrium price and decrease the equilibrium quantity.

An unanticipated cut in supply will, in the short run, lead to a sharp increase in price, but in the long run demand will respond to the price change. Similarly an unanticipated surge in demand for a product will initially push up prices but longer-term supply will be increased.

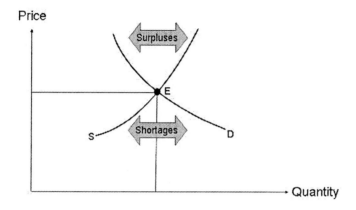

The **invisible hand principle** says that market prices act as an inducement to individuals to pursue productive activities that also promote the economic well being of society.

Supply and Demand: Applications and Extensions CH 4

Introduction

This chapter examines some of the applications of supply and demand analysis covered in the previous Reading. First we look at the impact of wage rates, interest rates and foreign exchange on supply and demand. Then we look at the impact of government action, including price controls on markets, and of black markets which are operating outside the legal system. Finally we consider taxation and how it relates to elasticity of supply and demand.

Resources

The first step in a firm's production process is the purchase of **resources**. Resources include raw materials, labor etc. Resource markets generally have downward-sloping demand curves and upward-sloping supply curves. There is a close link between the markets for the end-product and the resources used to make the product. For example, when the price of a resource increases, costs increase leading to a reduction in supply and higher prices for the end-product.

The **loanable funds** market refers to the market that coordinates the borrowing and lending decisions of firms and households. Participants in the market include commercial banks, and stock and bond markets. The interest rate is the price of loanable funds.

The demand curve will slope downwards to the right since firms and households will borrow more at low interest rates. On the other hand, low interest rates will make it less attractive to save so the supply curve will be upward sloping to the right. Market forces will drive interest rates to a level, E, where the quantity of funds demanded will equal the quantity of funds supplied.

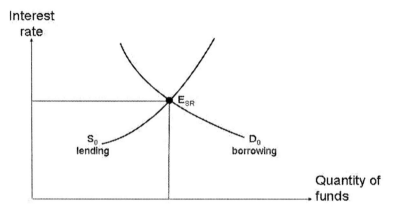

The interest rate is important because it is the link between the price of something today with its price in the future.

The **foreign exchange market** is the market in which different currencies are bought and sold. Exchange rates between currencies are very important since they determine the price of all goods and services that are traded in international markets. They will also influence decision makers who are looking at producing goods in different countries, although other issues such as transport costs, legal issues will be factors to consider before a decision is made to move production overseas.

A **price ceiling** is a legal restriction that establishes a maximum price that a good can be sold at. If the price ceiling is set below the equilibrium price it will increase demand and reduce the quantity supplied creating a **shortage** of the good. Non-price factors (e.g. waiting lists) will determine who is able to buy the product. Suppliers will be tempted to reduce the quality of the good supplied if they cannot increase prices.

Price floors establish a minimum price that can be charged for a good. If the price is fixed above the equilibrium price then a **surplus** of the good will appear.

The minimum wage is an example of a price floor, and has led to the substitution of machines or more highly-skilled workers for low-paid workers. Also employers will have little incentive to offer non-wage benefits to workers on the minimum wage.

A **black market** is a market that operates outside the legal system, either the sale of illegal goods or goods at illegal prices or terms. Black markets are characterized by higher profit margins for suppliers who do not get caught (to compensate the supplier for the higher risk), defective products and violence (to settle disputes). The point is made that a legal system that allows for settlement of disputes is essential for the smooth operation of markets.

Tax incidence refers to how the burden of a tax is distributed between buyers and sellers and related parties (the actual incidence). This will often be quite different to the **statutory incidence** which is the legal assignment of the responsibility to pay the tax. It can be shown that the actual incidence is independent of its statutory incidence, i.e. whether it is imposed on the buyer or the seller.

Looking at the example of when a tax is imposed on the seller of a product, this will shift the supply curve up by the amount of the tax. The intersection of the demand curve and supply curve will move, splitting the tax burden between the buyer and seller. The reduction in overall trade (and loss of benefit of this trade to both parties) results in a deadweight loss; this is the loss over and above the actual payment of tax to the government.

Elasticity and the incidence of tax

In the case that demand is inelastic and supply elastic the burden of tax will largely fall on the buyer (e.g. when oil prices rise). Conversely when demand is relatively elastic compared to supply, the sellers will bear the largest burden.

If either demand or supply is relatively inelastic fewer trades will be eliminated so a rise in tax will result in a relatively small deadweight loss.

Taking the Nation's Economic Pulse CH 7

Introduction

The focus of this chapter is on the measurement of GDP as the most commonly quoted measure of economic performance. Candidates need to know how to calculate GDP using both the expenditure and the resources cost-income approaches. They also need to be familiar with the differences between GDP and GNP, and how to switch between nominal and real GDP given the rate of inflation. At the end of the chapter we look at alternative measures for the performance of the economy.

Gross domestic product

Gross domestic product (GDP) is defined as the total market value of all final goods and services produced within a country's borders during a specific time period. GDP is a broad measure of current production of goods and services, and GDP calculations exclude second-hand goods, intermediate goods, and financial transactions.

There are two main approaches to measuring GDP:

1.   Expenditure approach, where GDP is the sum of:
     Consumption (C)
     Gross private investment (Ig)
     Government expenditure (G)
     Net Exports (NX)

The expenditure approach is commonly stated as:

$$GDP = C + I_g + G + NX$$

Gross private investment includes depreciation expense; gross investment is the sum of net investment (I_n) plus depreciation. Net exports (NX) is equal to exports minus imports (X – IM), and NX can be either positive or negative. If exports are higher than imports, NX will be positive and added to GDP; if imports are higher than exports, NX will be negative and subtracted from GDP.

2.   Cost resource-income approach, where GDP is the sum of:
     Wages, salaries, self-employed income
     Rents, profits, and interest
     Indirect business taxes
     Depreciation
     Net income of foreigners

Net income of foreigners can be positive or negative. If foreigners bring in more investment income into a country than the residents of the same country pay abroad, then net income will be positive.

GDP calculated by the expenditure approach and GDP calculated by the cost-income approach must be equal.

Example Int-1 Calculating GDP

The fictitious country of Euphoria has the following expenditure and income categories and amounts (in millions):

- Imports $95
- Net investment $100
- Wages and salaries $295
- Government expenditure $70
- Depreciation $25
- Indirect business taxes $60
- Issuance of corporate bonds $35
- Self-employed income $95
- Exports $150
- Rents, profits, and interest $140
- Net income of foreigners   -$40
- Consumption expenditure $325

The trick to calculating GDP is to identify expenditure versus cost-income components.

To use the GDP expenditure approach, we must first compute two preliminary items:

$$I_g = \text{net investment} + \text{depreciation} = \$100 + \$25 = \$125$$

$$NX = \text{exports} - \text{imports} = \$150 - \$95 = \$55$$

$$GDP = C + I_g + G + NX$$

$$GDP = \$325 + \$125 + \$70 + \$55$$

$$GDP = \$575$$

To use the GDP cost-income approach, sum up all cost-income components:

$$GDP = \text{wages and salaries} + \text{self-employed income} + \text{rents, profits, and interest} + \text{depreciation} + \text{indirect business taxes} + \text{net income of foreigners}$$

$$GDP = \$295 + \$95 + \$140 + \$25 + \$60 + (-\$40)$$

$$GDP = \$575$$

Notice that GDP is equal using either approach. The issuance of bonds is a financial flow, which is excluded from GDP calculations. (Assume that the asset financed by the bond flotation has already been counted under gross business investment).

GDP counts the value of goods and services produced inside a nation by residents of that nation and by foreigners living there, too. Whereas, GNP counts the value of goods and services produced by the citizens of a country, whether they are living in the country itself or living abroad. GDP and GNP will be equal only when net income of foreigners is zero.

GDP is measured in the U.S. in dollars. In simple terms, GDP is the sum of price multiplied by quantity (P × Q) of all final goods and services produced. Quantity represents real production within an economy; if quantity (or output) changes, then economic activity reported by GDP will change. However, GDP can change, even if there is no change in output, if prices by themselves change.

Nominal GDP measures economic activity by multiplying current prices with current output; nominal GDP can increase because of either increasing prices and/or increasing output. Whereas, real GDP measures economic activity by multiplying historical prices referenced to a particular year by current output; because prices are held constant, real GDP can only change because of output changes.

When newspapers or television report GDP forecasts, they almost always mean real GDP.

Inflation is the increase in prices over time, and there are two main ways in which inflation can be measured. The Consumer Price Index (CPI) measures narrow price changes in a typical "basket" of goods bought by consumers, captured in the consumption component of GDP calculations. The GDP deflator measures broad price changes across all categories of economic activity, captured by consumption, investment, government, and net exports.

Both CPI and the GDP deflator are referenced to a base year, which is assigned a value of 100.0. As inflation rises, so does the index value of the CPI or the GDP deflator.

The Equation below is used to calculate real GDP when we are given nominal GDP and the GDP deflator for any given year:

Equation Int-1

$$\text{real GDP}_{\text{period } t} = \text{nominal GDP}_{\text{period } t} \times \frac{\text{GDP deflator}_{\text{base year}}}{\text{GDP deflator}_{\text{period } t}}$$

Recall that the GDP deflator in the base year is equal to 100.0. Therefore, real GDP will always equal nominal GDP in the base year.

Example Int-2 Calculating real GDP

Given the following information:

- Nominal GDP in 2005 = $11,381.2 billion
- GDP deflator in 2005 = 121.4
- GDP base year is 1986

Calculate real GDP in 2005:

$$\text{real GDP}_{\text{period t}} = \text{nominal GDP}_{\text{period t}} \times \frac{\text{GDP deflator}_{\text{base year}}}{\text{GDP deflator}_{\text{period t}}}$$

$$= \$11,381.2 \text{ billion} \times \frac{100.0}{121.4}$$

$$= \$9,375.0 \text{ billion}$$

Although GDP attempts to capture a nation's economic activity, some activities will elude statisticians and will be excluded from any measure. Such excluded activities include:

- Leisure and human costs;
- Unreported and illegal activities, such as the underground economy;
- Value of unpaid household production, including chores;
- Harmful side effects of production, including pollution of air, water, soil; and
- Quality and variety of product improvements which occur through innovation.

GDP and GNP are the broadest measures of output. However, there are several alternative measures of economic performance:

- National income (NI) is the earnings of all resource owners, which is the sum of employment compensation (salaries), rents, corporate profits, interest, and self-employment income. However, not all of this income is available for personal use.
- Personal income (PI) adjusts NI by subtracting corporate profits and social insurance taxes and adding transfer payments and dividends. PI can be spent on consumption, saving, or paying of personal taxes.
- Disposable income (DI) strips away personal taxes from PI. Out of the five output measures, DI is the narrowest. DI can either be consumed or saved.

Working with Our Basic Aggregate Demand/ Aggregate Supply Model CH 10

Introduction

We now look at the effects of changes in aggregate demand and supply on other economic indicators, such as growth, prices and employment. First of all we examine the factors that change supply and demand and then differentiate between the short-run and long-run impact of anticipated versus unanticipated changes on the economy. We also consider the self-correcting mechanisms that will help stabilise the economy.

Aggregate demand

There are, in fact, three separate curves: aggregate demand, short-run aggregate supply, and long-run aggregate supply

The aggregate demand (AD) curve is a downward-sloping curve, with the price level (P) plotted on the vertical axis and real GDP (Y) plotted on the horizontal axis. There are six factors that will shift AD to the right (AD_1), also known as an increase in aggregate demand:

- Increase in real wealth
- Decrease in real interest rates
- Increased optimism in the economy
- Higher expected inflation in the future
- Higher incomes abroad, thereby boosting exports
- Domestic currency depreciation, thereby boosting exports and restricting imports

The opposite of these factors will cause the AD curve to shift to the left, also known as a decrease in aggregate demand (AD_2). The diagram below depicts the shape of the original aggregate demand curve (AD_0) and the shifted curves.

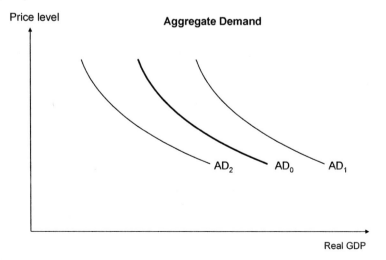

The short-run aggregate supply (SRAS) curve is an upward-sloping curve, with the price level (P) plotted on the vertical axis and real GDP (Y) plotted on the horizontal axis. There are five factors that will shift SRAS to the right (SRAS₁), also known as an increase in short-run aggregate supply:

- Increase in the stock of capital
- Technological improvements
- Reduction in input prices
- Lower expected inflation in the future
- Favourable shocks, such as good weather

The opposite of these factors will cause the SRAS curve to shift to the left, also known as a decrease in short-run aggregate supply (SRAS₂). The diagram below depicts the shape of the original short-run aggregate supply curve (SRAS₀) and the shifted curves.

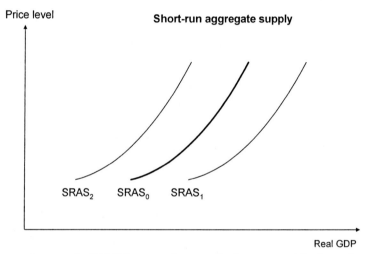

The long-run aggregate supply (LRAS) curve is a vertical curve, with the price level (P) plotted on the vertical axis and real GDP (Y) plotted on the horizontal axis. There are two factors that will shift LRAS to the right (SRAS₁), also known as an increase in long-run aggregate supply:

- Increase in the stock of capital
- Technological improvements

Observe that these factors are common to SRAS, which means that whenever the LRAS curve shifts, the SRAS curve will move with it in the same direction. The opposite of these factors will cause the LRAS curve to shift to the left, also known as a decrease in long-run aggregate supply (LRAS₂). The diagram below depicts the shape of the original long-run aggregate supply curve (LRAS₀) and the shifted curves.

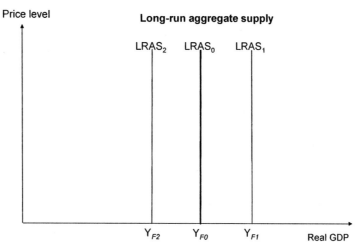

The LRAS curve plays a significant role in regulating the macro economy: the position of LRAS determines the level of economic activity corresponding to full employment (Y_{F0}). Full employment can only be achieved when an economy is operating somewhere along the LRAS curve.

An unanticipated change in macroeconomics suggests that people are caught off guard by the change, but over time, the market will react to it. When people initially react to unanticipated changes in either AD or SRAS, then output can change, but only in the short run. (Remember that LRAS represents the limit of production in the economy in the long run.)

Consider an unanticipated increase in government expenditure, a component of AD. If the AD curve shifts upwards, then the new short-run equilibrium will occur at the intersection of the new AD curve and the original SRAS curve. Thus, output (Y) and price level (P) will be higher in the short run. However, the economy is now operating beyond its capacity, which exerts pressure on resource prices. As resource prices increase, SRAS will shift to the left until equilibrium is restored along LRAS. Thus, output (Y) is restored to full employment and the price level is higher. In the long run, unanticipated changes in AD result in changes to the price level only.

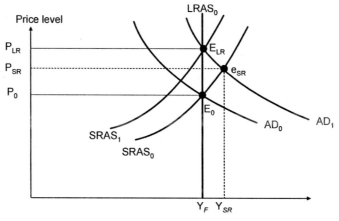

Unanticipated changes in SRAS will only affect the short-run position of the SRAS curve itself; there will be no affect on aggregate demand. Consider an economy dependent on agriculture, and an unexpected warm summer boosts the economy's main crop. In the short run, the favorable boost in production will shift the SRAS curve to the right, leading to a lower price level but a higher level of output. However, the economy is operating beyond its long-run capacity, and there is upward pressure on resource prices. As resource prices increase, SRAS will shift to the left until long-run equilibrium is restored along the LRAS curve. In the long run, unanticipated changes in SRAS result in neither a change to the price level nor change in output.

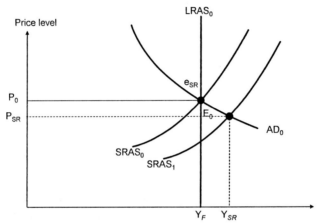

Market economies respond when they operate at an output level above or below full employment (along the LRAS curve). There are two self-correcting mechanisms that tend to restore long-run equilibrium:

- Changes in resource prices affect the SRAS curve. We have discussed this in the previous LOS. For example, when output is higher than full employment, increasing resource prices tends to decrease SRAS, causing higher price levels and eventually restoring the economy to full employment.
- Changes in real interest rates affect the AD curve. For example, when output is higher than full employment, real (inflation-adjusted) interest rates will increase as the demand for money increases. Higher real interest rates depress business investment, which is a component of AD. Thus, there is a tendency for AD to automatically decrease, which can help restore the economy to its full employment level of output.

The third self-correcting mechanism relates to consumption expenditure, which is a large component of AD. (Consumption represents approximately 65 percent of GDP in most developed economies.) Compared with other components of AD, consumption is the most stable component of GDP. The inherent stability of consumption expenditure helps to mitigate changes to other less stable components of GDP, such as net exports (tied to the exchange rate) and business investment (tied to interest rates and fickle business sentiment).

Keynesian Foundations of Modern Macroeconomics CH 11

Introduction

In this section we explore the main principles of Keynesian theory which was developed by a British economist to explain the prolonged unemployment in the 1930s; it has had a major influence on subsequent economic thinking. Keynes focused on demand rather than supply and the role of the government's fiscal policy in taking an economy out of recession. He believed that the government should run a budget deficit in order to stimulate demand and bring the economy back to full employment. This chapter examines the rationale behind his thinking including the importance of the expenditure multiplier.

Keynesian economics

The distinction between classical and Keynesian economics stems from the assumptions made on the length of recessions. The classical school assumed that the economy operated mostly at or near its long-run level of output; recessions tended to be short lived as the economy automatically reverted to long-run output and employment through the SRAS mechanism discussed in the previous Reading.

Keynesians are followers of John Maynard Keynes, a British economist of the early 20th century. Writing during the Great Depression, Keynes (hence Keynesians) believed that the economy could get stuck in prolonged recession, with reduced output and widespread unemployment. Keynesians do not believe that adjustments to SRAS will restore equilibrium. Rather, they believe that recessions stem from a deficiency of AD, and the government can only restore long-run output and employment levels by boosting AD. According to the Keynesians, SRAS adjustments are too slow, if indeed they operate at all.

The Keynesian model explains the output level at which an economy can operate, in the absence of either an explicit SRAS or LRAS curve.

The model distinguishes between autonomous verses induced expenditure. (Recall the major components of expenditure: C, I, G, and NX.) Autonomous expenditure has no relationship with levels of income; whereas induced expenditure is a function of income. For example, consumption expenditure increases as disposable income increases (induced). However, even when disposable income is equal to zero, the economy will maintain a level of consumption by drawing down assets (autonomous).

In a simplified economy consisting of consumers, total expenditure is equal to consumption expenditure. Total expenditure is an upward sloping function of GDP (output), and even when GDP is zero, there will be autonomous expenditure. The aggregate expenditure curve is shown as the AE curve in the graph below.

Businesses plan for a certain level of expenditure, and they build inventories to meet consumption expenditure. In the graph below, businesses wish to operate along a 45-degree line, where planned aggregate expenditure is equal to actual output. If people consume more than is planned, then businesses inventories will be depleted faster than expected. Businesses increase production to meet the unanticipated expenditure, which boosts output. Alternatively, if people consume less than is planned, then businesses inventories will be unexpectedly increased. In response, businesses decrease their production, resulting in lower output.

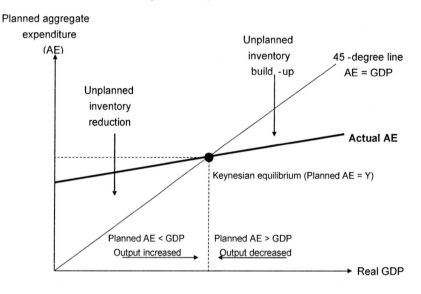

Keynesian equilibrium

Keynesian macro-equilibrium occurs along the 45-degree line, when real GDP is equal to planned aggregate expenditure.

The marginal propensity to consume (MPC) is additional consumption related to an additional unit of disposable income, is shown in the Equation Int-2 below:

Equation Int-2

$$\text{marginal propensity to consume} = \frac{\Delta \text{ consumption expenditure}}{\Delta \text{ disposable income}}$$

where Δ is uppercase Greek letter delta meaning change.

The MPC is a number greater than zero but less than one ($0 < MPC < 1$). Recall that disposable income can be either consumed or saved; therefore, we can define the marginal propensity to save (MPS) as $1 - MPC$. Note that $MPC + MPS = 1$.

The expenditure multiplier is related to the MPC and MPS, as shown below:

Equation Int-3

$$\text{expenditure multiplier} = \frac{1}{1 - \text{MPC}} = \frac{1}{\text{MPS}}$$

Example Int-3 Marginal propensity to consume and expenditure multiplier

When disposable income is $150, consumption expenditure is $120; and when disposable income is $200, consumption expenditure is $157.50. Calculate the marginal propensity to consume and the expenditure multiplier.

Use Equations Int-2 and Int-3, respectively:

marginal propensity to consume

$$= \frac{\Delta \text{ consump. exp.}}{\Delta \text{ disposable income}} = \frac{\$157.50 - \$120}{\$200 - \$150} = \frac{\$37.5}{\$50} = 0.75$$

Note that the MPS = 1 – MPC = 1 – 0.75 = 0.25

$$\text{expenditure multiplier} = \frac{1}{1 - \text{MPC}} = \frac{1}{1 - 0.75} = \frac{1}{0.25} = 4$$

The expenditure multiplier explains the total increase in output caused by an initial change in autonomous expenditure. The expenditure multiplier is positively related to the MPC and negatively related to MPS. Intuitively, if some of the increase in autonomous expenditure is saved rather than spent, the effect of the autonomous stimulus on the economy will be reduced.

Assume that the MPC = 0.75, which yields an expenditure multiplier of 4. If the government increased autonomous expenditure by $10, then the total effect of the government's increased expenditure would be a $10 × 4 = $40 increase in total output (Y).

If, however, people had a tendency to consume more of the autonomous increase (MPC = 0.80), then the new expenditure multiplier would be:

$$\text{expenditure multiplier} = \frac{1}{1 - \text{MPC}} = \frac{1}{1 - 0.80} = \frac{1}{0.20} = 5$$

If the government increased autonomous expenditure by $10, then the total effect of the government's increased expenditure would be a $10 × 5 = $50 increase in total output (Y).

In terms of the Keynesian model, an increase in autonomous expenditure would shift the actual AE curve upwards, resulting in a multiplied increase in output (Y) until planned aggregate expenditure equals output.

Keynesians believe that private investment is the most volatile component of aggregate expenditure. An unexplained decline in business confidence results in an autonomous decrease in private investment, which reverberates throughout the entire economy by the multiplier effect.

The decrease in aggregate demand causes a decline in output and employment levels. The economy's built-in stabilizers might not be enough to offset the decline in AD, so Keynesian believe that the government ought to increase expenditure to restore full employment.

Alternatively, an increase in business confidence would result in an autonomous increase in investment expenditure, which would reverberate throughout the economy via the expenditure multiplier. If output expands beyond full employment, inflation pressures would emerge.

Introductory Readings   Concept Check Questions

1.   It is noticed that a small change in price has a big impact on demand for a product. This means the demand is:

    A.   elastic, with a flat demand curve.

    B.   elastic, with a steep demand curve.

    C.   inelastic, with a flat demand curve.

    D.   inelastic, with a steep demand curve.

---

2.   A natural disaster will often cause:

    A.   a shift in the supply curve to the left.

    B.   a shift in the supply curve to the right.

    C.   a move to the left along the supply curve.

    D.   a move to the right along the supply curve.

---

3.   If the GDP deflator in a country has risen from 100 in 1985, to 130 in 2005 and nominal GDP has risen from $85 billion to $125 billion then the change in real GDP over the period is *closest* to:

    A.   a fall of 3.9%.

    B.   an increase of 13.1%.

    C.   an increase of 17.1%.

    D.   an increase of 62.5%.

4.   Which of the following statements is **CORRECT** regarding gross national product (GNP) and gross domestic product (GDP)?

A.   GNP and GDP are both the same, but different terms are used in different countries.

B.   GNP is GDP less the income of foreigners in the country plus the income earned by the country's citizens overseas.

C.   GNP is GDP less depreciation costs.

D.   GNP is calculated using the expenditure approach and GDP using the income approach.

5.   Which of the following would cause a shift in aggregate demand?

I.   An increase in real interest rates.
II.   New technology increasing productivity.
III.   A change in inflationary expectations.
IV.   A significant change in the exchange rate.

A.   II only.

B.   I and III only.

C.   I, III and IV only.

D.   All of the above.

6.   When economic output is less than the economy's potential, which of the following will act as a self-correcting mechanism?

A.   Fiscal stimulus.

B.   Real interest rates will decline.

C.   Real resource prices will rise.

D.   Rising inflation.

7.   The Keynesian model implies that:

A.   market forces are sufficient to ensure that the economy operates at the full employment level in the long term.

B.   adjusting money supply is the primary tool that should be used to stimulate aggregate demand.

C.   adjusting interest rates is the primary tool that should be used to stimulate aggregate demand.

D.   macroeconomic policy should focus on maintaining aggregate expenditures at the level that leads to full employment .

8.   If the marginal propensity to consume (MPC) is 0.7 and investment spending is increased by $3 billion then the additional income generated is closest to:

A. $3.33 billion.

B. $4.28 billion.

C. $7.00 billion.

D. $10.00 billion

Introductory Readings   Concept Check Answers

1.   It is noticed that a small change in price has a big impact on demand for a product. This means the demand is:

A.   elastic, with a flat demand curve.

B.   elastic, with a steep demand curve.

C.   inelastic, with a flat demand curve.

D.   inelastic, with a steep demand curve.

Correct Answer: 1.   A
Demand is elastic since it is highly responsive to a change in price, this will lead to a flat demand
  curve.

---

2.   A natural disaster will often cause:

A.   a shift in the supply curve to the left.

B.   a shift in the supply curve to the right.

C.   a move to the left along the supply curve.

D.   a move to the right along the supply curve.

Correct Answer: 2.   A
The supply curve shifts to the left as supply is decreased. This will in turn increase the
  equilibrium price.

3.   If the GDP deflator in a country has risen from 100 in 1985, to 130 in 2005 and nominal GDP has risen from $85 billion to $125 billion then the change in real GDP over the period is *closest* to:

    A.   a fall of 3.9%.

    B.   an increase of 13.1%.

    C.   an increase of 17.1%.

    D.   an increase of 62.5%.

Correct Answer: 3.   B
Real GDP (2004) = $125 billion x (100/130) = $96.15 billion
This is an increase of 13.1%

4.   Which of the following statements is **CORRECT** regarding gross national product (GNP) and gross domestic product (GDP)?

    A.   GNP and GDP are both the same, but different terms are used in different countries.

    B.   GNP is GDP less the income of foreigners in the country plus the income earned by the country's citizens overseas.

    C.   GNP is GDP less depreciation costs.

    D.   GNP is calculated using the expenditure approach and GDP using the income approach.

Correct Answer: 4.   B

5.   Which of the following would cause a shift in aggregate demand?
I.   An increase in real interest rates.
II.   New technology increasing productivity.
III.   A change in inflationary expectations.
IV.   A significant change in the exchange rate.
    A.   II only.

    B.   I and III only.

    C.   I, III and IV only.

    D.   All of the above.

Correct Answer: 5.   C
Item II would lead to a shift in the supply curve.

---

6.   When economic output is less than the economy's potential, which of the following will act as a self-correcting mechanism?
    A.   Fiscal stimulus.

    B.   Real interest rates will decline.

    C.   Real resource prices will rise.

    D.   Rising inflation.

Correct Answer: 6.   B
The main self-correcting mechanisms will be the fall in real interest rates and resource prices (including labor costs).

7.   The Keynesian model implies that:

A.   market forces are sufficient to ensure that the economy operates at the full employment level in the long term.

B.   adjusting money supply is the primary tool that should be used to stimulate aggregate demand.

C.   adjusting interest rates is the primary tool that should be used to stimulate aggregate demand.

D.   macroeconomic policy should focus on maintaining aggregate expenditures at the level that leads to full employment .

Correct Answer: 7.   D

---

8.   If the marginal propensity to consume (MPC) is 0.7 and investment spending is increased by $3 billion then the additional income generated is closest to:

A. $3.33 billion.

B. $4.28 billion.

C. $7.00 billion.

D. $10.00 billion

Correct Answer: 8.   D
The expenditure multiplier is 1/(1 – 0.7) or 3.33. Therefore the additional income is $3 billion x 3.33 or $10 billion.

STUDY SESSION 4

Economics: Macroeconomic Analysis

Overview

Economics have a guideline weighting of 10% of the exam questions. That is not a lot of questions for three study sessions but the material is relatively straightforward. Study Session 4 focuses on macroeconomics, 5 on microeconomics and 6 on global economic analysis.

For candidates who have studied economics or have knowledge of the basic concepts you will not need to spend much time on the Introduction. The Introduction is based on five chapters and covers the laws of supply and demand, market equilibrium, the markets for labor, loanable funds and foreign exchange, and the impact of government controls, black markets and taxes on supply and demand, measuring GDP and other measures of output and income, inflation, factors that affect aggregate demand and supply, and the basics of Keynesian economics.

It is important to note that the CFA Institute states that examination questions are drawn mainly from the subsequent Reading Assignments.

In Study Session 4 the Reading Assignments look at the key issues in macroeconomics – the study of economic growth and changes in levels of output, employment and prices. Initially we define and explain how the main indicators of the state of the economy are measured: the main indicators include demand and supply, inflation and unemployment. We then move on to examining how government policy can affect stability and economic growth. This is a key part of the Study Session, candidates need to understand the impact of changes in fiscal and monetary policies on the economy in both the short and long run, and be able to differentiate between the impact when policy changes are anticipated or unanticipated.

Reading Assignments

Economics: Private and Public Choice, 10th edition, James D. Gwartney, Richard L. Stroup, Russell S. Sobel, and David A. Macpherson (South-Western, 2003)

14.	"Economic Fluctuations, Unemployment, and Inflation," Ch. 8
15.	"Fiscal Policy," Ch. 12, pp. 269-283
16.	"Money and the Banking System," Ch. 13
17.	"Modern Macroeconomics: Monetary Policy," Ch. 14
18.	"Stabilization Policy, Output, and Employment," Ch. 15, pp. 348–362

14   Economic Fluctuations, Unemployment and Inflation

Learning Outcome Statements (LOS)

14-a	**Explain** the phases of the business cycle.
14-b	**Discuss** the problems in measuring unemployment and **describe** the three types of unemployment.
14-c	**Explain** full employment and the natural rate of unemployment.
14-d	**Define** inflation, **discuss** its causes, **distinguish** between anticipated and unanticipated inflation, and **discuss** the harmful effects of both on economic activity.

Introduction

This Reading identifies the different phases of the business cycle and how GDP, inflation and unemployment are key indicators of the stage in the business cycle. We look at how inflation and unemployment are defined and measured. Candidates will need to be define inflation and describe the harmful effects of unanticipated inflation.

14   Concept Check Questions

1.   Which of the following is **NOT** a stage of the business cycle?

    A.   Contraction.

    B.   Expansion.

    C.   Maturity.

    D.   Trough.

---

2.   If the CPI price index was 75 last year and 82 this year, then the annual inflation rate is *closest* to:

    A.   7.0%.

    B.   8.2%.

    C.   8.5%.

    D.   9.3%.

---

3.   Identify the a single stage of the business cycle?

    A.   Peak.

    B.   Inflation.

    C.   Maturity.

    D.   Activity.

14   Concept Check Answers

1.   Which of the following is **NOT** a stage of the business cycle?

   A.   Contraction.

   B.   Expansion.

   C.   Maturity.

   D.   Trough.

Correct Answer: 1.   C
The four stages are: peak, contraction, trough and expansion.

---

2.   If the CPI price index was 75 last year and 82 this year, then the annual inflation rate is *closest* to:

   A.   7.0%.

   B.   8.2%.

   C.   8.5%.

   D.   9.3%.

Correct Answer: 2.   D
The inflation rate is [(82 - 75)/75] x 100 = 9.33%

3.   Which of the following is a stage of the business cycle?

   A.   Peak.

   B.   Inflation.

   C.   Maturity.

   D.   Activity.

Correct Answer: 3.   A
The four stages are: peak, contraction, trough and expansion.

15   Fiscal Policy

Learning Outcome Statements (LOS)

15-a	**Explain** the process by which, according to the Keynesian view, fiscal policy affects aggregate demand and aggregate supply.
15-b	**Explain** the importance of the timing of changes in fiscal policy and the difficulties in achieving proper timing.
15-c	**Discuss** the impact of expansionary and restrictive fiscal policies based on the basic Keynesian model, the crowding-out model, the new classical model, and supply-side model.
15-d	**Identify** automatic stabilizers and **explain** how such stabilizers work.

Introduction

This Reading investigates the impact of changes in fiscal policy on output, prices and employment, assuming monetary policy is constant. Different economic models – Keynesian, crowding-out, new classical and supply-side models disagree on the impact of an expansionary or restrictive fiscal policy and the candidate needs to be familiar with the effectiveness of fiscal policy according to the four models. This section also looks at automatic stabilizers that take effect without a change in fiscal policy.

15   Concept Check Questions

1.   New classical economists believe that:

A.   increasing the budget deficit to stimulate growth will be less effective than the Keynesian model suggests since interest rates will rise.

B.   increasing the budget deficit will not increase aggregate demand since consumers anticipate increases in future tax rates.

C.   changing marginal tax rates has an important effect on aggregate supply.

D.   the government should adopt a restrictive fiscal policy when an inflationary boom is anticipated.

2.   Which of the following is an automatic stabilizer?

A.   Corporate profit tax.

B.   Interest rates.

C.   Exchange rates.

D.   Inflation rates.

3.   The crowding-out model says:

A.   increasing budget deficits to stimulate growth has no effect on economic activity.

B.   increasing budget deficits to stimulate growth will be lead to a decline in net exports.

C.   increasing budget deficits to stimulate growth will be financed by higher savings rates.

D.   the effect of increasing budget deficits to stimulate growth will be dampened by the negative impact of higher interest rates on private spending.

15   Concept Check Answers

1.   New classical economists believe that:

A.   increasing the budget deficit to stimulate growth will be less effective than the Keynesian model suggests since interest rates will rise.

B.   increasing the budget deficit will not increase aggregate demand since consumers anticipate increases in future tax rates.

C.   changing marginal tax rates has an important effect on aggregate supply.

D.   the government should adopt a restrictive fiscal policy when an inflationary boom is anticipated.

Correct Answer: 1.   B
A. is the crowding-out effect, C is supply-side economics, D. is the Keynesian model.

---

2.   Which of the following is an automatic stabilizer?

A.   Corporate profit tax.

B.   Interest rates.

C.   Exchange rates.

D.   Inflation rates.

Correct Answer: 2.   A
Automatic stabilizers will tend to expand a budget deficit during a recession and contract a budget deficit in a boom. They include unemployment benefits, corporate and personal taxes.

3.   The crowding-out model says:

   A.   increasing budget deficits to stimulate growth has no effect on economic activity.

   B.   increasing budget deficits to stimulate growth will be lead to a decline in net exports.

   C.   increasing budget deficits to stimulate growth will be financed by higher savings rates.

   D.   the effect of increasing budget deficits to stimulate growth will be dampened by the negative impact of higher interest rates on private spending.

Correct Answer: 3.   **D**

16   Money and the Banking System

Learning Outcome Statements (LOS)

16-a	**Explain** the relationship among the required reserve ratio, the potential deposit expansion multiplier, and deposit expansion multiplier.
16-b	**Describe** the role of a country's central bank and the tools that a central bank can use to control the money supply, and **explain** how a central bank can use monetary tools to implement monetary policy.
16-c	**Discuss** potential problems in measuring an economy's money supply.

Introduction

We now look at how money supply is defined and how the banking system operates. In particular we examine how the central bank in the US, the Federal Reserve System, controls money supply. This section provides the foundation for the next two Readings when we focus on monetary policy and its impact on an economy.

Money supply

Two of the most widely used measures of money supply are:

M1 = currency in circulation + demand and other checkable deposits + travelers' checks

M1 is essentially money and assets that can be converted into money at parity.

M2 = M1 + savings and time deposits (less than $100,000) + money market mutual funds

M2 is a broader definition that includes assets that can be easily converted to checking deposits or cash.

The banking system

The banking system in the US is under the jurisdiction of the Federal Reserve System.

The three institutions in the banking sector are:

1. Commercial banks.
2. Savings and loans - accept deposits in exchange for shares that pay dividends.
3. Credit unions - cooperative financial institutions for groups of individuals.

16   Concept Check Questions

1.   If the reserve ratio is lowered from 5% to 3% then the new potential deposit multiplier is *closest* to:

     A.   3.0.

     B.   20.0.

     C.   33.3.

     D.   50.0.

---

2.   If the central bank wishes to implement an expansionary monetary policy it would consider:

     A.   selling US securities.

     B.   raising the discount rate.

     C.   increasing the budget deficit.

     D.   reducing reserve requirements.

16   Concept Check Answers

1.   If the reserve ratio is lowered from 5% to 3% then the new potential deposit multiplier is *closest* to:

    A.   3.0.

    B.   20.0.

    C.   33.3.

    D.   50.0.

Correct Answer: 1.   **C**
The potential deposit expansion multiplier is the reciprocal of the reserve ratio which is $1/0.03 =$ 33.33

---

2.   If the central bank wishes to implement an expansionary monetary policy it would consider:

    A.   selling US securities.

    B.   raising the discount rate.

    C.   increasing the budget deficit.

    D.   reducing reserve requirements.

Correct Answer: 2.   **D**
The principal tools that the Fed has to expand the money supply are to reduce the reserve requirements, purchase U.S. securities and lower the discount rate.

17   Modern Macroeconomics: Monetary Policy

Learning Outcome Statements (LOS)

17-a	**Discuss** the determinants of money demand and supply.
17-b	**Discuss** how anticipation of the effects of monetary policy can influence the policy's effectiveness.
17-c	**Identify** the components of the equation of exchange, and **discuss** the implications of the equation for monetary policy, **describe** the quantity theory of money, and **discuss** its implications for the determination of inflation.
17-d	**Compare** and **contrast** the impact of anticipated or unanticipated monetary policy on the inflation rate, real output, employment and interest rates.

Introduction

A successful monetary policy is critical to providing a stable environment for an economy to grow and to provide high levels of employment. We start the section with looking at the factors that affect the demand and supply of money. We then examine how changes in monetary policy affect the economy in terms of interest rates, output, prices and employment. It is important that candidates understand the short and long-run effects of expansionary and restrictive monetary policies.

17   Concept Check Questions

1.   The demand for money curve shows that the quantity of money demanded is:
   A.   positively related to GDP growth.
   B.   inversely related to GDP growth.
   C.   positively related to interest rates.
   D.   inversely related to interest rates.

---

2.   The short-term impact of a move to a restrictive monetary policy, when the policy is anticipated, include:
   A.   an increase in short-term interest rates.
   B.   no change in real interest rates.
   C.   an increase in the inflation rate.
   D.   a decrease in real output.

3.   The quantity theory of money says that an increase in money supply will lead to:

   A.   an increase in the velocity of money.

   B.   an increase in prices.

   C.   an increase in output.

   D.   an increase in employment.

17   Concept Check Answers

1.   The demand for money curve shows that the quantity of money demanded is:
   A.   positively related to GDP growth.
   B.   inversely related to GDP growth.
   C.   positively related to interest rates.
   D.   inversely related to interest rates.

Correct Answer: 1.   D
Demand for money measures the relationship between interest rates and the amount of money that people want to hold.

---

2.   The short-term impact of a move to a restrictive monetary policy, when the policy is anticipated, include:
   A.   an increase in short-term interest rates.
   B.   no change in real interest rates.
   C.   an increase in the inflation rate.
   D.   a decrease in real output.

Correct Answer: 2.   B

---

3.   The quantity theory of money says that an increase in money supply will lead to:
   A.   an increase in the velocity of money.
   B.   an increase in prices.
   C.   an increase in output.
   D.   an increase in employment.

Correct Answer: 3.   B
The quantity theory of money says a change in money supply will lead to the same change in price levels, since velocity and output are unaffected by the quantity of money. This is derived from $MV = PY$.

18   Stabilization Policy, Output and Employment

Learning Outcome Statements (LOS)

18-a	**Describe** the composition and use of the index of leading economic indicators.
18-b	**Discuss** the time lags that may influence the performance of discretionary monetary and fiscal policy.
18-c	**Contrast** the adaptive expectations hypothesis to the rational expectations hypothesis and **discuss** implications on prices and output under the two hypotheses when there are changes in macroeconomic policies.
18-d	**Distinguish** between an activist and a non-activist strategy for stabilization policy.

Introduction

We can now build on the earlier Readings on fiscal and monetary policy to study the impact of expansionary and restrictive policies and discuss the effectiveness of policies in stabilizing the economy. We examine the different theories on how expectations are formed and how expectations decide the effectiveness of policy changes. Candidates also need to be able to differentiate between activist and non-activist approaches to stabilizing the economy.

18   Concept Check Questions

1.   GDP has been growing at an average of 0.5% annualized over the last four quarters but economic indicators suggest that the rate of growth is about to slow down. Under the rational-expectations hypothesis GDP in the next quarter is forecast to be:

    A.   lower than 0.5%.

    B.   0.5%.

    C.   higher than 0.5%.

    D.   we cannot forecast GDP using the rational-expectations hypothesis.

---

2.   If the growth rate in the economy is decelerating then, under the adaptive expectations hypothesis, people are most likely to:

    A.   overestimate the future growth rate.

    B.   underestimate the future growth rate.

18   Concept Check Answers

1.   GDP has been growing at an average of 0.5% annualized over the last four quarters but economic indicators suggest that the rate of growth is about to slow down. Under the rational-expectations hypothesis GDP in the next quarter is forecast to be:

    A.   lower than 0.5%.

    B.   0.5%.

    C.   higher than 0.5%.

    D.   we cannot forecast GDP using the rational-expectations hypothesis.

Correct Answer: 1.   A

---

2.   If the growth rate in the economy is decelerating then, under the adaptive expectations hypothesis, people are most likely to:

    A.   overestimate the future growth rate.

    B.   underestimate the future growth rate.

Correct Answer: 2.   A

Under adaptive expectations most people will expect past growth rates to continue so they will overestimate the future growth rate.

STUDY SESSION 5

Economics: Microeconomic Analysis

Overview

In this Study Session the Reading Assignments focus on the key issues in microeconomics - the study of consumers' choices and their influence on demand, how firms operate and their competitive environment, and the choices of resource suppliers. Different market structures are covered - their characteristics and how they determine firms' decision-making on pricing their products and the optimum output levels.

In the final Reading we consider the relationship between the demand for funds and interest rates, and how market interest rates are determined.

Reading Assignments

Economics: Private and Public Choice, 10th edition, James D. Gwartney, Richard L. Stroup, Russell S. Sobel, and David A. Macpherson (South-Western, 2003)

19.   "Demand and Consumer Choice," Ch. 19, including addendum "Consumer Choice and Indifference Curves"

20.   "Costs and the Supply of Goods," Ch. 20

21.   "Price Takers and the Competitive Process," Ch. 21

22.   "Price-Searcher Markets with Low Entry Barriers," Ch. 22

23.   "Price-Searcher Markets with High Entry Barriers," Ch. 23

24.   "The Supply of and Demand for Productive Resources" Ch. 24

Fundamentals of Financial Management, 10th edition, Eugene F. Brigham and Joel F. Houston (Dryden, 1998)

25.   "The Financial Environment: Markets, Institutions, and Interest Rates," Ch. 4, pp. 130-143

19 Demand and Consumer Choice, including Consumer Choice and Indifference Curves

Learning Outcome Statements (LOS)

19-a	**Explain** the fundamental principles of consumer choice and **discuss** marginal utility, marginal benefit, and the demand curve.
19-b	**Distinguish** between the income effect and the substitution effect.
19-c	**Discuss** the determinants of price and income elasticity of demand, and **explain** the concepts of price and income elasticity of supply.
19-d	**Calculate** and **interpret** price and income elasticity of demand, and **explain** why the price elasticity of demand tends to increase in the long run.
19-e	**Discuss** the characteristics of consumer indifference curves, the role of the consumption-opportunity constraint, and the budget constraint in indifference curve analysis.

Introduction

This Reading looks at consumer choice and the factors that affect consumer demand. Candidates need to understand the concepts of elasticity and be able to compute price elasticity (change in quantity demanded when the price changes) and income elasticity (change in quantity demanded when income changes) of demand. The Reading finishes with a discussion of indifference curves (points on an indifference curve are of equal benefit to a consumer) and how they determine optimal combinations of goods for a consumer to purchase.

19   Concept Check Questions

1.   Which of the following would lead to an increase in demand for wine?
      I.   An increase in consumer incomes.

      II.   Beer prices increase.

      III.   An increase in bottling costs.

      IV.   A rapid increase in the volumes of wine being produced in Eastern Europe.

      V.   An increase in the price of wine.

      A.   I and II only.

      B.   II and IV only.

      C.   I, II and V only.

      D.   All of the above.

---

2.   If the demand elasticity for a good is relatively inelastic it means that:
      A.   a percentage increase in price will result in a smaller percentage reduction in sales volume.

      B.   a percentage increase in price will result in the same percentage reduction in sales volume.

      C.   a percentage increase in price will result in a larger percentage reduction in sales volume.

      D.   a percentage increase in price will result in no sales being made.

---

3.   Points on a consumer indifference curve represent:
      A.   the consumption-opportunity constraint.

      B.   combinations of goods that are equally preferred by the consumer.

      C.   the demand for a product at different price levels.

      D.   the demand for a product at different income levels.

19   Concept Check Answers

1.   Which of the following would lead to an increase in demand for wine?

I.   An increase in consumer incomes.

II.   Beer prices increase.

III.   An increase in bottling costs.

IV.   A rapid increase in the volumes of wine being produced in Eastern Europe.

V.   An increase in the price of wine.

A.   I and II only.

B.   II and IV only.

C.   I, II and V only.

D.   All of the above.

Correct Answer: 1.   A
III and IV mainly affect the supply of wine. V affects the change in quantity demanded and
     therefore leads to a movement along the same demand curve.

---

2.   If the demand elasticity for a good is relatively inelastic it means that:

A.   a percentage increase in price will result in a smaller percentage reduction in sales
     volume.

B.   a percentage increase in price will result in the same percentage reduction in sales
     volume.

C.   a percentage increase in price will result in a larger percentage reduction in sales
     volume.

D.   a percentage increase in price will result in no sales being made.

Correct Answer: 2.   A
B. is unitary elasticity, C. is relatively elastic, D. is perfectly elastic.

3.   Points on a consumer indifference curve represent:

    A.   the consumption-opportunity constraint.

    B.   combinations of goods that are equally preferred by the consumer.

    C.   the demand for a product at different price levels.

    D.   the demand for a product at different income levels.

Correct Answer: 3.   **B**

20 Costs and the Supply of Goods

Learning Outcome Statements (LOS)

20-a	**Describe** the principal-agent problem of the firm, **distinguish** among the types of business firm, and **discuss** the major factors promoting cost efficiency and customer service.
20-b	**Distinguish** between 1) explicit costs and implicit costs, 2) economic profit and accounting profit, and 3) the short run and the long run in production.
20-c	**Define** and **identify** opportunity costs, fixed costs, variable costs, marginal costs, average costs, and sunk costs, and **differentiate** between economic costs and accounting costs.
20-d	**State** the law of diminishing returns and **explain** its impact on a company's costs.
20-e	**Describe** the shapes of the short-run marginal cost, average variable cost, average fixed cost, and average total cost curves.
20-f	**Define** economies and diseconomies of scale, **explain** how each is possible, and **relate** each to shapes of long-run average total cost curves.
20-g	**Describe** both the factors that cause cost curves to shift and the economic way of thinking about costs.

Introduction

We now move on to looking at firms and their cost bases. First of all candidates have to be able to distinguish between different types of costs, in particular explicit and implicit costs, and the difference between accounting and economic profits. They also have to be able to interpret the components of short-run and long-run costs and relate these to a firm's total cost curves. Finally they need to be able to make the link between the cost structure of firms and the impact on supply.

20   Concept Check Questions

1.   Economic profit:

    A.   takes into account explicit costs only.

    B.   takes into account implicit costs only.

    C.   is accounting profit less implicit costs.

    D.   is accounting profit less explicit costs.

---

2.   The average total cost will generally be:

    A.   high for small output levels due to high marginal costs.

    B.   high for small output levels due to high average fixed costs.

    C.   low for small output levels due to low marginal costs.

    D.   low for small output levels due to low average fixed costs.

---

3.   Which of the following factors would NOT lead to a shift in a firm's cost curve?

    A.   Increase in the annual business license fee.

    B.   Increase in production volumes.

    C.   Stricter regulations affecting the firm.

    D.   Improvements in technology.

20   Concept Check Answers

1.   Economic profit:

    A.   takes into account explicit costs only.

    B.   takes into account implicit costs only.

    C.   is accounting profit less implicit costs.

    D.   is accounting profit less explicit costs.

Correct Answer: 1.   C

Economic profit is after explicit and implicit costs have been taken into account, accounting profit
    is usually after explicit costs only.

---

2.   The average total cost will generally be:

    A.   high for small output levels due to high marginal costs.

    B.   high for small output levels due to high average fixed costs.

    C.   low for small output levels due to low marginal costs.

    D.   low for small output levels due to low average fixed costs.

Correct Answer: 2.   B

The average total cost curve is usually U-shaped.

---

3.   Which of the following factors would NOT lead to a shift in a firm's cost curve?

    A.   Increase in the annual business license fee.

    B.   Increase in production volumes.

    C.   Stricter regulations affecting the firm.

    D.   Improvements in technology.

Correct Answer: 3.   B

Changes in resource prices, tax and regulations and technology advances are the major reasons
    for a shift in the cost curve.

21   Price Takers and the Competitive Process

Learning Outcome Statements (LOS)

21-a	**Discuss** the conditions that characterize pure competition (a price taker market) and **explain** how and why price takers maximize profits at the quantity for which marginal cost, price, and marginal revenue are equal.
21-b	**Calculate** and **interpret** the total revenue and the marginal revenue for a price taker, **explain** the relationship between total revenue, total cost, price, marginal revenue, marginal cost, and the profit maximizing out put level.
21-c	**Explain** the decision by price takers to continue to operate, temporarily shut down, or go out of business, when faced with price below average total cost.
21-d	**Describe** the short-run supply curves for a company and for a competitive market.
21-e	**Explain** the impact on prices and output of increases or decreases in demand in a competitive market.
21-f	**Contrast** the role of constant-cost, increasing-cost, and decreasing-cost industries in determining the shape of a long-run market supply curve.
21-g	**Explain** the impact of time on the elasticity of market supply and **discuss** the role of profits and losses in a purely competitive market.

Introduction

We continue our analysis of firms by examining price-taker firms, these are firms who have to accept the market price for their products, otherwise their sales will disappear, so they face a perfectly elastic demand curve.   Candidates need to understand at what production level price-taker firms maximize profits and be able to describe the short-run and long-run supply curves for different types of price-taker industry.

21   Concept Check Questions

1.   A price-taker market is characterized by each of the following **EXCEPT**:

    A.   a large number of participants.

    B.   each participant has a small market share.

    C.   high entry barriers.

    D.   identical products.

---

2.   A profit maximizing price taker will expand output until marginal revenue equals:

    A.   market price.

    B.   average variable cost.

    C.   average total cost.

    D.   marginal cost.

3.   A decreasing-cost industry has a supply curve that:

   A.   slopes upwards to the right.

   B.   is horizontal.

   C.   slopes downwards to the right.

21   Concept Check Answers

1.   A price-taker market is characterized by each of the following **EXCEPT**:
    A.   a large number of participants.
    B.   each participant has a small market share.
    C.   high entry barriers.
    D.   identical products.

Correct Answer: 1.   C

---

2.   A profit maximizing price taker will expand output until marginal revenue equals:
    A.   market price.
    B.   average variable cost.
    C.   average total cost.
    D.   marginal cost.

Correct Answer: 2.   D
Output will be expanded until $P = MR = MC$. Marginal revenue always equals market price.

---

3.   A decreasing-cost industry has a supply curve that:
    A.   slopes upwards to the right.
    B.   is horizontal.
    C.   slopes downwards to the right.

Correct Answer: 3.   C
Decreasing-cost industries often have suppliers that use mass production techniques leading to lower costs as volumes expand.

22   Price-Searcher Markets with Low Entry Barriers

Learning Outcome Statements (LOS)

22-a	**Describe** the conditions that characterize monopolistic competition (a competitive price-searcher market).
22-b	**Explain** how firms choose price and output combinations in monopolistic competition.
22-c	**Summarize** the debate about the allocative efficiency of monopolistic competition with low barriers to entry, including the implications of contestable markets and entrepreneurship.
22-d	**Discuss** the principle of price discrimination and **illustrate** how a firm might apply this principle to gain from such a practice.

Introduction

Price–searcher markets are ones which face downward–sloping demand curves for their products, so if they increase prices they will see demand fall but not completely disappear. Most firms are price searchers, they are looking to maximise profit and they decide what price to charge and how much to produce of their product. In this Reading we look at price-searcher markets with low entry barriers which can lead to a highly competitive environment. Again candidates have to understand how firms make decisions on levels of output and evaluate the efficiency of price-searcher markets.

22   Concept Check Questions

1.   Which of the following is a characteristic of a competitive price-searcher market?

    A.   firms produce identical products.

    B.   firms cannot sell products above the market price.

    C.   the market is purely competitive.

    D.   firms have downward sloping demand curves.

2.   A profit maximizing firm in a competitive price-searcher market will expand output until marginal revenue equals:

    A.   market price.

    B.   average variable cost.

    C.   average total cost.

    D.   marginal cost.

3.   Long-run economic profits can be made by:

    A.   price takers and price searchers in competitive markets.

    B.   price takers only.

    C.   price searchers in competitive markets only.

    D.   neither price takers nor price searchers in competitive markets.

22   Concept Check Answers

1.   Which of the following is a characteristic of a competitive price-searcher market?
   A.   firms produce identical products.
   B.   firms cannot sell products above the market price.
   C.   the market is purely competitive.
   D.   firms have downward sloping demand curves.

Correct Answer: 1.   D
A, B and C are all characteristics of a price-taker market.

---

2.   A profit maximizing firm in a competitive price-searcher market will expand output until marginal revenue equals:
   A.   market price.
   B.   average variable cost.
   C.   average total cost.
   D.   marginal cost.

Correct Answer: 2.   D
Output will be expanded until MR = MC.

---

3.   Long-run economic profits can be made by:
   A.   price takers and price searchers in competitive markets.
   B.   price takers only.
   C.   price searchers in competitive markets only.
   D.   neither price takers nor price searchers in competitive markets.

Correct Answer: 3.   D

23   Price-Searcher Markets with High Entry Barriers

Learning Outcome Statements (LOS)

23-a	**Discuss** entry barriers that may protect companies against competition from potential market entrants.
23-b	**Differentiate** between a monopoly and an oligopoly.
23-c	**Describe** how a profit-maximizing monopolist sets prices and determines output and **discuss** price and output under oligopoly, with and without collusion.
23-d	**Discuss** why oligopolists have a strong incentive to collude and to cheat on collusive agreements and **discuss** the obstacles to collusion among oligopolistic companies.
23-e	**Describe** the different defects that can occur in a market with high entry barriers.
23-f	**Describe** government policy alternatives that are intended to reduce the problems stemming from high barriers to entry.
23-g	**Contrast** the pricing and output decisions of firms in pure competition, monopolistic competition, oligopoly, and monopoly with reference to quantity produced, price, marginal revenue, marginal cost, demand and average total cost.

Introduction

Price-searcher markets with high entry barriers (such as legal barriers, patents or economies of scale) have a limited number of participants in the market. In the case of only one participant it is a monopoly, in the case of a few firms it is an oligopoly. Candidates need to recognise the characteristics of monopolies and oligopolies and discuss how they set output levels. Additionally they need to understand the inefficiencies created by entry barriers and look at the rationale behind government policies that protect industries.

23   Concept Check Questions

1.   Which of the following statements regarding a monopoly is **FALSE**?

    A.   There are high barriers to entry.

    B.   There is a single seller of a well-defined product.

    C.   It is a price-searcher market.

    D.   The demand curve is horizontal.

---

2.   Which of the following statements regarding an oligopoly is **FALSE**?

    A.   There are high barriers to entry.

    B.   There is a single producer of a well-defined product.

    C.   There are substantial economies of scale.

    D.   It is a price-searcher market.

3.   Which of the following is a government response to the problems arising from high barriers to entry to a market?

    A.   I.   Reduce tariffs that limit competition.

    B.   II.   Break up the monopoly into smaller companies.

    C.   III.   Regulate the price charged by the monopoly.

    D.   I.   Reduce tariffs that limit competition.

          II.   Break up the monopoly into smaller companies.

          III.   Regulate the price charged by the monopoly.

23 Concept Check Answers

1. Which of the following statements regarding a monopoly is **FALSE**?

    A. There are high barriers to entry.

    B. There is a single seller of a well-defined product.

    C. It is a price-searcher market.

    D. The demand curve is horizontal.

Correct Answer: 1.   D
The demand curve is downward sloping.

---

2. Which of the following statements regarding an oligopoly is **FALSE**?

    A. There are high barriers to entry.

    B. There is a single producer of a well-defined product.

    C. There are substantial economies of scale.

    D. It is a price-searcher market.

Correct Answer: 2.   B
In an oligopoly there are a few producers who are interdependent.

---

3. Which of the following is a government response to the problems arising from high barriers to entry to a market?

    A. I.   Reduce tariffs that limit competition.

    B. II.   Break up the monopoly into smaller companies.

    C. III. Regulate the price charged by the monopoly.

    D. I.   Reduce tariffs that limit competition.

    II.   Break up the monopoly into smaller companies.

    III. Regulate the price charged by the monopoly.

Correct Answer: 3.   D

24   The Supply of and Demand for Productive Resources

Learning Outcome Statements (LOS)

24-a	**Explain** the relationship between the price of a resource and the quantity demanded of that resource with reference to supply, demand, and derived demand.
24-b	**Identify** and **describe** three factors that may cause shifts in the demand curve for a resource.
24-c	**Define** marginal product, marginal revenue, value of marginal product (VMP), the marginal revenue product (MRP) of a resource and **explain** the relation between MRD and demand for that resource.
24-d	**Explain** the necessary conditions to achieve the cost-minimizing employment levels for two or more variable resources.
24-e	**Discuss** the factors that influence resource supply and demand in the short run and long run.

Introduction

Having examined the choices of consumers and firms, we turn to the suppliers of resources. These are individuals or firms that are motivated by the income they receive for supplying the resource. Supply and demand for the resource decide the price that they can charge. The candidate is expected to understand the factors that drive demand and how the marginal revenue product from a resource determines demand.

24 Concept Check Questions

1. The short-run supply curve for accountants is generally:

    A.   elastic.

    B.   inelastic.

---

2. If the price of a resource increases then the quantity demanded will be:

    A.   lower in the long run than short run.

    B.   lower in the short run than long run.

3.   The following table provides data on the number of units produced per day depending on the number of workers employed, other costs are fixed.

Number of Workers	Units produced
1	15
2	28
3	39
4	48
5	55

Units are sold at $10 each. If wage rates are $100 per day how many workers should the firm employ to maximize profits?

A.   1

B.   2

C.   3

D.   4

4.   Using the data in the previous question, if wage rates increase to $120 per day how many workers should the firm employ to maximize profits?

A.   1

B.   2

C.   3

D.   4

24   Concept Check Answers

1.   The short-run supply curve for accountants is generally:

   A.   elastic.

   B.   inelastic.

Correct Answer: 1.   B
In the short run the availability of new accountants, even if wages paid to accountant increase, will be limited. In the long run the supply is more elastic as more people will train to be accountants.

---

2.   If the price of a resource increases then the quantity demanded will be:

   A.   lower in the long run than short run.

   B.   lower in the short run than long run.

Correct Answer: 2.   A
In the long run producers have more time to adapt to the change in price and find substitute resources.

3.   The following table provides data on the number of units produced per day depending on the number of workers employed, other costs are fixed.

Number of Workers	Units produced
1	15
2	28
3	39
4	48
5	55

Units are sold at $10 each. If wage rates are $100 per day how many workers should the firm employ to maximize profits?

    A.   1

    B.   2

    C.   3

    D.   4

Correct Answer: 3.   C

Number of Workers	Units produced	MRP
1	15	$150
2	28	$130
3	39	$110
4	48	$90
5	55	$70

The MRP of the fourth worker is less than his wage, therefore the firm will employ three workers.

---

4.   Using the data in the previous question, if wage rates increase to $120 per day how many workers should the firm employ to maximize profits?

    A.   1

    B.   2

    C.   3

    D.   4

Correct Answer: 4.   B
The MRP of the third worker is less than his wage, therefore the firm will employ two workers.

25   The Financial Environment: Markets, Institutions and Interest Rates

Learning Outcome Statements (LOS)

25-a	**Identify** and **explain** the factors that influence the supply of and demand for capital.
25-b	**Describe** the role of interest rates in allocating capital.
25-c	**Explain** how the supply of and demand for funds determine interest rates.
25-d	**Discuss** the factors that cause the supply of and demand curves for funds to shift.
25-e	**Distinguish** between the real and the nominal risk-free rate of interest.
25-f	**Discuss** economic conditions that can change the real risk-free rate of interest.
25-g	**Explain** the effect of inflation on the real rate of return earned by financial securities and by physical assets.
25-h	**Describe** default risk, liquidity risk, and maturity risk premiums.
25-i	**Explain** interest rate risk and reinvestment rate risk.
25-j	**Explain** how inflation-indexed bonds can protect investors from inflation and maturity risk.

Introduction

This Reading looks at the supply and demand for funds and the link to interest rates. Candidates should be able to differentiate between nominal and real interest rates and the effect of inflation on required returns. We also explore how market interest rates are determined and the premium required for default risk, liquidity risk and maturity risk.

25 Concept Check Questions

1. If the current inflation rate is 5% per annum but inflation rates are expected to decline to an average of 3% over the next five years then the inflation premium on a five year bond will be:

    A. 2%.

    B. 3%.

    C. 5%.

    D. 15%.

2. The return on short-term U.S. Treasury bills is closest to:

    A. the real risk-free rate.

    B. the nominal risk-free rate.

3. In an economic recession which of the following is the most likely to be at high levels relative to its historic average?

    A. the risk-free rate.

    B. the real risk-free rate.

    C. the inflation premium.

    D. the default risk premium on AAA bonds.

25 Concept Check Answers

1. If the current inflation rate is 5% per annum but inflation rates are expected to decline to an average of 3% over the next five years then the inflation premium on a five year bond will be:

   A. 2%

   B. 3%

   C. 5%

   D. 15%

Correct Answer: 1.   B
The inflation premium is the expected annual inflation rate over the life of the bond of 3%.

---

2. The return on short-term U.S. Treasury bills is closest to:

   A. the real risk-free rate

   B. the nominal risk-free rate.

Correct Answer: 2.   B

---

3. In an economic recession which of the following is the most likely to be at high levels relative to its historic average?

   A. the risk-free rate.

   B. the real risk-free rate.

   C. the inflation premium.

   D. the default risk premium on AAA bonds.

Correct Answer: 3.   D
The risk of bankruptcy will be relatively high increasing the default risk premium. Interest rates and inflation rates will be a low levels reflecting low demand for capital.

STUDY SESSION 6

Economics: Global Economic Analysis

Overview

This is a relatively short Study Session focusing on international trade. There has been rapid growth in the number of cross border transactions and the Session starts with an explanation of the benefits of international trade and the largely negative impact of trade barriers (tariffs, quotas etc.) which are widely used to restrict international trade. It also looks at the mechanics of the foreign exchange markets, how exchange rates are quoted and the main theories explaining forward exchange rates including interest rate and purchasing power parity. Candidates are also expected to understand the impact of government monetary and fiscal policies on currencies and the other factors that make currencies depreciate or appreciate.

Reading Assignments

Economics: Private and Public Choice, 10th edition, James D. Gwartney, Richard L. Stroup, Russell S. Sobel, and David A. Macpherson (South-Western, 2003)

26.   "Gaining from International Trade," Ch. 17

International Investments, 5th edition, Bruno Solnik and Dennis McLeavey (Addison Wesley, 2004)

27.   "Foreign Exchange," Ch. 1

28.   "Foreign Exchange Parity Relations" Ch. 2, pp. 31–48

26. Gaining from International Trade

Learning Outcome Statements (LOS)

26-a	**State** the conditions under which a nation can gain from international trade in the context of both comparative and absolute advantage, and **describe** the benefits of international trade.
26-b	**Discuss** the effects of international trade on domestic supply and demand.
26-c	**Distinguish** between commonly used trade-restricting devices, including tariffs, quotas, voluntary export restraints, and exchange-rate controls and **explain** their impact on the domestic economy.
26-d	**Identify** who benefits and loses from the imposition of a tariff.
26-e	**Discuss** the three arguments to adopt trade restrictions and discuss popular fallacies related to trade restrictions.

Introduction

This Reading Assignment concentrates on the benefits for a nation if it exports goods where it has a comparative advantage (can produce goods at a lower opportunity cost than other nations) and import goods where it has a comparative disadvantage. This contributes to economic efficiency for the trading partners. However countries frequently impose trading barriers to protect domestic industries and candidates need to be aware of the beneficiaries and losers (usually the consumer) of barriers such as quotas, tariffs, export constraint and exchange-rate controls.

26 Concept Check Questions

1. The following data has been provided regarding the output per worker in Nation A and Nation B:

	Output per Worker per Day	
	Clothing	Electronics
A	1	2
B	2	3

Assume that other production costs are constant in each country and transportation costs are low. Which of the following statement(s) is/are **TRUE**?

I.   Nation B has an absolute advantage in the production of both clothing and electronics.

II. Both countries will gain if Nation A focuses on the production of clothing and Nation B on the production of electronics.

III. Both countries will gain if Nation A focuses on the production of electronics and Nation B on the production of clothing.

IV. Only Nation B can gain from trade between the two countries because it is a lower cost producer of radios and televisions.

    A.   II only.

    B.   I and II only.

    C.   I and III only.

    D.   I and IV only.

---

2. The following are all examples of trade restrictions **EXCEPT**:

    A.   import quotas.

    B.   special interest groups.

    C.   exchange rate controls.

    D.   tariffs.

---

3. Which of the following is a **CORRECT** statement regarding import quotas?

    A.   An import quota means that the government earns extra revenue from taxation.

    B.   Imports are taxed as a percentage of value.

    C.   Domestic producers can sell their products at a higher price.

    D.   Consumers will benefit from lower prices for the imported goods.

26 Concept Check Answers

1. The following data has been provided regarding the output per worker in Nation A and Nation B:

	Output per Worker per Day	
	Clothing	Electronics
A	1	2
B	2	3

Assume that other production costs are constant in each country and transportation costs are low. Which of the following statement(s) is/are **TRUE**?

I. Nation B has an absolute advantage in the production of both clothing and electronics.

II. Both countries will gain if Nation A focuses on the production of clothing and Nation B on the production of electronics.

III. Both countries will gain if Nation A focuses on the production of electronics and Nation B on the production of clothing.

IV. Only Nation B can gain from trade between the two countries because it is a lower cost producer of radios and televisions.

    A. II only.

    B. I and II only.

    C. I and III only.

    D. I and IV only.

Correct Answer: 1.   C

Although Nation B has the absolute advantage in the production of both products (i.e. it can produce both products more cheaply in terms of man hours), Nation A has a comparative advantage in the production of electronics. If Nation A switched its workers to producing electronics and Nation B switched its workers to producing clothing there will be an expansion in total output and both countries will gain.

---

2. The following are all examples of trade restrictions **EXCEPT**:

    A. import quotas.

    B. special interest groups.

    C. exchange rate controls.

    D. tariffs.

Correct Answer: 2.   B

3.   Which of the following is a **CORRECT** statement regarding import quotas?

   A.   An import quota means that the government earns extra revenue from taxation.

   B.   Imports are taxed as a percentage of value.

   C.   Domestic producers can sell their products at a higher price.

   D.   Consumers will benefit from lower prices for the imported goods.

Correct Answer: 3.   C
A and B refer to tariffs, not import quotas.

27 Foreign Exchange

Learning Outcome Statements (LOS)

27-a	**Define** direct and indirect methods of foreign exchange quotations and **convert** direct (indirect) foreign exchange quotations into indirect (direct) foreign exchange quotations.
27-b	**Calculate** and **interpret** the spread on a foreign currency quotation and **explain** how spreads on foreign currency quotations can differ as a result of market conditions, bank/dealer positions, and trading volume.
27-c	**Calculate** and **interpret** currency cross rates, given two spot exchange quotations involving three currencies.
27-d	**Distinguish** between the spot and forward markets for foreign exchange.
27-e	**Calculate** and **interpret** the spread on a forward foreign currency quotation and **explain** how spreads on forward foreign currency quotations can differ as a result of market conditions, bank/dealer positions, trading volume, and maturity/length of contract.
27-f	**Calculate** and **interpret** a forward discount or premium and **express** it as an annualized rate.
27-g	**Explain** interest rate parity and **illustrate** covered interest arbitrage.

Introduction

This Reading focuses on the mechanics of the foreign exchange markets or the interbank market where most transactions take place. Candidates have to be familiar with the ways that foreign exchange rates are quoted, and whether they are on a direct or indirect basis. Reasonably simple computations of cross rates, spreads on spot and forward exchange rates, and discounts and premiums on forward rates need to be mastered. Finally, it is important that you understand the relationship between interest rate differentials and forward and spot rates which is called interest rate parity. Again you must be prepared to do calculations based on the interest rate parity equation.

27   Concept Check Questions

1.   If, in the U.K., the quotation for Australian dollars is Aus\$/£ = 2.70 this is an example of:

    A.   a direct quotation.

    B.   an indirect quotation.

---

2.   The U.S. dollar is quoted against the Singapore dollar as S\$/US\$ = 1.7405 to 1.7420. The bid-ask percent spread is *closest* to:

    A.   0.0015%

    B.   0.0861%

    C.   0.1500%

    D.   8.6000%

3.   In a forward foreign exchange contract the contracted forward price:

    A.   is the spot rate when the contract is agreed.

    B.   is the spot rate when the contract matures.

    C.   reflects both the spot rate when the contract is agreed and the interest rate differential between the two currencies.

    D.   reflects both the spot rate when the contract matures and the interest rate differential between the two currencies.

---

4.   Which of the following statement(s) is/are **CORRECT** with respect to interest rate parity?

I.   Interest rate parity gives the opportunity for covered interest arbitrage.

II.   Countries with relatively high interest rates will have currencies that trade at forward premiums to currencies of countries with low interest rates.

III.   Interest differentials should be equal to the forward differentials.

    A.   I only.

    B.   III only.

    C.   II and III only

    D.   All of the above.

27   Concept Check Answers

1.   If, in the U.K., the quotation for Australian dollars is Aus\$/£ = 2.70 this is an example of:

   A.   a direct quotation.

   B.   an indirect quotation.

Correct Answer: 1.   B

An indirect quotation is when the home currency unit is quoted in terms of the foreign currency.

---

2.   The U.S. dollar is quoted against the Singapore dollar as S\$/US\$ = 1.7405 to 1.7420. The bid-ask percent spread is *closest* to:

   A.   0.0015%

   B.   0.0861%

   C.   0.1500%

   D.   8.6000%

Correct Answer: 2.   B

$$\text{spread} = \frac{\text{ask} - \text{bid}}{\text{ask}} \times 100 = \frac{(1.7420 - 1.7405)}{1.7420} \times 100 = 0.0861$$

3.   In a forward foreign exchange contract the contracted forward price:
   A.   is the spot rate when the contract is agreed.

   B.   is the spot rate when the contract matures.

   C.   reflects both the spot rate when the contract is agreed and the interest rate differential between the two currencies.

   D.   reflects both the spot rate when the contract matures and the interest rate differential between the two currencies.

Correct Answer: 3.   C

---

4.   Which of the following statement(s) is/are **CORRECT** with respect to interest rate parity?
I.   Interest rate parity gives the opportunity for covered interest arbitrage.
II.   Countries with relatively high interest rates will have currencies that trade at forward premiums to currencies of countries with low interest rates.
III.   Interest differentials should be equal to the forward differentials.
   A.   I only.

   B.   III only.

   C.   II and III only

   D.   All of the above.

Correct Answer: 4.   B

28   Foreign Exchange Parity Relations

Learning Outcome Statements (LOS)

28-a	**Explain** how exchange rates are determined in a flexible or floating exchange rate system.
28-b	**Explain** the role of each component of the balance-of-payments accounts.
28-c	**Explain** how current account deficits or surpluses and financial account deficits or surpluses affect an economy.
28-d	**Describe** the factors that cause a nation's currency to appreciate or depreciate.
28-e	**Explain** how monetary and fiscal policies affect the exchange rate and balance-of-payments components.
28-f	**Describe** a fixed exchange rate and a pegged exchange rate system.
28-g	**Discuss** absolute purchasing power parity and relative purchasing power parity.

Introduction

We now look at different exchange rate systems before focusing on flexible or floating-rate systems where the rate is determined by supply and demand for the currency. Candidates need to be familiar with the main factors (growth in income, inflation and interest rates) that drive exchange rates and the impact of fiscal and monetary policy on exchange rates. The chapter finishes with the review of another parity relationship, the link between relative inflation rates and spot and forward rates.

28   Concept Check Questions

1.   In a flexible exchange rate system:

A.   exchange rates are managed by a currency board.

B.   exchange rates are determined by supply and demand for the currency.

C.   the currency moves in a narrow pre-determined band against another currency.

D.   the country cannot set its own monetary policy.

---

2.   One of the most likely effects of an unanticipated move to a restrictive fiscal policy is:

A.   an inflow of capital.

B.   a rise in real interest rates.

C.   depreciation of the currency.

D.   a larger current-account deficit, or smaller surplus.

3.　One of the most likely effects of an unanticipated move to a restrictive monetary policy is:

　　A.　depreciation of the currency.

　　B.　a fall in real interest rates.

　　C.　a capital outflow.

　　D.　a shift towards a current-account deficit.

4.　The balance-of-payments account is made up of:

　　A.　current-account balance plus capital-account balance plus the official reserve account balance.

　　B.　balance of merchandise trade plus invisible services plus the official reserve account balance.

　　C.　current-account balance plus capital-account balance plus unilateral transfers.

　　D.　balance of merchandise goods and services plus net investment income plus unilateral transfers.

28   Concept Check Answers

1.   In a flexible exchange rate system:
   A.   exchange rates are managed by a currency board.
   B.   exchange rates are determined by supply and demand for the currency.
   C.   the currency moves in a narrow pre-determined band against another currency.
   D.   the country cannot set its own monetary policy.

Correct Answer: 1.   B

---

2.   One of the most likely effects of an unanticipated move to a restrictive fiscal policy is:
   A.   an inflow of capital.
   B.   a rise in real interest rates.
   C.   depreciation of the currency.
   D.   a larger current-account deficit, or smaller surplus.

Correct Answer: 2.   C
The dominant impact is likely to be a fall in real interest rates due to reduced government borrowing which will lead to a decline in real interest rates, an outflow of capital, depreciation of the currency and a move towards a current-account surplus.

3.   One of the most likely effects of an unanticipated move to a restrictive monetary policy is:

    A.   depreciation of the currency.

    B.   a fall in real interest rates.

    C.   a capital outflow.

    D.   a shift towards a current-account deficit.

Correct Answer: 3.   D

A restrictive monetary policy will slow growth and inflation, which will increase real interest rates. This will lead to an inflow of capital, appreciation of the currency, and move towards a current account deficit.

---

4.   The balance-of-payments account is made up of:

    A.   current-account balance plus capital-account balance plus the official reserve account balance.

    B.   balance of merchandise trade plus invisible services plus the official reserve account balance.

    C.   current-account balance plus capital-account balance plus unilateral transfers.

    D.   balance of merchandise goods and services plus net investment income plus unilateral transfers.

Correct Answer: 4.   A

STUDY SESSION 7 Introduction

Introductory Readings

Financial Accounting, 8th edition, Belverd E. Needles, Jr., and Marian Powers, (Houghton Mifflin, 2004)

"Measuring Business Income," Ch. 3

"Financial Reporting and Analysis," Ch. 5, pp. 246–258

"Inventories," Ch. 8

"Current Liabilities and the Time Value of Money," Ch. 9, pp. 412–426

"Contributed Capital," Ch. 12, pp. 543-553

"The Corporate Income Statement and the Statement of Stockholders' Equity," Ch.13, pp. 584-591

Measuring Business Income

Introduction

This section looks at the concept of net income which is used to measure a company's profitability. Candidates need to be familiar with the accrual basis of accounting and the matching principle and why they are used, rather than accounting simply on a cash basis.

Accounting methods

Financial statements are prepared at the end of regular accounting periods to make comparisons between different accounting periods easier. A fiscal year refers to the twelve-month period used by a company (which in many cases is not the same as the calendar year).

Although revenues and expenses can be accounted for on a cash basis for tax purposes, this is generally regarded as unsatisfactory since revenues are often earned in a different period from which the payments are received, and expenses paid in a different period from which they are incurred. The **matching rule** states that revenues must be assigned to the periods when the services are performed or the goods are sold, and expenses must be assigned to the period in which they produce the revenue.

Accrual accounting refers to methods that accountants use to apply the matching rule, i.e. that revenues are recognized when they are earned and expenses when they are incurred rather than when they are actually paid. Accounts are likely to need adjustment. For example transactions may occur in one accounting period but the benefits may spread over more than one accounting period.

Financial Reporting and Analysis

Introduction

In this section Candidates learn the definition of each category or component on the balance sheet and income statement. We will refer to balance sheet and income statement items throughout the rest of the Financial Statement Analysis notes so it is essential you are comfortable with the structure, presentation and contents of financial statements.

Balance Sheet

The major categories of a balance sheet are as follows:

ASSETS	LIABILITIES
Current Assets	Current Liabilities
Investments	Long-term Liabilities
Property, Plant and Equipment	
Intangible Assets	**STOCKHOLDERS' EQUITY**
	Contributed Capital
	Retained Earnings

Current Assets – cash and other assets which can reasonably be expected to be realized in cash or used within one year, or within the normal operating cycle of the business, whichever is longer.

Investments – assets that are not used in the normal operation of the business and are not expected to be converted into cash within one year.

Property, Plant and Equipment – long-term assets used in the continuing operation of the business. These assets are depreciated to allocate the cost of the assets over the period when they are used.

Intangible Assets – long-term assets with no physical substance – e.g. patents, goodwill.

Current Liabilities – obligations due to be paid or performed within one year, or within the normal operating cycle of the business, whichever is longer.

Long-Term Liabilities – debts that are due to be paid out in more than one year or beyond the normal operating cycle.

Contributed Capital – the par value of issued stock plus the amounts paid-in in excess of the par value.

Retained Earnings – earnings that have been retained by the company, rather than distributed to stockholders.

Income statement

The components of a multi-step income statement are as follows:

	Net Sales
–	Cost of Goods Sold
=	Gross Profit
–	Operating Expenses
=	Income from Operations
+/-	Other Revenue and Expenses
=	Income before Income Taxes
–	Income Taxes
=	Net Income

Net Sales – gross proceeds from sales, less sales returned and discounts offered.

Cost of Goods Sold – amount paid for the goods that were sold.

Operating Expenses – costs other than the cost of goods sold, often broken down into selling expenses and general and administrative expenses.

Other Revenue and Expenses – revenues and expenses that are not a result of operating activities, these include interest income and interest expenses.

Inventories

Introduction

Inventory is another short-term asset appearing on the balance sheet and the cost of inventory will also affect the income statement. There are four methods of accounting for inventory and the candidate needs to understand the impact on the balance sheet and income statement of the method used. This Reading is covered in more detail in Study Session 9, Reading 39.

Inventory

Inventory is a current asset and consists of goods held for sale in the normal course of business. The cost of inventory will include the costs of raw materials used, cost of labor and overhead costs. The cost of goods sold (COGS) is measured as the cost of goods available for sale less the value of inventory at the end of the accounting period. The valuation method used to value inventory is critical since it will decide the COGS and gross profit of the company and the value of inventory on the balance sheet.

Inventory cost

Inventory cost is the price or consideration paid to acquire an asset. There are three components to inventory cost:

- Invoice price less purchase discounts.
- Freight or transportation including insurance costs when in transit.
- Applicable taxes and tariffs.

It could be argued that other costs, such as storage costs, should also be included in the cost of inventory. Allocation of these costs is difficult so they are usually expensed.

When assigning costs to items that are sold, different methods can be used. These methods make different assumptions on the order in which items are sold. The four most commonly used methods are shown below.

Specific Identification Method

This method can be used when it is possible to match units left in inventory with a specific purchase. This might be used by an art dealer where there are high priced items for sale that are all unique.

Average-Cost Method

Under this method inventory is priced at the average cost of items available for sale during the period.

First-In, First-Out Method (FIFO)

This is based on the assumption that the cost of goods sold is associated with the earliest purchases in inventory. This means that the cost of goods held in inventory is associated with those that have been purchased most recently.

Last-In, First-Out Method (LIFO)

The assumption under LIFO is that the cost of goods sold is associated with the most recently purchased, the cost of goods held in inventory are associated with those that have been purchased the earliest.

Example Int-1   Calculating cost of inventory

On December 31st a company holds 200 units in inventory with an assigned total value of $1,000, or $5.00 per unit. On January 10th it purchases 30 additional units at a cost of $5.50 per unit and on January 20th it purchases 70 additional units at a cost of $6.00 per unit. 50 units are sold over the month so 250 units are left in inventory at the end of January.

Specific Identification Method

This requires additional information. If we are told that the specific cost of the 50 units sold was $4.50 each, then

Cost of Goods Sold (COGS) $= 50 \times \$4.50 = \$225.00$

January 31st inventory   = Costs of goods available for sale – COGS

$$= \$1,000 + (30 \times \$5.50) + (70 \times \$6.00) -- \$225 = \$1,360.00$$

Average-Cost Method

Average unit cost of goods available for sale

$$= \text{Cost of goods available for sale/units available}$$

$$= \$1,585/(200 + 30 + 70) = \$5.28$$

Cost of goods available $= \$1,585.00$

less January 31st inventory $= 250 \times \$5.28$

$$= \$1,320.00$$

COGS $= \$265.00$

First-In, First-Out Method (FIFO)

In this case the 50 units sold are those that were purchased first at a cost of $5.00 per unit

Cost of goods available $= \$1,585.00$

less January 31st inventory $= (150 \times \$5.00) + (30 \times \$5.50) + (70 \times \$6.00)$

$$= \$1,335.00$$

COGS $= \$250.00$

Example Int-1 (continued) Calculating cost of inventory

Last-In, First-Out Method (LIFO)

In this case the 50 units sold are those that were purchased last at a cost of $6.00 per unit.

Costs of goods available   = $1,585.00

less January 31st inventory $= (200 \times \$5.00) + (30 \times \$5.50) + (20 \times \$6.00)$

                                 = $1,285.00

COGS   = $300.00

Effect of inventory accounting method

In the above example, where prices are rising, we can see that LIFO gives the highest COGS and FIFO the lowest COGS, so LIFO will give the lowest gross margin. For income statement items LIFO is generally considered the best method since it more closely follows the matching rule, the current value of costs is used. However, looking at the balance sheet, the inventory value recorded is higher under FIFO than LIFO. In this case FIFO could be considered a better method since inventory values are closer to current values.

When the replacement cost of inventory falls below the historic cost, perhaps due to a decline in price levels or obsolescence, then the inventory should be written down to the lower-of-cost-or-market. There are two methods for doing this:

Item-by-Item Method

Cost and market values are computed for each item in inventory.

Major Category Method

Total cost and total market values are computed for each category of goods.

Example Int-2   Calculating inventory values

Item-by-Item Method

	Quantity	Cost per Unit	Market Value per Unit	Lower of Cost or Market
Category 1				
Item a	100	$4.00	$4.50	$400.00
Item b	100	$5.00	$3.50	$350.00
Category 2				
Item c	100	$2.00	$1.00	$100.00
Item d	100	$6.00	$5.00	$500.00
Inventory at the lower of cost or market				$1,350.00

Major Category Method

Category 1	Quantity	Total Cost	Total Market Value	Lower of Cost or Market
Item a	100	$400.00	$450.00	
Item b	100	$500.00	$350.00	
Total		$900.00	$800.00	$800.00
Category 2				
Item c	100	$200.00	$100.00	
Item d	100	$600.00	$500.00	
Total		$800.00	$600.00	$600.00
Inventory at the lower of cost or market				$1,400.00

Current Liabilities and the Time Value of Money

Introduction

We now move on to look at the liability side of the balance sheet. Candidates need to be able to differentiate between current liabilities and long-term liabilities and know how to treat liabilities when the amount or likelihood of payment is uncertain.

Liabilities

A liability is a legal obligation to make a future payment of assets, or perform a service in the future, as a result of a past transaction. Current liabilities are liabilities that are expected to be paid within a year, or within a normal operating cycle, whichever is longer. Long-term liabilities are due after one year or operating cycle. Generally, current liabilities are paid from the current assets or from the proceeds of current operations whereas long-term liabilities represent the financing of long-term assets.

Liabilities are usually valued at the amount of money need to pay the debt or the value of goods or services to be delivered. Whilst in some cases the amount is definitely known in other cases an estimate is made, perhaps based on past experience. An example is when a sale is made but there remains a liability to service the item sold.

Current liabilities can be broken down into:

(i) Definitely Determinable Liabilities

- Accounts payable
- Bank loans and commercial paper
- Notes payable
- Accrued liabilities
- Dividends payable
- Sales and excise tax payable
- Current portion of long-term debt
- Payroll liabilities
- Unearned revenues

(ii) Estimated Liabilities

The existence of a liability is clear but often the amount will not be known until later. These items include:

- Income taxes – a company's managers will usually only know the profits after the year-end so an estimated figure must be used.
- Property tax payable – these are usually paid to the local governments in the U.S., and the assessment dates are unlikely to match a firm's year-end. Therefore an estimated figure should be used.
- Product warranty liability – whilst a warranty or guarantee is outstanding on a product there is a liability and a firm should estimate how much the warranty is likely to cost.
- Vacation pay liability – not all employees will collect vacation pay so this should also be recorded as an estimated liability.

(iii) Contingent liabilities

A contingent liability is not an existing liability but a potential liability in the sense that it depends on the outcome of a future event that arises because of a past transaction.

It should be entered in the accounts if it is both (i) probable and (ii) can be reasonably estimated. Potential liabilities that do not meet these conditions should be referred to in the notes to the accounts.

Contributed Capital

Introduction

Candidates are expected to know the breakdown of contributed capital and the difference between preferred stock and ordinary stock. We also look at payments to stockholders in the form of cash dividends or repurchase of stock and the impact on the balance sheet. Dividends are revisited in Study Session 13.

Contributed capital

This is made up of three components:

1. Preferred Stock – par value, amount authorized and amount issued and outstanding.
2. Common Stock – par value, amount authorized and amount issued and outstanding.
3. Paid-in Capital in excess of par value.

Accounting for dividends

There are three dates to consider:

1. Date of declaration – when the directors declare that a dividend is going to be paid, the issuer will record a cash dividend payable item as a liability.
2. Date of record – when ownership of the stock entitles the owner to receive the dividend. After this, and prior to payment, the stock is ex-dividend. No accounting entries are needed.
3. Date of payment – the date the dividend is paid, and the liability is settled.

Common stock

This is the residual equity which means that the holders have the last claim on assets in the case that the company goes into liquidation. It is usually the only stock that carries voting rights. Dividends may be paid to stockholders which means that part of the stockholders' equity, usually earnings, is being paid out to stockholders.

Preferred stock

This has preference over common stock, usually in terms of both dividends and claim on assets in the case of liquidation. Dividends are often quoted as a percentage of par value and in this sense the characteristics of preferred stock are similar to those of a fixed-income instrument. Different types of preferred stock are:

Cumulative preferred stock – if a dividend is missed then it accumulates and must be paid before a dividend can be paid to common stock holders.

Convertible preferred stock – can be exchanged into common stock.

Callable preferred stock – the issuer can redeem the stock at a pre-specified price.

Stock issuance

Par value stock – the par value is credited to the Common Stock (or Preferred Stock) account and any surplus, or deficit, to the 'Paid-in Capital in Excess of Par Value' account, or debited to the 'Discount on Capital Stock' account respectively.

No-par stock – the proceeds of the issue are credited to the Common Stock account.

Treasury stock

This is stock that has been bought back by the issuer, usually in the stock market, and not been resold or retired.

It is treated as stock that has been issued but is no longer outstanding, and therefore does not have voting rights, rights to dividends etc.

The Corporate Income Statement and the Statement of Stockholders' Equity

Introduction

Here we consider stock dividends and stock splits which are corporate actions that do not affect a company's income or asset value.

Retained earnings

Retained earnings are the part of stockholders' equity that represents the stockholders' claim on assets generated by the firm's earnings. It is the profits (or losses) since inception less any dividends paid to stockholders or transfers to contributed capital.

Accounting for stock dividends and stock splits

Stock dividends

This is a distribution of shares to existing common stockholders in proportion to the size of their holding. This does not involve a cash payment and leads only to a transfer of funds from retained earnings to the contributed capital account. The amount transferred is determined by the market value of the shares issued.

Stock splits

This is when a corporation increases the number of issued shares and reduces the par value accordingly. Again this does not involve a cash payment. The motivation is usually to reduce the market price and increase liquidity of the shares.

Introduction   Concept Check Questions

1.   In a firm's financial statements expenses should be recorded:

    A.   when they occur.

    B.   when they are paid.

    C.   once they can be reasonably estimated.

    D.   in the same period that related revenues are recorded.

---

2.   When inventory costs are increasing due to inflation, the decision to use LIFO rather than FIFO will lead to:

    A.   lower net income and lower inventory balances.

    B.   lower net income and higher inventory balances.

    C.   higher net income and lower inventory balances.

    D.   higher net income and higher inventory balances.

3.   A stock dividend:

    A.   Has no impact on the financial statements.

    B.   Reduces the par value of stock outstanding.

    C.   Transfers an amount from retained earnings to contributed capital.

    D.   On the declaration date reduces stockholders' equity by the size of the dividend payable.

---

4.   If Treasury stock is included in a firm's balance sheet as part of stockholders' equity it means that:

    A.   the firm has issued preferred shares.

    B.   the firm has repurchased its own stock.

    C.   the firm has invested in Treasury notes or Treasury bonds.

    D.   the firm has issued stock where the dividends are linked to Treasury bill yields.

Introduction   Concept Check Answers

1.   In a firm's financial statements expenses should be recorded:

    A.   when they occur.

    B.   when they are paid.

    C.   once they can be reasonably estimated.

    D.   in the same period that related revenues are recorded.

Correct Answer 1:   D

The matching rule says that related revenues and expenses should be recorded in the same accounting period.

---

2.   When inventory costs are increasing due to inflation, the decision to use LIFO rather than FIFO will lead to:

    A.   lower net income and lower inventory balances.

    B.   lower net income and higher inventory balances.

    C.   higher net income and lower inventory balances.

    D.   higher net income and higher inventory balances.

Correct Answer 2:   A

COGS will be higher under LIFO reducing net income. Ending inventory will be lower since it will include 'old' inventory bought at lower prices.

3.   A stock dividend:

   A.   has no impact on the financial statements.

   B.   reduces the par value of stock outstanding.

   C.   transfers an amount from retained earnings to contributed capital.

   D.   on the declaration date reduces stockholders' equity by the size of the dividend payable.

Correct Answer 3:   C

   B refers to a stock split. D is not true since no cash is paid out.

---

4.   If Treasury stock is included in a firm's balance sheet as part of stockholders' equity it means that:

   A.   the firm has issued preferred shares.

   B.   the firm has repurchased its own stock.

   C.   the firm has invested in Treasury notes or Treasury bonds.

   D.   the firm has issued stock where the dividends are linked to Treasury bill yields.

   3.

Correct Answer 4:   B

   Treasury stock refers to repurchased stock. This is likely to have happened because the managers believed the stock was undervalued in the market or as a defense against a takeover.

STUDY SESSION 7

Financial Statement Analysis: Basic Concepts

Overview

Financial Statement Analysis and Corporate Finance have a guideline weighting of 28% of the exam questions so this is a topic you must do well on. Candidates who are not financial analysts may well find they are not sufficiently familiar with the details of accounting practices such as the treatment of inventory, leases, deferred tax and depreciation. None of the material is difficult but you will need to spend time working through the text and applying your knowledge to practice questions. In many cases you will be required to do calculations but more importantly you must be able to interpret the numbers or ratios computed. The objective of building up knowledge of financial statements and accounting principles is to allow you to use financial statement data to better understand a company's operations and position relative to its competitors and in order to make investment decisions.

In Study Session 7 the main Reading Assignments cover two key topics. The first topic is accounting for income and assets including when items should be recognized on the income statement and balance sheet. The second topic is analyzing cash flows and being able to differentiate between operating, investing and financing cash flows. The Study Session ends with a discussion of the changes in accounting methods that can be expected from efforts to harmonize standards worldwide.

Candidates who have studied accounting at an introductory level and are familiar with the relationship between the items on the income statement, balance sheet and cash flow statement and have knowledge of the basic concepts used in financial reporting will not need to spend much time on the Introductory Readings. It is important to note that the CFA Institute states that examination questions are drawn mainly from the subsequent Reading Assignments.

Readings Assignments

29.   "Framework for Financial Statement Analysis," Ch. 1, The Analysis and Use of Financial Statements, 3rd edition, Gerald I. White, Ashwinpaul C. Sondhi, and Dov Fried (Wiley, 2003)

30.   "Long-Term Assets," Ch. 10, Financial Accounting, 8th edition, Belverd E. Needles, Jr., and Marian Powers, (Houghton Mifflin, 2004)

31.   "Accounting Income and Assets: The Accrual Concept," Ch. 2, (including Box 2-5), The Analysis and Use of Financial Statements, 3rd edition, Gerald I. White, Ashwinpaul C. Sondhi, and Dov Fried (Wiley, 2003)

32.   "The Statement of Cash Flows," Ch. 14, Financial Accounting, 8th edition, Belverd E. Needles, Jr., and Marian Powers, (Houghton Mifflin, 2004)

33.   "Analysis of Cash Flows," Ch. 3, pp. 74–82, 84 (Box 3-1) and 87–99, The Analysis and Use of Financial Statements, 3rd edition, Gerald I. White, Ashwinpaul C. Sondhi, and Dov Fried (Wiley, 2003)

34.   Future FASB Changes and the Analytical Challenges of GAAP, Patricia A. Mc Connell (AIMR 2004), pp. 18–20 and 23-24

29   Framework for Financial Statement Analysis

Learning Outcome Statements (LOS)

29-a	**Discuss** the general principles of the financial reporting system and **explain** the objectives of financial reporting according to the Financial Accounting Standards Board (FASB) conceptual framework.
29-b	**Identify** the accounting qualities (e.g., relevance, reliability, predictive value, timeliness) set forth in Statement of Financial Accounting Concepts (SFAC) 2, and **discuss** how these qualities provide useful information to an analyst.
29-c	**Discuss** the roles of the International Organization of Securities Commissions (IOSCO) and the International Accounting Standards Board (IASB) in setting and enforcing global accounting standards.
29-d	**Describe** and **distinguish** between the principal financial statements: Balance Sheet, Income Statement, Statement of Comprehensive Income, Statement of Cash Flows and Statement of Stockholders' Equity and **discuss** the additional sources of information accompanying the financial statements, including the financial footnotes, supplementary schedules, Management Discussion and Analysis (MD&A) and Proxy statements.
29-e	**Discuss** the role of the auditor and the meaning of the audit opinion.

Introduction

In the Reading we look at how accounting standards are set in the U.S. and internationally, and the objectives of financial reporting. We also consider the relationship between the different statements and additional information that is provided. Finally the role of the auditor is discussed.

29   Concept Check Questions

1.   Which of the following is least likely to be important to an analyst when using financial reports?

    A.   Detail.

    B.   Relevance.

    C.   Materiality.

    D.   Consistency.

---

2.   The IASB was established in order to:

    A.   harmonize accounting standards worldwide.

    B.   review disclosure standards for publicly owned companies.

    C.   provide an alternative set of accounting standards to U.S. GAAP.

    D.   investigate regulatory issues with respect to accounting standards.

29   Concept Check Answers

1.   Which of the following is least likely to be important to an analyst when using financial reports?

    A.   Detail.

    B.   Relevance.

    C.   Materiality.

    D.   Consistency.

Correct Answer 1:.   **A**

If the financial reports are to be relevant and timely it is not practical for them to include every detail of the financial data.

---

2.   The IASB was established in order to:

    A.   harmonize accounting standards worldwide.

    B.   review disclosure standards for publicly owned companies.

    C.   provide an alternative set of accounting standards to U.S. GAAP.

    D.   investigate regulatory issues with respect to accounting standards.

Correct Answer 2:   **A**

IASB was set up to coordinate the accounting standards followed by companies worldwide.

30   Long-Term Assets

Learning Outcome Statements (LOS)

30-a	**Describe** the factors that distinguish long-term assets from other assets, and **identify** the common types of long-term assets and their carrying values on the balance sheet.
30-b	**Determine** the cost, and **record** the purchase, of property, plant and equipment.
30-c	**Explain** depreciation accounting (including the reasons for depreciation), **calculate** depreciation using the straight-line, production (also known as units-of-production), and declining-balance methods, and **calculate** depreciation after revising the estimated useful life of an asset.
30-d	**Describe** how to account for the sale, exchange, or disposal of depreciable assets, and **determine** whether a gain or loss is recorded.
30-e	**Identify** assets that should be classified as natural resources, and **prepare** entries to account for such assets, including entries to record depletion.
30-f	**Identify** the types of intangible assets, and **describe** how the accounting treatment for goodwill under U.S. GAAP differs from the accounting treatment for other intangible assets.

Introduction

In this Reading we consider how the cost of long-term assets, which are used for more than one year or business cycle, are allocated over their useful life. For tangible assets, such as plant and equipment, the allocation of the cost is called depreciation and it can be calculated in a number of ways. This topic is covered in more detail in Study Session 9.

30 Concept Check Questions

1. Depreciation is a method of:

  A. allocating the cost of an asset over its useful life.
  B. adjusting the historic cost of an asset to its market value.
  C. adjusting the historic cost of an asset to its replacement value.
  D. recognizing impairment of an asset when it has no further value to a firm.

---

2. Intangible assets are generally:

  A. depleted.
  B. amortized.
  C. depreciated.
  D. held in the balance sheet at cost.

3.   When an asset is sold for an amount below its book value (asset value net of depreciation) which of the following will be recognized?

A.   A loss on the income statement.

B.   A profit on the income statement.

C.   An increase in the asset value on the balance sheet.

D.   A write down of the asset value on the balance sheet.

30 Concept Check Answers

1.   Depreciation is a method of:

    A.   allocating the cost of an asset over its useful life.

    B.   adjusting the historic cost of an asset to its market value.

    C.   adjusting the historic cost of an asset to its replacement value.

    D.   recognizing impairment of an asset when it has no further value to a firm.

Correct Answer 1.   **A**

Depreciation is a way of spreading the cost of an asset over its life, it is based on historic cost and there is no attempt to recognize market or replacement value. Impairment refers to writing down the value of an asset if its book value is above the value of the cash flows it will generate in the future.

---

2.   Intangible assets are generally:

    A.   depleted.

    B.   amortized.

    C.   depreciated.

    D.   held in the balance sheet at cost.

Correct Answer 2.   **B**

Tangible assets are generally depreciated, natural resources depleted, and intangibles (but not goodwill) amortized.

---

3.   When an asset is sold for an amount below its book value (asset value net of depreciation) which of the following will be recognized?

    A.   A loss on the income statement.

    B.   A profit on the income statement.

    C.   An increase in the asset value on the balance sheet.

    D.   A write down of the asset value on the balance sheet.

Correct Answer 3.   **A**

The asset will no longer be shown on the balance sheet and the difference between the book value and the realized value will be recorded as a loss on the income statement.

31   Accounting Income and Assets: The Accrual Concept

Learning Outcome Statements (LOS)

31-a	**Describe** the format of the income statement and **describe** the components of net income.
31-b	**Explain** the importance of the matching principle for revenue and expense recognition, **identify** the requirements for revenue recognition to occur, **identify** and **describe** the appropriate revenue recognition, given the status of completion of the earning process and the assurance of payment, and **discuss** different revenue recognition methods and their implications for financial analysis.
31-c	**Identify** the appropriate income statement and balance sheet entries using the percentage-of-completion method and the completed contract method and **describe** and **calculate** the effects on cash flows and selected financial ratios that result from using the percentage-of-completion method versus the completed contract method.
31-d	**Describe** the types and analysis of unusual or infrequent items, extraordinary items, discontinued operations, accounting changes, and prior period adjustments.
31-e	**Discuss** managerial discretion in areas such as classification of good news/bad news, income smoothing, big bath behavior, and accounting changes, and **explain** how this discretion can affect the financial statements.
31-f	**Describe** the format and the components of the balance sheet and the format, classification, and use of each component of the statement of stockholders' equity.

Introduction

This Reading looks at the income statement (using accounting income as opposed to economic or other forms of income) and the balance sheet. The Reading focuses on the different methods for revenue recognition and discusses the areas where management has the most discretion with respect to revenue recognition. The balance sheet is also analyzed and in particular the components of stockholders' equity identified. The trickiest part of this Reading concerns accounting for long-term projects using the percentage-of-completion method or completed contract methods. You need to be familiar with the calculations using either method and also understand the impact on the financial statements of the choice of method used.

31   Concept Check Questions

1.   Which of the following is **NOT** a condition for revenues to be recorded in the income statement?

   A.   Payment has been received.
   B.   The related cost can be reliably determined.
   C.   There are no remaining contingent liabilities.
   D.   Almost all of the goods or services have been provided.

---

2.   Which of the following is **NOT** a component of stockholders' equity?

   A.   Capital leases.
   B.   Treasury stock.
   C.   Preferred stock.
   D.   Retained earnings.

3.   A company is selling golf club memberships before the golf course has finished being constructed and the total cost is uncertain. An appropriate method for recording revenues is the:

  A.   Installment method.

  B.   Cost recovery method.

  C.   Completed contract method.

  D.   Percentage-of-completion method.

---

4.   The completed contract method is used rather than the percentage-of-completion method to account for a project. Prior to completion this will lead to:

  I.   Lower cash flows.

  II.   Higher stockholders' equity.

  III.   Earlier revenue recognition.

  A.   I only.

  B.   I and II only.

  C.   All of the above.

  D.   None of the above.

31   Concept Check Answers

1.   Which of the following is **NOT** a condition for revenues to be recorded in the income statement?

   A.   Payment has been received.

   B.   The related cost can be reliably determined.

   C.   There are no remaining contingent liabilities.

   D.   Almost all of the goods or services have been provided.

Correct Answer 1.   A

   Assurance of payment is required rather than actual payment.

---

2.   Which of the following is **NOT** a component of stockholders' equity?

   A.   Capital leases.

   B.   Treasury stock.

   C.   Preferred stock.

   D.   Retained earnings.

Correct Answer 2.   A

   Capital lease obligations are a liability.

3.   A company is selling golf club memberships before the golf course has finished being constructed and the total cost is uncertain. An appropriate method for recording revenues is the:

    A.   Installment method.

    B.   Cost recovery method.

    C.   Completed contract method.

    D.   Percentage-of-completion method.

Correct Answer 3.   **B**

When costs are uncertain the cost recovery method should be used.

---

4.   The completed contract method is used rather than the percentage-of-completion method to account for a project. Prior to completion this will lead to:

    I.   Lower cash flows.

    II.   Higher stockholders' equity.

    III.   Earlier revenue recognition.

    A.   I only.

    B.   I and II only.

    C.   All of the above.

    D.   None of the above.

Correct Answer4.   **D**

Cash flows will be the same (ignoring tax) and revenue recognition (and increased equity) will only occur in the final year.

32   The Statement of Cash Flows

Learning Outcome Statements (LOS)

32-a	**Identify** the types of important information for investment decision making presented in the statement of cash flows.
32-b	**Compare** and **contrast** the categories (i.e., cash provided or used by operating activities, investing activities, and financing activities) in a statement of cash flows, and **describe** how noncash investing and financing transactions are reported.
32-c	**Calculate** and **interpret,** using the indirect method, the net cash provided or used by operating activities.
32-d	**Prepare** and **interpret,** using the indirect method, the statement of cash flows for investing activities and financing activities.

Introduction

Candidates are required to have an in-depth knowledge of the cash flow statements and how items are classified as either cash from operations, investing and financing. At this stage we provide a very brief introduction, but in Reading 33 cash flows are considered in much greater detail.

33   Analysis of Cash Flows

Learning Outcome Statements (LOS)

33-a	**Classify** a particular transaction or item as cash flow from 1) operations, 2) investing, or 3) financing.
33-b	**Compute** and **interpret** a statement of cash flows, using the direct method and the indirect method.
33-c	**Convert** an indirect statement of cash flows to a direct basis.
33-d	**Explain** the two primary factors that may cause discrepancies between balances of operating assets and liabilities reported on the balance sheet and those reported in the cash flow statements.
33-e	**Describe** and **compute** free cash flow.
33-f	**Distinguish** between the U.S. GAAP and IAS GAAP classifications of dividends paid or received and interest paid or received for statement of cash flow purposes.

Introduction

Cash flows are critical. Not only do they provide the link between the income statement and balance sheet but they provide data which is less susceptible to being distorted by management choices on accounting methods. A net cash flow number is not particularly helpful; to understand the dynamics of a company the breakdown of the cash flow into cash flow from operating, financing and investing activities is far more useful. Most cash flows fall into the operating category and reflect the ability of the company to generate funds internally. Investing cash flows provide information on the cash being used to buy assets which will maintain current capacity and support future growth. Financing cash flows reflect the capital structure of the company and the cash that is being paid, or collected, from providers of capital (but be careful, interest paid, interest and dividends received are operating cash flows under U.S. GAAP).

For the exam, candidates need to be comfortable using the direct and indirect methods to compute a statement of operating cash flows.

Statement of cash flows

The statement of cash flows reports the cash inflows and outflows for a company over a period. It provides a link between the beginning and end-period balance sheets and provides additional information to that provided by the balance sheet and income statement.

The cash flow is broken into three components:

Cash Flow from Operations (CFO) – this is the amount of cash generated by a firm as a result of its production of goods and services. A company undergoing rapid growth might show negative cash flow from operations. Longer term a company should be able to achieve positive cash flow from operations in order to pay dividends, repay debt and fund expansion.

Cash Flow from Investing (CFI) – this is the amount of cash generated from the purchase and sale of productive assets and investments. This is necessary to maintain and expand a company's operating capacity.

Cash Flow from Financing (CFF) – this is the amount of cash used to pay dividends and repurchase shares, repay borrowings and the cash received from the issue of equity and debt.

32 & 33   Concept Check Questions

1.   When a company decides to use a straight-line method rather than an accelerated method for accounting for depreciation for a major asset purchase this will:

   A.   not have an impact on cash flows.
   C.   lead to lower cash flow from financing.
   B.   lead to lower cash flow from operations.
   D.   lead to higher cash flow from operations.

---

2.   When a company makes an interest payment to bond holders this would be recorded under U.S. GAAP as:

   A.   a cash flow from financing.
   B.   a cash flow from operations.
   C.   a cash flow from investment.
   D.   having no impact on cash flows.

3.   Which of the following will lead to the largest increase in free cash flow?

   A.   A decrease in cash flow from operations and a decrease in capital expenditure.

   B.   An increase in cash flow from operations and a decrease in capital expenditure.

   C.   A decrease in cash flow from operations and an increase in capital expenditure.

   D.   An increase in cash flow from operations and an increase in capital expenditure.

---

4.   Cash flow from operations will tend to increase if:

   A.   Inventories increase.

   B.   Trade payables increase.

   C.   Accounts receivables increase.

   D.   Amortization expense increases.

32 & 33   Concept Check Answers

1.   When a company decides to use a straight-line method rather than an accelerated method for accounting for depreciation for a major asset purchase this will:

     A.   not have an impact on cash flows.

     C.   lead to lower cash flow from financing.

     B.   lead to lower cash flow from operations.

     D.   lead to higher cash flow from operations.

Correct Answer1.   A

Depreciation does not lead to a movement in cash so it does not have an impact on cash flows (ignoring any tax effects).

---

2.   When a company makes an interest payment to bond holders this would be recorded under U.S. GAAP as:

     A.   a cash flow from financing.

     B.   a cash flow from operations.

     C.   a cash flow from investment.

     D.   having no impact on cash flows.

Correct Answer 2.   B
Interest payments are operating cash flows.

3.   Which of the following will lead to the largest increase in free cash flow?

  A.   A decrease in cash flow from operations and a decrease in capital expenditure.

  B.   An increase in cash flow from operations and a decrease in capital expenditure.

  C.   A decrease in cash flow from operations and an increase in capital expenditure.

  D.   An increase in cash flow from operations and an increase in capital expenditure.

Correct Answer3.   B
Free cash flow = cash flow from operations – capital expenditure

---

4.   Cash flow from operations will tend to increase if:

  A.   Inventories increase.

  B.   Trade payables increase.

  C.   Accounts receivables increase.

  D.   Amortization expense increases.

Correct Answer4.   B

An increase in inventory levels or client receivables means that more cash is tied up in the business reducing operating cash flows. Amortization is a non cash item. If trade payables increase it indicates that the company has been able to delay paying suppliers which will increase operating cash flow.

34   Future FASB Changes and the Analytical Challenges of GAAP

Learning Outcome Statements (LOS)

34-a	**Identify** the projects on the FASB agenda that were/are related to international convergence.
34-b	**Describe** two different guidance rules for revenue recognition discussed by the FASB and IASB.

Introduction

The Financial Accounting Standards Board (FASB) is in the process of harmonizing U.S. GAAP with International Accounting Standards (IAS), with the aim of achieving harmonization in 2007. There are a number of areas that are key, including stock compensation, business combinations and revenue recognition. The changes to accounting methods will not only affect how companies produce financial reports but also the stock valuation by analysts and the market. This is of particular relevance to companies who are listing in both U.S. and European markets (and other world markets) and will need to provide financial statements complying with different standards.

34   Concept Check Questions

1.   Which one of the following is not one of the projects listed as being on the agenda to harmonize U.S. GAAP and IAS GAAP?

    A.   Fair-value measurement.

    B.   Accounting for stock compensation.

    C.   Accounting for depreciation expense.

    D.   Accounting treatment for convertible bonds.

---

2.   Which of the following is most likely to create a conflict between current standards on the recognition of revenue?

    A.   A five-year office cleaning contract which can be terminated at one month's notice by either party.

    B.   A five-year credit card agreement when the credit card is paid for by the user on a monthly basis.

    C.   A short-term building contract which will be accounted for using the completed contract method.

    D.   The sale of a two-year magazine subscription which is non refundable, paid for at the beginning of the period.

34   Concept Check Answers

1.   Which one of the following is not one of the projects listed as being on the agenda to harmonize U.S. GAAP and IAS GAAP?

   A.   Fair-value measurement.

   B.   Accounting for stock compensation.

   C.   Accounting for depreciation expense.

   D.   Accounting treatment for convertible bonds.

Correct Answer

   Depreciation does not lead to a movement in cash so it does not have an impact on cash flows (ignoring any tax effects).

Correct Answer 1.   **C**
Depreciation is not one of the items listed.

2.   Which of the following is most likely to create a conflict between current standards on the recognition of revenue?

A.   A five-year office cleaning contract which can be terminated at one month's notice by either party.

B.   A five-year credit card agreement when the credit card is paid for by the user on a monthly basis.

C.   A short-term building contract which will be accounted for using the completed contract method.

D.   The sale of a two-year magazine subscription which is non refundable, paid for at the beginning of the period.

Correct Answer 2.   **D**
The conflict will arise between the net asset method for recognizing revenues and Statement 5, which says that the earnings process should be completed. In A the payment is not assured for the whole period, in B the payment is not received upfront and C is a short-term project using a recognized accounting method, so conflict is most likely to arise in case D.

STUDY SESSION 8

Financial Statement Analysis: Financial Ratios and Earnings per Share

Overview

Analyzing financial statements through the use of ratios is the backbone of this Study Session. Numbers taken from financial statements are, on their own, fairly meaningless. It is only when the relationship between the numbers or ratios are computed that we can start to get an idea of the financial strength and profitability of a company. When we start comparing the ratios of a company with its own past ratios or with ratios of other companies in the industry we get a much clearer idea of the company's relative performance.

The next Reading Assignment looks at the calculation of earnings per share and how to accommodate potentially dilutive securities which, if exercised or converted, would lead to lower earnings per share. Finally there are two Readings on financial shenanigans which are used by companies to manipulate reported earnings. These Readings identify the most commonly used tricks and the effect on revenues, income and liabilities.

Reading Assignments

35.   "Analysis of Financial Statements," Ch. 10, pp. 319–358 and Exhibits 10.1, 10.2, and 10.3, *Investment Analysis and Portfolio Management*, 7th edition, Frank K. Reilly and Keith C. Brown (Dryden, 2003)

36.   "Dilutive Securities and Earnings per Share," Ch. 16, pp. 788–801 and Appendix 16B pp. 809-814, *Intermediate Accounting*, 11th edition, Donald E. Kieso, Jerry J. Weygandt and Terry D. Warfield (Wiley, 2004)

Financial Shenanigans, 2nd edition, Howard Schilit (McGraw-Hill, 2002)

37.   "Seek and Ye Shall Find," Ch. 2

38.   "Searching for Shenanigans," Ch. 3

35 Analysis of Financial Statements

Learning Outcome Statements (LOS)

35-a	**Interpret** common-size balance sheets and common-size income statements and **discuss** the circumstances under which the use of common-size financial statements is appropriate.
35-b	**Calculate**, **interpret**, and **discuss** the uses of measures of a company's internal liquidity, operating performance (i.e. operating efficiency (activity) and operating profitability), risk profile, and growth potential.
35-c	**Calculate** and **interpret** the various components of the company's return on equity using the original and extended DuPont systems and a company's financial ratios relative to its industry, to the aggregate economy, and to the company's own performance over time.

Introduction

This Reading includes the definitions of a large number of ratios and candidates should attempt to memorize the ratios. Although some of the definitions may differ from those you are familiar with, the definitions given in the source text and used in these notes, should be the ones applied in the exam. Candidates will not only be expected to calculate ratios but more importantly to be able to use ratios to draw conclusions about a company's performance both over time and relative to other participants in the market and industry. Ratios not only reflect the profitability of a company and its growth prospects but also its capital structure and the risk inherent in its business and as a result of financing decisions. Finally, the DuPont analysis of return on equity and the calculation of the sustainable growth rate of a company are important topics to revise.

The main categories of analysis where financial ratios are used are as follows:

1. Common size statements
2. Internal liquidity (solvency)
3. Operating performance
   a. Operating efficiency
   b. Operating profitability
4. Risk Analysis
   a. Business risk
   b. Financial risk
   c. Liquidity risk
5. Growth analysis

We will discuss the definition of the ratios used and the application and interpretation of the ratios one by one for Ripley Corporation, whose financial statements are shown below. It is important to always consider ratios in the context of the firm's industry, its major competitors, the market and the overall economy as well as against the company's own history.

Financial information used in Examples 35-1 to 35-7

RIPLEY CORPORATION BALANCE SHEET		
Year end December 31st 2004 and 2005, US$ million		
	2004	2005
Assets		
Current Assets		
Cash and cash equivalents	950	1,350
Accounts receivable	14,200	13,600
Inventories	2,500	4,600
Other current assets	235	765
Total Current Assets	17,885	20,315
Property, plant and equipment (net of accumulated depreciation)	124,000	128,050
Other noncurrent assets	36,600	35,700
Total Assets	178,485	184,065
Liabilities and Shareholders' Equity		
Current Liabilities		
Short-term debt	500	455
Trade accounts payable	8,100	7,345
Accrued expenses and other liabilities	17,885	9,756
Income taxes payable	827	956
Total Current Liabilities	27,312	18,512
Long-term debt	25,000	25,000
Other noncurrent liabilities	0	0
Deferred income taxes	1,050	1,065
Common shareholders' equity		
Common stock	87,000	98,000
Paid-in capital	15,000	18,000
Retained earnings	23,123	23,488
Total Common Shareholders' Equity	125,123	139,488

Total Liabilities Common Shareholders' Equity	178,485	184,065

RIPLEY CORPORATION INCOME STATEMENT
Year end December 31st 2005, US$ million

	2005
Net sales	184,235
Cost of goods sold	(163,910)
Gross profit	20,325
Selling, general and administrative expenses	(15,424)
Operating profit (EBIT)	4,901
Interest income	60
Interest expense	(1,972)
Operating income before tax	2,989
Provision for income taxes	(1,136)
Reported net income	1,853
Dividends declared	1,488

1.   The quick ratio is *closest* to:
   A.   0.34.
   B.   0.63.
   C.   0.76.
   D.   1.45.

---

2.   The average receivables collection period for Islington Corporation is *closest* to:
   A.   1.4 days.
   B.   5.0 days.
   C.   73.5 days.
   D.   109.5 days.

3. The return on total capital for Islington Corporation is *closest* to:
   A. 3.8%.
   B. 5.0%.
   C. 7.0%.
   D. 12.2%.

---

4. Islington Corporation's interest coverage is *closest* to:
   A. 0.15 times.
   B. 3.16 times.
   C. 6.33 times.
   D. 16.33 times.

---

5. If the payables payment period for a firm increases this will tend to:
   A. increase the cash conversion cycle.
   B. decrease the cash conversion cycle.
   C. leave the cash conversion cycle unchanged.

6   Business risk is the variability of:

    A.   sales.

    B.   net income.

    C.   gross profit.

    D.   operating profit.

---

7.   A firm has a dividend pay out ratio of 60%, a return on total capital of 12% and a return on equity of 15%. The sustainable growth rate is *closest* to:

    A.   4.8%.

    B.   6.0%.

    C.   7.2%.

    D.   9.0%.

---

8.   Using common sized financial statements is useful when:

    I.   Comparing companies that are different sizes.

    II.   Looking at historic trends for a company's performance.

    III.   Comparing companies that use different accounting principles.

    A.   I only.

    B.   I and II only.

    C.   II and III only.

    D.   All of the above.

35 Concept Check Answers

Islington Corporation provides you with the following information (use for questions 1 to 4):

Income Statement			Balance Sheet			
$ million			Average over period		$ million	
Sales	298	Cash	50	Accounts Payable		80
COGS	(200)	Accounts Receivable	60	Accrued Expenses		65
Gross Profit	98	Inventory	100	Long-term Debt		150
SGA Expenses	(60)	Property, P & E	375			
Op. Profit	38	Depreciation	(85)	Common Stock		140
Interest expense	(6)			Retained Earnings		65
Tax	(13)					
Net Income	19	Total Assets	500	Total Liabilities & Equity		500

1.   The quick ratio is *closest* to:

    A.   0.34.

    B.   0.63.

    C.   0.76.

    D.   1.45.

Correct Answer 1.   C

Quick ratio   = (cash + marketable securities + receivables)/current liabilities
                = (50 + 60)/145
                = 0.76

---

2.   The average receivables collection period for Islington Corporation is *closest* to:

    A.   1.4 days.

    B.   5.0 days.

    C.   73.5 days.

    D.   109.5 days.

Correct Answer 2.   C

Receivables turnover
   = net sales/average receivables
   = 298/60
   = 4.966
Average receivables collection period
   = 365/receivables turnover
   = 73.5 days

3.   The return on total capital for Islington Corporation is *closest* to:
   A.   3.8%.
   B.   5.0%.
   C.   7.0%.
   D.   12.2%.

Correct Answer 3.   B
Return on total capital
   = (net income + interest expense)/average total capital
   = 25/500
   = 5%

---

4.   Islington Corporation's interest coverage is *closest* to:
   A.   0.15 times.
   B.   3.16 times.
   C.   6.33 times.
   D.   16.33 times.

Correct Answer 4.   C
Interest coverage
   = EBIT /interest expense
   = 38/6
   = 6.33 times

---

5.   If the payables payment period for a firm increases this will tend to:
   A.   increase the cash conversion cycle.
   B.   decrease the cash conversion cycle.
   C.   leave the cash conversion cycle unchanged.

Correct Answer 5.   B
Cash conversion cycle = receivables collection period + inventory period – payables payment period.

6   Business risk is the variability of:

    A.   sales.

    B.   net income.

    C.   gross profit.

    D.   operating profit.

Correct Answer 6.   **D**

---

7.   A firm has a dividend pay out ratio of 60%, a return on total capital of 12% and a return on equity of 15%. The sustainable growth rate is *closest* to:

    A.   4.8%.

    B.   6.0%.

    C.   7.2%.

    D.   9.0%.

Correct Answer 7.   **B**

Sustainable growth rate
  = earnings retention rate x return on equity
  = 0.4 x 15%
  = 6%

---

8.   Using common sized financial statements is useful when:

    I.   Comparing companies that are different sizes.

    II.   Looking at historic trends for a company's performance.

    III.   Comparing companies that use different accounting principles.

    A.   I only.

    B.   I and II only.

    C.   II and III only.

    D.   All of the above.

Correct Answer 8.   **B**

36   Dilutive Securities and Earnings per Share

Learning Outcome Statements (LOS)

36-a	**Differentiate** between simple and complex capital structures for purposes of calculating earnings per share (EPS), **describe** the components of EPS, and **calculate** a company's EPS in a simple capital structure.
36-b	**Calculate** a company's weighted average number of shares outstanding.
36-c	**Describe** stock dividends and stock splits, and **determine** the effect of each on a company's weighted average number of shares outstanding.
36-d	**Distinguish** between dilutive and antidilutive securities and **calculate** a company's basic and diluted EPS in a complex capital structure and **describe** and **determine** the effects of convertible securities, options, and warrants on a company's EPS.
36-e	**Compare** and **contrast** the requirements for EPS reporting in simple versus complex capital structures.

Introduction

This Reading looks at the computation of basic and diluted earnings per share. Candidates need to be comfortable calculating weighted-average numbers of shares outstanding and adjusting for complex capital structures when there are potentially dilutive securities such as convertible bonds or options outstanding. The calculations are not difficult but remember to adjust for tax on interest payments on convertible bonds and use the Treasury stock method (not a particularly intuitive method) when there are options or warrants outstanding.

36 Concept Check Questions

1.   A company has 250,000 common stock shares outstanding on January 1st. On July 1st a 1 for 1 stock dividend is announced and on October 1st the company raises cash through the sale of 50,000 shares. The weighted average number of shares outstanding over the year is *closest* to:

    A.   387,500.
    B.   433,333.
    C.   512,500.
    D.   550,000.

---

2.   Esher Corporation had net income last year of $1 million and the weighted average of common shares outstanding was 800,000. There was $100,000 of a convertible bond outstanding with each bond convertible into one share. The coupon on the bond is 10% and the company's marginal tax rate is 30%. The diluted earnings per share are *closest* to:

    A. $1.11.
    B. $1.12.
    C. $1.19.
    D. $1.25.

3.   If a firm has warrants outstanding, earnings per share dilution will occur if the exercise price is:

  A.   below the end market price for the period.
  B.   above the end market price for the period.
  C.   below the average market price for the period.
  D.   above the average market price for the period.

---

4.   A firm has 1 million options outstanding at an exercise price of $26 and the market price per common share is $30. For the purpose of calculating diluted earnings per share then the potential additional shares that are outstanding due to the options is *closest* to:

  A.   33,333.
  B.   38,462.
  C.   133,334.
  D.   1,000,000.

36   Concept Check Answers

1.   A company has 250,000 common stock shares outstanding on January 1st. On July 1st a 1 for 1 stock dividend is announced and on October 1st the company raises cash through the sale of 50,000 shares. The weighted average number of shares outstanding over the year is *closest* to:

    A.   387,500.

    B.   433,333.

    C.   512,500.

    D.   550,000.

Correct Answer 1.   C
Adjusted shares outstanding are shown below:

January 1st	500,000	6 months
July 1st	500,000	3 months
October 1st	550,000	3 months

2.   Esher Corporation had net income last year of $1 million and the weighted average of common shares outstanding was 800,000. There was $100,000 of a convertible bond outstanding with each bond convertible into one share. The coupon on the bond is 10% and the company's marginal tax rate is 30%. The diluted earnings per share are *closest* to:

    A. $1.11.

    B. $1.12.

    C. $1.19.

    D. $1.25.

Correct Answer 2.   B
Diluted EPS = ($1,000,000 + $7,000)/900,000 = $1.12

3.   If a firm has warrants outstanding, earnings per share dilution will occur if the exercise price is:

    A.   below the end market price for the period.

    B.   above the end market price for the period.

    C.   below the average market price for the period.

    D.   above the average market price for the period.

Correct Answer 3.   C

---

4.   A firm has 1 million options outstanding at an exercise price of $26 and the market price per common share is $30. For the purpose of calculating diluted earnings per share then the potential additional shares that are outstanding due to the options is *closest* to:

    A.   33,333.

    B.   38,462.

    C.   133,334.

    D.   1,000,000.

Correct Answer 4.   C

37   Seek and Ye Shall Find

38   Searching for Shenanigans

Learning Outcome Statements (LOS)

37-a	**Explain** the two basic strategies underlying all accounting "shenanigans," and **describe** seven categories of technique that may be used by management to distort a company's reported financial performance and financial condition.
37-b	**Identify** conservative and aggressive accounting policies.
37-c	**Describe** why "shenanigans" exist and **explain** where they are most likely to occur.
38-d	**List** the documents that an analyst should use to identify "shenanigans" and **explain** what information to look for in such documents.

Introduction

These Readings look at tricks or shenanigans that companies use to ensure that their reported earnings are in line with expectations. Obviously the intention is often to hide potentially disappointing earnings. The candidate has to be familiar with specific tricks that are used and the impact on the financial statements, and where they need to look for clues that such shenanigans are being used.

37 & 38 Concept Check Questions

1.   Which of the following is usually classified as "financial shenanigans"?

   A.   A change in accounting policies.

   B.   Extended footnotes in the company accounts.

   C.   An optimistic letter from the company president.

   D.   Steps to distort a company's reported financial statements.

---

2.   Which of the following would indicate a company is using conservative accounting policies?

   A.   Advertising costs are being capitalized.

   B.   Amortization periods are being extended.

   C.   Investment income is reported as part of revenue.

   D.   A policy of expensing start-up costs for new businesses.

---

3.   Which of the following would not be a warning signal for an analyst reviewing the audit of a company?

   A.   A qualified auditor's report.

   B.   The appointment of a new auditor.

   C.   Independent members on the audit committee.

   D.   A small number of reservations on the audit report.

37 & 38 Concept Check Answers

1.   Which of the following is usually classified as "financial shenanigans"?

    A.   A change in accounting policies.

    B.   Extended footnotes in the company accounts.

    C.   An optimistic letter from the company president.

    D.   Steps to distort a company's reported financial statements.

Correct Answer 1.   **D**

---

2.   Which of the following would indicate a company is using conservative accounting policies?

    A.   Advertising costs are being capitalized.

    B.   Amortization periods are being extended.

    C.   Investment income is reported as part of revenue.

    D.   A policy of expensing start-up costs for new businesses.

Correct Answer 2.   **D**

3.   Which of the following would not be a warning signal for an analyst reviewing the audit of a company?

     A.   A qualified auditor's report.

     B.   The appointment of a new auditor.

     C.   Independent members on the audit committee.

     D.   A small number of reservations on the audit report.

Correct Answer 3.   C

An analyst would expect to see a clean auditor's report, any qualifications or reservations would send a warning signal. The appointment of a new auditor would raise the question of whether there had been a disagreement regarding accounting policies with the previous auditor. The existence of an audit committee with independent members is a positive sign.

STUDY SESSION 9

Financial Statement Analysis: Assets

Overview

This Study Session looks at some important issues concerning the reporting of assets in financial statements and how different accounting methods can be used. Often the choice of method makes a substantial difference to the reported financial position and profitability of the company. It can also impact on actual cash flows in the form of taxes paid. An analyst needs to consider the necessary adjustments to the reported figures to better understand the underlying position of the company.

In the following Readings we look at two specific issues relating to assets on the balance sheet, these are accounting for inventory and long-lived assets.

Reading Assignments

The Analysis and Use of Financial Statements, 3rd edition, Gerald I. White, Ashwinpaul C. Sondhi, and Dov Fried (Wiley, 2003)

39.   "Analysis of Inventories," Ch. 6, pp. 192–215 and pp. 219-220

40.   "Analysis of Long-Lived Assets: Part I – The Capitalization Decision," Ch. 7, pp. 227–240, including Box 7-1 and pp. 242–244

41.   "Analysis of Long-Lived Assets: Part II – Analysis of Depreciation and Impairment," Ch. 8, pp. 257–278 and pp. 280–282

39 Analysis of Inventories

Learning Outcome Statements (LOS)

39-a	**Compute** ending inventory balances and cost of goods sold using the LIFO, FIFO, and average cost methods to account for product inventory and **explain** the relationship among and the usefulness of inventory and cost-of-goods-sold data provided by the LIFO, FIFO, and average cost methods when prices are 1) stable or 2) changing.
39-b	**Adjust** the financial statements of companies using different inventory accounting methods to **compare** and **describe** the effect of the different methods on cost of goods sold and inventory balances. **Discuss** how a company's choice of inventory accounting method affects other financial items such as income, cash flow, and working capital, and **compute** and **describe** the effects of the choice of inventory method on profitability, liquidity, activity, and solvency ratios.
39-c	**Discuss** the reasons why a LIFO reserve might decline during a given period and **discuss** the implications of such a decline for financial analysis.
39-d	**Discuss** how inventories are reported in the financial statements and how cost, market and net realizable value are generally determined.

Introduction

When a company sells an item of inventory they must assign a cost to the item. In some cases the company records the cost as that of replacing the item of inventory or, more precisely, as that of the last unit of inventory purchased (last-in, first-out or LIFO). In other cases they record it as the cost of the first unit of inventory purchased (first-in, first-out, or FIFO). Another method is to use the average cost of items in inventory. The choice of method will not only have a direct impact on the cost assigned to each unit of inventory sold in the income statement but also on the value of the remaining inventory in the balance sheet. It can also have a real (as opposed to only an accounting) effect on the company since cash flows will reflect the tax paid by the company under the different methods. Candidates will need to able to compute financial statement items using the different methods and to work out the effect on financial ratios.

The material is relatively straightforward and will hopefully provide some easy marks in the exam.

39   Concept Check Questions

1.   A firm has inventory of 200 units at the beginning of the period, at a cost of $10 each. Over the year it purchases another 500 units at $9 each, and then another 600 units at $8 each. The ending inventory is 300 units. The value of the inventory using FIFO and LIFO reporting is *closest* to:

	LIFO	FIFO
A.	$2,400	$2,900
B.	$2,400	$2,608
C.	$2,608	$2,900
D.	$2,900	$2,400

2.   LIFO reserve is:

A.   the amount that must be added to COGS calculated under FIFO to calculate COGS under LIFO.

B.   the amount that must be added to COGS calculated under LIFO to calculate COGS under FIFO.

C.   the amount that must be added to inventories calculated under FIFO to calculate inventories under LIFO.

D.   the amount that must be added to inventories calculated under LIFO to calculate inventories under FIFO.

3.   If the size of inventories is increasing and prices are rising then using LIFO rather than FIFO for inventory accounting will report:

    A.   lower cash flows and lower working capital.

    B.   lower cash flows and higher working capital.

    C.   higher cash flows and lower working capital.

    D.   higher cash flows and higher working capital.

---

4.   A company reports under LIFO the following information:

LIFO reserve	$5 million
Increase in LIFO reserve	$2 million
Sales	$50 million
COGS	$30 million

The gross profit margin if the company had used FIFO accounting would be:

    A.   40%.

    B.   44%.

    C.   50%.

    D.   56%.

---

5.   An analyst should generally use:

    A.   LIFO when analyzing a balance sheet and FIFO when analyzing an income statement.

    B.   FIFO when analyzing a balance sheet and LIFO when analyzing an income statement.

    C.   FIFO when analyzing a balance sheet and FIFO when analyzing an income statement.

    D.   LIFO when analyzing a balance sheet and LIFO when analyzing an income statement.

39   Concept Check Answers

1.   A firm has inventory of 200 units at the beginning of the period, at a cost of $10 each. Over the year it purchases another 500 units at $9 each, and then another 600 units at $8 each. The ending inventory is 300 units. The value of the inventory using FIFO and LIFO reporting is *closest* to:

	LIFO	FIFO
A.	$2,400	$2,900
B.	$2,400	$2,608
C.	$2,608	$2,900
D.	$2,900	$2,400

Correct Answer 1.   D

Under FIFO the remaining 300 units are the ones purchased last so have a value of:

$$(300 \times \$8) = \$2,400$$

Under LIFO they are the ones purchased first so have a value of:

$$(200 \times \$10) + (100 \times \$9) = \$2,900$$

---

2.   LIFO reserve is:

A.   the amount that must be added to COGS calculated under FIFO to calculate COGS under LIFO.

B.   the amount that must be added to COGS calculated under LIFO to calculate COGS under FIFO.

C.   the amount that must be added to inventories calculated under FIFO to calculate inventories under LIFO.

D.   the amount that must be added to inventories calculated under LIFO to calculate inventories under FIFO.

Correct Answer 2.   D

3.   If the size of inventories is increasing and prices are rising then using LIFO rather than FIFO for inventory accounting will report:

    A.   lower cash flows and lower working capital.

    B.   lower cash flows and higher working capital.

    C.   higher cash flows and lower working capital.

    D.   higher cash flows and higher working capital.

Correct Answer 3.   C

---

4.   A company reports under LIFO the following information:

LIFO reserve	$5 million
Increase in LIFO reserve	$2 million
Sales	$50 million
COGS	$30 million

The gross profit margin if the company had used FIFO accounting would be:

    A.   40%.

    B.   44%.

    C.   50%.

    D.   56%.

Correct Answer 4.   B

COGS under FIFO is ($30 million - $2 million) = $28 million Gross profit margin

$$= \left(\frac{50-28}{50}\right) = 44\%$$

---

5.   An analyst should generally use:

    A.   LIFO when analyzing a balance sheet and FIFO when analyzing an income statement.

    B.   FIFO when analyzing a balance sheet and LIFO when analyzing an income statement.

    C.   FIFO when analyzing a balance sheet and FIFO when analyzing an income statement.

    D.   LIFO when analyzing a balance sheet and LIFO when analyzing an income statement.

Correct Answer 5.   B

LIFO is more accurate for income statements since, if prices are changing, the costs will better represent current costs.

FIFO is more accurate for balance sheets since the value of inventory will be closer to market value.

40   Analysis of Long-Lived Assets, Part 1 – The Capitalization Decision

Learning Outcome Statements (LOS)

40-a	**Compute** and **describe** the effects of capitalizing versus expensing on net income, shareholders' equity, cash flow from operations, and financial ratios and **explain** the effects on financial statements and the interest coverage (times interest earned) of capitalizing interest costs, and **explain** the circumstances in which intangible assets, including software development costs and research and development costs, are capitalized.
40-b	**Calculate** and **describe** both the initial and long-term effects of asset revaluations on financial ratios.

Introduction

Now we turn to long-term assets which are not, as in the case of inventory, held for the purpose of selling to customers. Examples would be plant and machinery, computer software and patents. This Reading centers on the rationale behind, and the impact of, a decision to expense versus capitalize the cost of these assets. Candidates need to know the effects of these decisions on the financial statements and ratios.

40 Concept Check Questions

1. A company finances the construction of a new factory with borrowings. Which of the following statements is **CORRECT** regarding the interest costs during the construction period?

    A. Interest costs should be expensed.

    B. Interest costs should be capitalized.

    C. The company can choose whether to expense or capitalize the interest costs.

---

2. A decision by a new company to capitalize costs rather than expense them will initially lead to:

    A. lower profits.

    B. higher debt to equity ratios.

    C. lower operating profit margins.

    D. higher cash flow from operations.

3.   In the U.S. which of the following costs are expensed?

    A.   Acquisition of a brand name.

    B.   The purchase of franchise rights.

    C.   Research and development spending.

    D.   Software development costs once the feasibility of a project is established.

40   Concept Check Answers

1.   A company finances the construction of a new factory with borrowings. Which of the following statements is **CORRECT** regarding the interest costs during the construction period?

    A.   Interest costs should be expensed.

    B.   Interest costs should be capitalized.

    C.   The company can choose whether to expense or capitalize the interest costs.

Correct Answer 1.   **D**

2.   A decision by a new company to capitalize costs rather than expense them will initially lead to:

    A.   lower profits.

    B.   higher debt to equity ratios.

    C.   lower operating profit margins.

    D.   higher cash flow from operations.

Correct Answer 1.   **D**

3.   In the U.S. which of the following costs are expensed?

    A.   Acquisition of a brand name.

    B.   The purchase of franchise rights.

    C.   Research and development spending.

    D.   Software development costs once the feasibility of a project is established.

Correct Answer 1.   **D**

41   Analysis of Long-Lived Assets, Part 2 – Analysis of Depreciation and Impairment

Learning Outcome Statements (LOS)

41-a	**Identify** the different depreciation methods and **discuss** how the choice of depreciation method affects a company's financial statements, ratios, and taxes. **Explain** the role of depreciable lives and salvage values in the computation of depreciation expenses, and **compute** and **describe** how changing depreciation methods or changing the estimated useful life or salvage value of an asset affects financial statements and ratios.
41-b	**Discuss** the use of fixed asset disclosures to compare companies' average age of depreciable assets, and **calculate**, using such disclosures, the average age and average depreciable life of fixed assets.
41-c	**Define** impairment of long-lived assets and **explain** what effect such impairment has on a company's financial statements and ratios.
41-d	**List** the requirements of SFAS 143, Accounting for Asset Retirement Obligations (AROs), and **explain** the likely financial statement and ratio effects for most firms.

Introduction

Moving on from the previous Reading, we now look in more detail at the accounting treatment of long-lived assets on the balance sheet and income statements. We compare the effects of using different methods of depreciating, or allocating the cost, of tangible assets over their useful life. Candidates will need to be able to compute depreciation expense and net book values using straight-line and accelerated methods. Also candidates need to be familiar with the accounting treatment of impairment of assets which must be recognized when the value of an asset on the balance sheet is more than the cash flows that will be generated by the asset.

41   Concept Check Questions

1.   An asset costs $40,000 and has a depreciable life of eight years and an estimated salvage value of $5,000 at the end of the eight years (use data for questions 1 to 3).

The depreciation expense in the third year using the straight-line method is *closest* to:

    A. $4,000.

    B. $4,375.

    C. $5,000.

    D. $5,625.

2.   The depreciation expense in the third year using the double-declining-balance method is *closest* to:

    A. $4,375.

    B. $4,922.

    C. $5,000.

    D. $5,625.

3.   The depreciation expense in the third year using the sum-of-years'-digits method is *closest* to:

    A. $2,917.

    B. $4,861.

    C. $5,833.

    D. $6,666.

4.   A company has just completed a major capital expenditure program and has decided to use accelerated depreciation methods rather than straight-line depreciation methods. The impact of this decision on this year's financial statements is likely to be the following:

    A.   net income and return on equity will both be lower.

    B.   net income and return on equity will both be higher.

    C.   net income will be higher and return on equity will be lower.

    D.   net income will be lower and return on equity will be higher.

---

5.   If a company's gross investment in plant and equipment at year end is $10 million, accumulated depreciation is $4 million and the depreciation expense over the year is $1 million, then the estimated average age of the plant and equipment is:

    A.   1 year.

    B.   4 years.

    C.   6 years.

---

6.   SFAS 143 is important for all of the following reasons, except?

    A.   It standardizes accounting treatment of costs associated with retiring assets.

    B.   It allows companies to delay making provisions for environmental remediation.

    C.   It allocates the costs of environmental remediation to the period when it is incurred.

    D.   It requires companies to disclose details of liabilities related to environmental remediation.

41   Concept Check Answers

1.   An asset costs $40,000 and has a depreciable life of eight years and an estimated salvage value of $5,000 at the end of the eight years (use data for questions 1 to 3).

The depreciation expense in the third year using the straight-line method is *closest* to:

    A. $4,000.

    B. $4,375.

    C. $5,000.

    D. $5,625.

Correct Answer 1.   **D**

---

2.   The depreciation expense in the third year using the double-declining-balance method is *closest* to:

    A. $4,375.

    B. $4,922.

    C. $5,000.

    D. $5,625.

Correct Answer 1.   **D**

---

3.   The depreciation expense in the third year using the sum-of-years'-digits method is *closest* to:

    A. $2,917.

    B. $4,861.

    C. $5,833.

    D. $6,666.

4.   A company has just completed a major capital expenditure program and has decided to use accelerated depreciation methods rather than straight-line depreciation methods. The impact of this decision on this year's financial statements is likely to be the following:

    A.   net income and return on equity will both be lower.

    B.   net income and return on equity will both be higher.

    C.   net income will be higher and return on equity will be lower.

    D.   net income will be lower and return on equity will be higher.

Correct Answer 1.   **D**

---

5.   If a company's gross investment in plant and equipment at year end is $10 million, accumulated depreciation is $4 million and the depreciation expense over the year is $1 million, then the estimated average age of the plant and equipment is:

    A.   1 year.

    B.   4 years.

    C.   6 years.

Correct Answer 1.   **D**

---

6.   SFAS 143 is important for all of the following reasons, except?

    A.   It standardizes accounting treatment of costs associated with retiring assets.

    B.   It allows companies to delay making provisions for environmental remediation.

    C.   It allocates the costs of environmental remediation to the period when it is incurred.

    D.   It requires companies to disclose details of liabilities related to environmental remediation.

STUDY SESSION 10

Financial Statement Analysis: Liabilities

Overview

This is another Study Session containing important topics in financial statement analysis. The first Reading looks at tax and the differences between accounting for tax in financial statements and in tax reports. The differences give rise to deferred tax assets and liabilities when tax is 'overpaid' or 'underpaid' according to the financial statements. In addition to mastering the different terminology used in the reporting systems, candidates need to understand the details of how deferred tax items are created and recorded.

The last two Readings tackle analysis of liabilities. First we look at financial liabilities where there is debt as a result of a financing decision. Generally debt is recorded on the balance sheet as the present value of future cash flows (interest and principal repayment) that the company will need to pay on the debt. The Reading focuses on the impact on the financial statements of issuing bonds when they are issued at a premium or discount to par value. Next we look at contractual liabilities such as leases and other forms of off-balance-sheet debt. Candidates need to differentiate between the effect of companies using operating leases (which are an expense and not recorded on the balance sheet) and using capital leases (where the accounting treatment is similar to the company actually owning the asset).

Reading Assignments

The Analysis and Use of Financial Statements, 3rd edition, Gerald I. White, Ashwinpaul C. Sondhi, and Dov Fried (Wiley, 2003)

42.   "Analysis of Income Taxes," Ch. 9, pp. 290–314 (including Box 9-1 and 9-2)

43.   "Analysis of Financing Liabilities," Ch. 10, pp. 322–332, 337–343

44.   "Leases and Off-Balance-Sheet Debt," Ch. 11, pp. 363–383 (including Box 11-1) and pp. 386-393

42   Analysis of Income Taxes

Learning Outcome Statements (LOS)

42-a	**List** and **explain** the key terms used in income tax accounting, **explain** why and how deferred tax liabilities and assets are created, and **describe** the liability method of accounting for deferred taxes.
42-b	**Discuss** the implications of a valuation allocation (i.e. when it is required, what impact it has on the financial statements, and how it might affect an analyst's review of a company).
42-c	**Explain** the factors that determine whether a company's deferred tax liabilities should be treated as a liability or as equity for purposes of financial analysis.
42-d	**Distinguish** between temporary and permanent items in pretax financial income and taxable income.
42-e	**Compute** income tax expense, income taxes payable, deferred tax assets, and deferred tax liabilities.
42-f	**Calculate** the adjustment to the financial statements related to a change in the tax rate.

Introduction

The objectives of financial reporting are to produce statements that are useful to assess the financial position and performance of the company and there is an incentive to reduce the taxes that will have to be paid in the near term. However tax reporting is based on different objectives and often taxable income is calculated using modified cash methods. This, plus differences in reporting methods and estimates, results in differences between income tax expense on the financial statements and taxable income on tax reports. The differences give rise to deferred tax assets (which the company can reclaim in the future) or deferred tax liabilities (which the company must pay in the future). Candidates need to able to differentiate between temporary and permanent differences between the two reporting systems.

The Study Guide says that deferred taxes are applicable globally and therefore are the focus of the Reading Assignment. We look at accounting differences that create deferred tax assets and liabilities in the notes below.

42   Concept Check Questions

1.   If a deferred tax liability is very unlikely to be paid then it should be treated as:
   A.   a long-term liability.
   B.   stockholders' equity.
   C.   a short-term liability.
   D.   an extraordinary item.

---

2.   A firm's taxable income is $300,000 and pretax income is $400,000 and the tax rate is 25%, then the deferred tax expense is:
   A.   0.
   B. $ 25,000.
   C. $ 75,000.
   D. $100,000

---

3.   Tax loss carryforwards:
   A.   are a deferred tax liability and should be reduced by a valuation allowance if they are unlikely to be realized.
   B.   are a deferred tax asset and should be reduced by a valuation allowance if they are unlikely to be recovered.
   C.   are a potential asset since they may decrease future taxes payable, but they are not recognized under U.S. GAAP.
   D.   are a potential liability since they may increase future taxes payable, but they are not recognized under U.S. GAAP.

42   Concept Check Answers

1.   If a deferred tax liability is very unlikely to be paid then it should be treated as:

   A.   a long-term liability.

   B.   stockholders' equity.

   C.   a short-term liability.

   D.   an extraordinary item.

Correct Answer 1.   B
If the factors that created the deferred tax liability are unlikely to be reversed, than it is
   considered part of stockholders' equity.

---

2.   A firm's taxable income is $300,000 and pretax income is $400,000 and the tax rate is 25%,
then the deferred tax expense is:

   A.   0.

   B. $ 25,000.

   C. $ 75,000.

   D. $100,000

Correct Answer 2.   B
Taxes payable are $75,000 and the tax expense is $100,000, the difference is a deferred tax
   expense.

---

3.   Tax loss carryforwards:

   A.   are a deferred tax liability and should be reduced by a valuation allowance if they are
unlikely to be realized.

   B.   are a deferred tax asset and should be reduced by a valuation allowance if they are
unlikely to be recovered.

   C.   are a potential asset since they may decrease future taxes payable, but they are not
recognized under U.S. GAAP.

   D.   are a potential liability since they may increase future taxes payable, but they are not
recognized under U.S. GAAP.

Correct Answer 3.   B

43   Analysis of Financing Liabilities

Learning Outcome Statements (LOS)

43-a	**Compute** the effects of debt issuance and amortization of bond discounts and premiums on the financial statements and ratios; **discuss** the effect on reported cash flows of issuing zero-coupon debt. **Determine** the appropriate classification for debt with equity features and **calculate** the effect of issuance of such instruments on the debt to total capital ratio.
43-b	**Discuss** the effect of changing interest rates on the market value of debt and on financial statements and ratios.

Introduction

This Reading looks at the treatment of bonds on the issuer's financial statements. The liability and interest expense associated with the bond are based on interest rates at the time of issue, not the par value of the bond. The liability is the present value of the cash flows payable to the bond holders, and if a bond is issued at a discount or a premium this discount or premium is amortized over the life of the bond so the liability is equal to the par value at maturity. This method of accounting has an impact on cash flows reporting and candidates must understand the implications for the categorization of cash flow. Interest paid is based on the coupon rate and is a cash outflow from operations, whereas the repayment of capital or amortization of the premium is a cash flow from financing. This leads to inconsistencies in the treatment of cash flow for high versus low or zero coupon bonds.

43   Concept Check Questions

1.   If a bond is issued at a discount the interest expense:

    A.   increases over time.

    B.   decreases over time.

    C.   is constant over time.

---

2.   If interest rates rise after a firm issues long-term debt then the equity value of the firm will be:

    A.   overstated.

    B.   understated.

    C.   fairly stated.

3.   If the conversion price of a convertible bond is significantly lower than the market price of the underlying stock then an analyst should treat the convertible as:
    A.   equity.
    B.   long-term debt.

---

4.   Interest expense is lowest for:
    A.   bonds with warrants.
    B.   convertible bonds.
    C.   conventional bonds.
    D.   zero coupon bonds.

43   Concept Check Answers

1.   If a bond is issued at a discount the interest expense:

    A.   increases over time.

    B.   decreases over time.

    C.   is constant over time.

Correct Answer 1.   **A**

The balance sheet liability for the bond increases over time, interest expense is the balance sheet liability multiplied by the effective interest rate.

---

2.   If interest rates rise after a firm issues long-term debt then the equity value of the firm will be:

    A.   overstated.

    B.   understated.

    C.   fairly stated.

Correct Answer 2.   **B**

The market value of the debt will fall as interest rates rise leading to an economic gain for the firm, thereby increasing the real value to stockholders; this is not reflected in the financial statements.

3.   If the conversion price of a convertible bond is significantly lower than the market price of the underlying stock then an analyst should treat the convertible as:
   A.   equity.
   B.   long-term debt.

Correct Answer 3.   **A**
It is very likely that the convertible will be converted into equity, therefore the debt will not have to be repaid.

---

4.   Interest expense is lowest for:
   A.   bonds with warrants.
   B.   convertible bonds.
   C.   conventional bonds.
   D.   zero coupon bonds.

Correct Answer 4.   **B**
Interest expense is lower for bonds with equity features. It is lower for convertibles than bonds with warrants since bonds with warrants are issued at a discount.

44   Leases and Off-Balance-Sheet Debt

Learning Outcome Statements (LOS)

44-a	**Classify** a lease as capital or operating and **discuss** the factors that determine whether a company would tend to favor leasing over outright asset purchases and more specifically, factors that would favor capital or operating leases.
44-b	**Calculate** the effects of capital and operating leases on financial statements and ratios of the lessees.
44-c	**Explain** and **differentiate** the accounting treatment for a sale and leaseback of assets under U.S. and IASB GAAP.
44-d	**Describe** the types and economic consequences of off-balance-sheet financing and **determine** how take-or-pay contracts, throughput arrangements, and the sale of receivables affect selected financial ratios.
44-e	**Distinguish** between a sales-type lease and a direct-financing lease and **describe** the effects on the financial statements and ratios of sales-type and operating leases.

Introduction

This Reading starts with an analysis of leases and a discussion of why lessees generally prefer to structure and report leases as operating leases where they are essentially paying a rental expense for the use of an asset (the asset could be anything from an airplane to a photocopier). However, when a company effectively purchases an asset through a lease agreement the lease must be treated as a capital lease. The asset is then reported on the balance sheet and depreciated and a liability is also recorded which is the present value of future lease payments. Candidates need to study the impact on financial ratios of the different methods of lease accounting. Operating leases are often referred to as off-balance-sheet financing. Candidates are expected to be able to describe other forms of off-balance-sheet financing such as the sale of receivables and take-or-pay contracts.

44   Concept Check Questions

1.   A company that makes extensive use of operating leases, rather than capital leases, will report:

    A.   lower debt to equity ratios and lower operating expenses.

    B.   higher debt to equity ratios and lower operating expenses.

    C.   lower debt to equity ratios and higher operating expenses.

    D.   higher debt to equity ratios and higher operating expenses.

---

2.   A lease must be classified as a capital lease by a lessee if:

    A.   the lease term is 50% of the economic life of the asset.

    B.   the lessee is responsible for servicing and maintaining the asset.

    C.   the present value of lease payments is 75% of the fair value of the asset.

    D.   the lessee has the right to buy the asset at the end of the lease term at a heavily discounted price.

3.   The total expense of a capital lease is made up of:
    A.   deprecation plus interest.
    B.   interest plus principal repayment.
    C.   depreciation plus principal repayment.
    D.   depreciation plus interest plus principal repayment.

---

4.   Which of the following is not an example of off-balance-sheet financing?
    A.   Capital leases.
    B.   Sale of receivables.
    C.   Take-or-pay arrangements.
    D.   Equity accounting for affiliated finance companies.

44   Concept Check Answers

1.   A company that makes extensive use of operating leases, rather than capital leases, will report:

    A.   lower debt to equity ratios and lower operating expenses.

    B.   higher debt to equity ratios and lower operating expenses.

    C.   lower debt to equity ratios and higher operating expenses.

    D.   higher debt to equity ratios and higher operating expenses.

Correct Answer 1.   C

---

2.   A lease must be classified as a capital lease by a lessee if:

    A.   the lease term is 50% of the economic life of the asset.

    B.   the lessee is responsible for servicing and maintaining the asset.

    C.   the present value of lease payments is 75% of the fair value of the asset.

    D.   the lessee has the right to buy the asset at the end of the lease term at a heavily discounted price.

Correct Answer 2.   D

3.   The total expense of a capital lease is made up of:
   A.   deprecation plus interest.
   B.   interest plus principal repayment.
   C.   depreciation plus principal repayment.
   D.   depreciation plus interest plus principal repayment.

Correct Answer 3,   A

---

4.   Which of the following is not an example of off-balance-sheet financing?
   A.   Capital leases.
   B.   Sale of receivables.
   C.   Take-or-pay arrangements.
   D.   Equity accounting for affiliated finance companies.

Correct Answer 4.   A
Operating, rather than capital leases, are off-balance-sheet financing.

STUDY SESSION 11

Corporate Finance

Overview

This is a long Study Session covering important corporate finance concepts, including cash flow, leverage, cost of capital and how they impact on the value of a company. These concepts also appear in other Level I Study Sessions and throughout the CFA syllabus.

The first Reading looks at agency problems and then we move on to the core of the Study Session. The next four Readings deal with capital budgeting, and the decision-making process for whether potential investments or projects should be undertaken. This involves calculating the cost of capital, estimating the future cash flows from the investments and deciding whether the cash flows will cover the cost of capital. We also consider measures of risk for a company which will give an indication of the level of uncertainty surrounding the cash flow forecasts.

In the last two Readings we look at capital structure and dividend policy. We consider the issues that affect how a company should balance debt and equity financing to maximise its share price. We then look at dividends and how high or low dividend payout ratios will affect the company's share price.

Reading Assignments

Fundamentals of Financial Management, 8th edition, Eugene F. Brigham and Joel F. Houston (Dryden, 1998)

45. "An Overview of Financial Management," Ch. 1, pp. 18–22

46. "The Cost of Capital," Ch. 9

47. "The Basics of Capital Budgeting," Ch. 10

48. "Cash Flow Estimation and Other Topics in Capital Budgeting," Ch. 11

49. "Risk Analysis and the Optimal Capital Budget," Ch. 12

50. "Capital Structure and Leverage," Ch. 13, including Appendix 13A

51. "Dividend Policy," Ch. 14

45   An Overview of Financial Management

Learning Outcome Statements (LOS)

45-a	**Discuss** potential agency problems of stockholders versus 1) managers and 2) creditors and **describe** four mechanisms used to motivate managers to act in stockholders' best interests.

Introduction

This is a short Reading which discusses the potential problems that may arise when a principal (shareholder) appoints agents (managers) and gives authority to the latter to make decisions. Conflicts of interest may also occur between stockholders and creditors. Ways to alleviate these agency problems and conflicts of interest are discussed.

45   Concept Check Questions

1.   Which of the following is the mechanism *least likely* to be used for motivating managers to act in the best interests of stockholders?

    A.   High annual salaries.

    B.   Executive stock options.

    C.   The threat of hostile takeover.

    D.   Shareholder-sponsored proposals at annual stockholders' meetings.

---

2.   Which of the following is an example of an agency problem?

    A.   An owner/manager owns all of the outstanding company's common stock.

    B.   Different shareholders in a company prefer different levels of dividend payout-ratios.

    C.   Managers are awarded performance shares if they stay with the company for ten years.

    D.   A company's managers decide to maximize the stockholders' returns by increasing the company's gearing.

45   Concept Check Answers

1.   Which of the following is the mechanism *least likely* to be used for motivating managers to act in the best interests of stockholders?

    A.   High annual salaries.

    B.   Executive stock options.

    C.   The threat of hostile takeover.

    D.   Shareholder-sponsored proposals at annual stockholders' meetings.

Correct Answer 1.   A

---

2.   Which of the following is an example of an agency problem?

    A.   An owner/manager owns all of the outstanding company's common stock.

    B.   Different shareholders in a company prefer different levels of dividend payout-ratios.

    C.   Managers are awarded performance shares if they stay with the company for ten years.

    D.   A company's managers decide to maximize the stockholders' returns by increasing the company's gearing.

Correct Answer 2.   D

46   The Cost of Capital

Learning Outcome Statements (LOS)

46-a	**Explain** and **interpret** the cost of capital used in capital budgeting as a weighted average of the opportunity costs of various types of capital the company targets for use.
46-b	**Calculate** the component costs of 1) debt, 2) preferred stock, 3) retained earnings (three different methods), and 4) newly issued stock or external equity.
46-c	**Define** target (optimal) capital structure and **calculate** a company's weighted-average cost of capital, **calculate** a company's marginal cost of capital and **distinguish** between the weighted-average cost of capital and marginal cost of capital.
46-d	**Explain** the factors that affect the cost of capital, and **distinguish** between those factors that can and cannot be controlled by the company.

Introduction

All capital has a cost and the true cost of capital is not the same as the cash interest paid on debt or dividends paid to shareholders. This Reading deals with various components of capital in a target capital structure and candidates are expected to be able to calculate the cost of each component. A weighted-average calculation of the cost of capital is also presented, as well as the calculation for marginal cost of capital. Calculations are generally relatively simple but do not forget to adjust for tax in the cost of debt as interest is a tax deductible expense. Candidates are also expected to recognize the factors which affect the cost of capital and identify those which are within and beyond the control of the firm.

46   Questions

1.   A company has preferred stock outstanding whose current market price is $85; the par value is $100. The dividend is $8 per annum and the marginal corporate tax rate is 40%. The cost of preferred stock is *closest* to:

   A.   4.8%.

   B.   5.6%.

   C.   8.0%.

   D.   9.4%.

2.   A company has a 10% coupon bond outstanding that is trading in the market at a yield to maturity of 9%. The company's marginal corporate tax rate is 40%. The cost of debt is *closest* to:

   A.   5.4%.

   B.   6.0%.

   C.   9.0%.

   D.   10.0%.

3.   A company has a stock price of $25 and is expected to pay a dividend of $1 one year from now. The growth in dividends is forecast to be 5%. The company's marginal corporate tax rate is 40%. The cost of retained earnings is *closest* to:

   A.   2.4%.

   B.   4.0%.

   C.   5.4%.

   D.   9.0%.

4.   Company X has bonds outstanding that yield 6% and Company Y has bonds outstanding that yield 8%. The cost of equity is likely to be:

    A.   lower for Company X than Company Y.

    B.   higher for Company X than Company Y.

---

5.   A company has a target capital structure of 60% debt, 30% common equity and 10% preferred equity. If the after-tax cost of debt is 6%, common equity is 10% and preferred equity is 9%, the weighted-average cost of capital is *closest* to:

    A.   6.0%.

    B.   7.5%.

    C.   8.3%.

    D.   10.0%.

46   Concept Check Answers

1.   A company has preferred stock outstanding whose current market price is $85; the par value is $100. The dividend is $8 per annum and the marginal corporate tax rate is 40%. The cost of preferred stock is *closest* to:

    A.   4.8%.

    B.   5.6%.

    C.   8.0%.

    D.   9.4%.

Correct Answer 1.   D

k_{ps} = preferred dividend/current price = $8/$85 = 9.4%

---

2.   A company has a 10% coupon bond outstanding that is trading in the market at a yield to maturity of 9%. The company's marginal corporate tax rate is 40%. The cost of debt is *closest* to:

    A.   5.4%.

    B.   6.0%.

    C.   9.0%.

    D.   10.0%.

Correct Answer 2.   A

Cost of debt = $k_d(1-T) = 9\%(1.0 - 0.4) = 5.4\%$

---

3.   A company has a stock price of $25 and is expected to pay a dividend of $1 one year from now. The growth in dividends is forecast to be 5%. The company's marginal corporate tax rate is 40%. The cost of retained earnings is *closest* to:

    A.   2.4%.

    B.   4.0%.

    C.   5.4%.

    D.   9.0%.

Correct Answer 3.   D

$$k_e = \frac{D_1}{P} + g = \frac{\$1}{\$25} + 5\% = 9\%$$

4.   Company X has bonds outstanding that yield 6% and Company Y has bonds outstanding that yield 8%. The cost of equity is likely to be:
    A.   lower for Company X than Company Y.

    B.   higher for Company X than Company Y.

Correct Answer 4.   **A**
The bond-yield-plus-risk-premium approach states that the cost of equity for each company is the long-term bond yield on debt issued by each company plus a risk premium.

---

5.   A company has a target capital structure of 60% debt, 30% common equity and 10% preferred equity. If the after-tax cost of debt is 6%, common equity is 10% and preferred equity is 9%, the weighted-average cost of capital is *closest* to:
    A.   6.0%.

    B.   7.5%.

    C.   8.3%.

    D.   10.0%.

Correct Answer 5.   **B**

$$WACC = w_d k_d (1-T) + w_{ps} k_{ps} + w_s k_s$$
$$= (0.60 \times 6\%) + (0.30 \times 10\%) + (0.10 \times 9\%) = 7.5\%$$

47   The Basics of Capital Budgeting

Learning Outcome Statements (LOS)

47-a	**Calculate** and **interpret** payback period, discounted payback period, net present value (NPV), and internal rate of return (IRR), and **evaluate** capital projects using each method.
47-b	**Explain** the effect on shareholders of the adoption of investment opportunities with 1) zero net present values and 2) positive net present values.
47-c	**Explain** the NPV profile, the relative advantages and disadvantages of the NPV and IRR methods, particularly with respect to independent versus mutually exclusive projects, the "multiple IRR problem" and the cash flow pattern that causes the problem, and why NPV and IRR methods can produce conflicting rankings for capital projects.
47-d	**Describe** the role of the post-audit in the capital budgeting process.

Introduction

This is an important section and deals with capital budgeting and evaluation of projects. Four main methods of evaluating whether projects are attractive or not are the payback period, discounted payback period, net present value (NPV), and internal rate of return (IRR). Candidates should know how to evaluate projects using the different methods and identify the advantages and the disadvantages of each method. Using NPV is the preferred method and candidates should understand why the assumption made on the reinvestment of capital is considered more realistic in the NPV than in the IRR method. Calculations are frequently based on the concept of time value of money (NPV and IRR are already covered in Study Session 2) and candidates should practice the calculations using a CFA Institute approved calculator.

47   Concept Check Questions

1.   The following data is provided on the expected net cash flows from two projects:

Year	Project A ($mn)	Project B ($mn)
0	-100	-200
1	50	50
2	40	80
3	30	80

If the cost of capital for each project is 10% which of the following statements is *correct*?

    A.   Both project A and project B should be rejected.

    B.   Both project A and project B should be accepted.

    C.   Project B should be accepted and project A rejected.

    D.   Project A should be accepted and project B rejected.

---

2.   If the cash flows from a project are as follows:

Year	Project ($mn)
0	-100
1	75
2	50

The IRR is *closest* to:

    A.   10.0%.

    B.   12.5%.

    C.   15.0%.

    D.   17.5%.

---

3.   Which of the following statements is *correct* concerning the different methods for evaluating projects?

    A.   If the payback period is positive it indicates that a project should be accepted.

    B.   The NPV method can give multiple answers if there are non-normal cash flows.

    C.   The IRR method is preferred since it assumes reinvestment at the project's cost of capital.

    D.   The NPV method is preferred since it assumes reinvestment at the project's cost of capital.

47   Concept Check Answers

1.   The following data is provided on the expected net cash flows from two projects:

Year	Project A ($mn)	Project B ($mn)
0	-100	-200
1	50	50
2	40	80
3	30	80

If the cost of capital for each project is 10% which of the following statements is *correct*?

    A.   Both project A and project B should be rejected.

    B.   Both project A and project B should be accepted.

    C.   Project B should be accepted and project A rejected.

    D.   Project A should be accepted and project B rejected.

Correct Answer 1.   **D**

Year	A Discounted Net Cash Flow	B Discounted Net Cash Flow
0	-100.00	-200.00
1	45.50	45.50
2	33.10	66.10
3	22.50	60.10
	1.10	-28.30

2. If the cash flows from a project are as follows:

Year	Project ($mn)
0	-100
1	75
2	50

The IRR is *closest* to:

    A.   10.0%.

    B.   12.5%.

    C.   15.0%.

    D.   17.5%.

Correct Answer 2.   **D**

$$0 = CF_0 + \frac{CF_1}{(1+IRR)} + \frac{CF_2}{(1+IRR)^2} + \ldots\ldots + \frac{CF_n}{(1+IRR)^n}$$

$$= -100 + \frac{75}{(1+IRR)} + \frac{50}{(1+IRR)^2}$$

$IRR = 17.5\%$

Need to use financial calculator or alternatively use trial and error to select which answer is closest.

---

3. Which of the following statements is *correct* concerning the different methods for evaluating projects?

    A.   If the payback period is positive it indicates that a project should be accepted.

    B.   The NPV method can give multiple answers if there are non-normal cash flows.

    C.   The IRR method is preferred since it assumes reinvestment at the project's cost of capital.

    D.   The NPV method is preferred since it assumes reinvestment at the project's cost of capital.

Correct Answer 3.   **D**

48   Cash Flow Estimation and Other Topics in Capital Budgeting

Learning Outcome Statements (LOS)

48-a	**Distinguish** between cash flows and accounting profits and **discuss** the relevance to capital budgeting of the following: incremental cash flow, sunk cost, opportunity cost, externality, and cannibalization.
48-b	**Explain** the importance of changes in net working capital in the capital budgeting process.
48-c	**Determine** by NPV analysis whether a project (expansion or replacement) should be undertaken and **compute** and **interpret** each of the following for an expansion project and a replacement project: initial investment outlay, operating cash flow over a project's life, and terminal-year cash flow.
48-d	**Compare** two projects with unequal lives, using both the replacement chain and equivalent annual annuity approaches.
48-e	**Discuss** how the effects of inflation are reflected in capital budgeting analysis.

Introduction

Estimating the cash flows is a first step in applying NPV and IRR methods and the Reading identifies the cash flows which should be used in capital budgeting. Only incremental cash flows, and not sunk costs, are relevant in the process of capital budgeting and opportunity cost, externality and cannibalization need to be considered. Candidates also need to be able to rank a project, either an expansion or a replacement project, using NPV analysis. This will involve identifying three types of cash flows (initial investment outlay, operating cash flows over the project's life and the terminal year cash flows) and candidates have to avoid common pitfalls such as forgetting to adjust for additional working capital requirements at the beginning and end of projects and the impact of depreciation charges on tax.

48   Concept Check Questions

1.   In calculating incremental cash flows which of the following should **NOT** be included?

    A.   Sunk costs.

    B.   Externalities.

    C.   Opportunity costs.

---

2.   When capital projects require additional working capital, at the **end** of the project the increase in working capital should be treated as:

    A.   a cash inflow.

    B.   a cash outflow.

    C.   a cash inflow, after reducing by a factor of (1 – tax rate).

    D.   a cash outflow, after reducing by a factor of (1 – tax rate).

3.   Which of the following is a method for evaluating projects with different lives?
  A.   Replacement project analysis.
  B.   Incremental cash flow approach.
  C.   The replacement chain approach.

---

4.   A company provides the following information:

	$ million
Sales	25.0
Costs excluding depreciation	10.0
Depreciation	3.0
Operating income	12.0
Tax	4.8
Net income	7.2

The cash flow that should be used for capital budgeting purposes is:
  A. $7.2 million.
  B. $9.0 million.
  C. $10.2 million.
  D. $15.0 million.

48   Concept Check Answers

1.   In calculating incremental cash flows which of the following should **NOT** be included?
   A.   Sunk costs.

   B.   Externalities.

   C.   Opportunity costs.

Correct Answer 1.   **A**
Sunk costs should not be included since they cannot be recovered.

---

2.   When capital projects require additional working capital, at the **end** of the project the increase in working capital should be treated as:
   A.   a cash inflow.

   B.   a cash outflow.

   C.   a cash inflow, after reducing by a factor of (1 – tax rate).

   D.   a cash outflow, after reducing by a factor of (1 – tax rate).

Correct Answer 2.   **A**
Additional working capital will be a cash outflow at the beginning of the project and must be added back at the end of the project. Tax is not relevant.

3.   Which of the following is a method for evaluating projects with different lives?
   A.   Replacement project analysis.
   B.   Incremental cash flow approach.
   C.   The replacement chain approach.

Correct Answer 3.   C
The two methods discussed in the syllabus are the replacement chain approach and the equivalent annual annuity approach.

---

4.   A company provides the following information:

	$ million
Sales	25.0
Costs excluding depreciation	10.0
Depreciation	3.0
Operating income	12.0
Tax	4.8
Net income	7.2

The cash flow that should be used for capital budgeting purposes is:
   A. $7.2 million.
   B. $9.0 million.
   C. $10.2 million.
   D. $15.0 million.

Correct Answer 4.   C
Cash flow is net income plus depreciation, which equals $10.2 million.

49   Risk Analysis and the Optimal Capital Budget

Learning Outcome Statements (LOS)

49-a	**Distinguish** among three types of project risk: stand-alone, corporate, and market.
49-b	**Distinguish** among sensitivity analysis, scenario analysis, and Monte Carlo simulation as risk analysis techniques.
49-c	**Describe** how the security market line is used in the capital budgeting process and **describe** the pure play and accounting beta methods for estimating individual project betas.
49-d	**Discuss** the procedure for developing a risk-adjusted discount rate.
49-e	**Define** capital rationing.

Introduction

Up to now we have assumed that the actual cash flows of a project will match the estimated ones with certainty, but in reality they will not and we need a framework to analyze the risks. In this section we will look into three different types of project risk and we need to be able to distinguish between stand alone, corporate and market risks. Then we investigate three different types of risk analysis techniques which are commonly used, i.e. sensitivity analysis, scenario analysis and Monte Carlo simulation. Finally candidates need to be able to apply the Capital Asset Pricing Model (CAPM) to calculate required returns from projects to compensate for their beta-risk.

49   Concept Check Questions

1.   A well-diversified investor will be most concerned with a project's:

   A.   market risk.

   B.   corporate risk.

   C.   stand-alone risk.

---

2.   Scenario analysis is used to calculate:

   A.   market risk.

   B.   corporate risk.

   C.   sensitivity risk.

   D.   stand-alone risk.

3.   A company is considering investing 20% of its assets in a new project, the company is entirely equity financed. Its existing business has a beta of 1.0 and its cost of equity is 15%, the new project has an estimated beta of 1.5. The risk free rate is 5%. The overall rate of return that the company must earn if they decide to proceed with the new project is:

    A.   15.0%.

    B.   16.0%.

    C.   20.0%.

    D.   22.5%.

---

4.   Which of the following is a method for calculating an asset's beta?

    A.   Market method.

    B.   Scenario method.

    C.   Pure play method.

    D.   Monte Carlo simulation.

49   Concept Check Answers

1.   A well-diversified investor will be most concerned with a project's:

    A.   market risk.

    B.   corporate risk.

    C.   stand-alone risk.

Correct Answer 1.   **A**
Market risk cannot be diversified away.

---

2.   Scenario analysis is used to calculate:

    A.   market risk.

    B.   corporate risk.

    C.   sensitivity risk.

    D.   stand-alone risk.

Correct Answer 2.   **D**
Sensitivity analysis and scenario analysis are used to assess stand-alone risk

3.   A company is considering investing 20% of its assets in a new project, the company is entirely equity financed. Its existing business has a beta of 1.0 and its cost of equity is 15%, the new project has an estimated beta of 1.5. The risk free rate is 5%. The overall rate of return that the company must earn if they decide to proceed with the new project is:

    A.   15.0%.

    B.   16.0%.

    C.   20.0%.

    D.   22.5%.

Correct Answer 3.   **B**
The beta of the company if they proceed with the project will be 0.8(1.0) + 0.2(1.5) = 1.1
The market return is the same as the existing business, which has a beta of 1, so we can calculate the required rate of return from the project using CAPM:
R_p = 5% + 1.5(15% - 5%) = 20%
The overall rate of return that the company needs to earn if they take on the project is:
$$(0.80 \times 15\%) + (0.20 \times 20\%) = 16\%$$

---

4.   Which of the following is a method for calculating an asset's beta?
    A.   Market method.
    B.   Scenario method.
    C.   Pure play method.
    D.   Monte Carlo simulation.

Correct Answer 4.   **C**
The pure play method and the accounting beta method are the two methods discussed.

50   Capital Structure and Leverage

Learning Outcome Statements (LOS)

50-a	**Describe**, and **state** the impact of changes in factors that influence a company's capital structure decision.
50-b	**Explain** business risk, discuss factors that influence business risk, **calculate** and interpret the effect of changes in sales or earnings before interest and taxes (EBIT) on earnings per share for companies with different amounts of debt financing, **define** operating leverage, calculate and interpret degree of operating leverage, and **explain** how it affects a project's or company's expected rate of return.
50-c	**Calculate** the breakeven quantity of sales and determine the company's gain or loss at various sales levels.
50-d	**Explain** financial risk, define financial leverage, describe the relationship between financial leverage and financial risk, and calculate and **interpret** degree of financial leverage.
50-e	**Discuss** why the use of greater amounts of debt in the capital structure can raise both the cost of debt and the cost of equity capital and describe how changes in the use of debt can cause changes in the company's earnings per share and in the company's stock price.
50-f	**Distinguish** between the value of a company and the value of the company's common stock.
50-g	**Explain** the relationship between a firm's optimal capital structure and the firm's 1) weighted average cost of capital and 2) stock price.
50-h	**Explain** the effect of taxes and bankruptcy costs on the cost of capital, the optimal capital structure, and the Modigliani and Miller (MM) capital structure irrelevance proposition.
50-i	**Compare** the MM capital structure irrelevance proposition with the trade-off theory of leverage.
50-j	**Describe** how a company signals its prospects through its financing choices.
50-k	**Calculate** and **interpret** degree of total leverage.

Introduction

This Reading focuses on optimal capital structures or the balance between debt and equity financing that will maximize a company's share price. Although debt, since interest payments are tax-deductible, appears to be cheaper than equity, the situation is more complex. As a company increases its debt financing, the risk will increase pushing up the cost of both debt and equity. There is an optimal balance that can be achieved. Students are also required to know how to measure a company's operating and financial risk by computing degree of operating and financial leverage which, when multiplied together, will give the degree of total leverage.

Target capital structure

When a firm's management is deciding the target capital structure it must balance the following risk and return factors:

- Using more debt generally leads to a higher return.
- Using more debt increases the risk for stockholders.

The optimal capital structure will find a balance between these factors that will maximize the firm's stock price.

50   Concept Check Questions

1.   The expected returns to stockholders are:

A.   increased by a company having high operating leverage and low financial leverage.

B.   increased by a company having low operating leverage and high financial leverage.

C.   increased by a company having both low operating leverage and low financial leverage.

D.   increased by a company having both high operating leverage and high financial leverage.

---

2.   If a firm has no debt the degree of financial leverage will be:

A.   0.

B.   1.

C.   100.

D.   infinite.

---

3.   High fixed costs will generally indicate that a firm has:

A.   low financial leverage.

B.   low operating leverage.

C.   high financial leverage.

D.   high operating leverage.

4.   Which of the following statements about debt financing is *least accurate*?

A.   The cost of debt will increase if a company substantially increases its debt financing.

B.   Debt financing is usually cheaper than equity financing since interest is a tax-deductible expense.

C.   Firms with assets that are illiquid and with high business risk should avoid high financial leverage.

D.   Existing stockholders will always prefer that a company funds expansion using debt rather than equity finance.

---

5.   Signaling theory says that the announcement of a stock offering by a company should be viewed by investors as a:

A.   positive signal regarding the company's prospects.

B.   negative signal regarding the company's prospects.

---

6.   A company has sales of $2 million, fixed costs of $300,000, plus interest costs of $100,000. It sells 500,000 units a year and variable costs are $3 per unit. The degree of operating leverage is *closest* to:

A.   1.25.

B.   1.33.

C.   2.50.

D.   5.00.

50   Concept Check Answers

1.   The expected returns to stockholders are:

   A.   increased by a company having high operating leverage and low financial leverage.

   B.   increased by a company having low operating leverage and high financial leverage.

   C.   increased by a company having both low operating leverage and low financial leverage.

   D.   increased by a company having both high operating leverage and high financial leverage.

Correct Answer 1.   D
High operating leverage and financial leverage will increase the expected returns, but will also increase the risk of the returns.

---

2.   If a firm has no debt the degree of financial leverage will be:

   A.   0.

   B.   1.

   C.   100.

   D.   infinite.

Correct Answer 2.   B
The degree of financial leverage measures the percentage change in EPS for a percentage change in EBIT. If interest charges are zero then any change in EBIT will be reflected in the same change in EPS.

---

3.   High fixed costs will generally indicate that a firm has:

   A.   low financial leverage.

   B.   low operating leverage.

   C.   high financial leverage.

   D.   high operating leverage.

Correct Answer 3.   D
High fixed costs generally mean that a small change in sales will lead to a larger change in EBIT, this is high operating leverage.

4.   Which of the following statements about debt financing is *least accurate*?

A.   The cost of debt will increase if a company substantially increases its debt financing.

B.   Debt financing is usually cheaper than equity financing since interest is a tax-deductible expense.

C.   Firms with assets that are illiquid and with high business risk should avoid high financial leverage.

D.   Existing stockholders will always prefer that a company funds expansion using debt rather than equity finance.

Correct Answer 4.   D
Stockholders will generally have a higher expected return if debt financing is used since it is cheaper, but their risk will be higher if debt financing is used.

---

5.   Signaling theory says that the announcement of a stock offering by a company should be viewed by investors as a:

A.   positive signal regarding the company's prospects.

B.   negative signal regarding the company's prospects.

Correct Answer 5.   B
It is a negative signal since it suggests that the company's managers want to bring in new investors ahead of poor company results.

---

6.   A company has sales of $2 million, fixed costs of $300,000, plus interest costs of $100,000. It sells 500,000 units a year and variable costs are $3 per unit. The degree of operating leverage is *closest* to:

A.   1.25.

B.   1.33.

C.   2.50.

D.   5.00.

Correct Answer 6.   C

$$DOL = \frac{Q(P-V)}{Q(P-V)-F}$$

$$= \frac{500,000(\$4-\$3)}{500,000(\$4-\$3)-\$300,000} = 2.5 \text{ times}$$

51 Dividend Policy

Learning Outcome Statements (LOS)

51-a	**Explain** the relationship between a firm's optimal dividend policy and the firm's stock price.
51-b	**Describe** the dividend irrelevance theory, the "bird-in-the-hand" theory, and the tax-preference theory and **explain** the dividend irrelevance theory in the context of the determinants of the value of the company, and **discuss** the principal conclusion for dividend policy of the dividend irrelevance theory and **describe** how any shareholder can construct his or her own dividend policy.
51-c	**Calculate**, assuming a constant return on equity, a company's implied dividend growth rate, given the company's dividend payout rate.
51-d	**Describe** how managers signal their company's earnings forecast through changes in dividend policy **describe** the clientele effect.
51-e	**Describe** the residual dividend model and **discuss** the model's possible advantages or disadvantages to the company.
51-f	**Describe** dividend payment procedures, including the declaration, holder- of-record, ex-dividend, and payment dates.
51-g	**Describe** stock dividends and stock splits, and **explain** their likely pricing effects and **discuss** the advantages and disadvantages of stock repurchases, and **calculate** and **interpret** the price effect of a stock repurchase.

Introduction

We now move on to the optimal dividend policy and what proportion of earnings a company should pay out to maximize its share price. There are three dividend preference theories you need to be familiar with – the dividend irrelevance theory, the bird-in-the-hand theory and the tax preference theory. Candidates also need to be able to describe dividend payment procedures and the impact of stock dividends and stock splits. Finally the advantages and disadvantages of stock repurchases are discussed.

51   Concept Check Questions

1.   Miller and Modigliani's theory concerning investor preference regarding dividend payout ratios says that:

   A.   investors prefer to see a stable payout ratio.

   B.   investors prefer a high dividend payout ratio since it gives greater certainty of return.

   C.   investors prefer a low dividend payout ratio since it generally leads to lower taxes being paid.

   D.   investors are indifferent to the payout ratio since they can sell or buy shares if they require higher or lower current income.

2.   A company has a constant return on equity of 12% and net profit margin of 10% and the dividend payout ratio is 70%. The dividend growth rate will be:

   A.   3.0%.

   B.   3.6%.

   C.   7.0%.

   D.   8.4%.

3.   The residual dividend model says that:
   A.   dividends paid should be earnings less capital expenditure.

   B.   dividends paid should be cash flow from operations less cash flow from investment.

   C.   dividends paid should be earnings less the amount needed to finance the optimal capital budget.

   D.   dividends paid should be cash flow from operations less the amount needed to finance the optimal capital budget.

4.   A stock is likely to rise following the announcement of a stock dividend since:
   A.   stock dividends will increase the liquidity of the shares.

   B.   stockholders will benefit since they receive additional stock without paying.

   C.   it is a signal from the management that they are positive about the firm's prospects.

   D.   investors prefer to receive cash today rather than wait for uncertain gains in the future.

51 Concept Check Answers

1. Miller and Modigliani's theory concerning investor preference regarding dividend payout ratios says that:

    A.   investors prefer to see a stable payout ratio.

    B.   investors prefer a high dividend payout ratio since it gives greater certainty of return.

    C.   investors prefer a low dividend payout ratio since it generally leads to lower taxes being paid.

    D.   investors are indifferent to the payout ratio since they can sell or buy shares if they require higher or lower current income.

Correct Answer 1.   **D**
A is supported by empirical evidence, B is the bird-in-the-hand theory and C is the tax preference theory.

---

2. A company has a constant return on equity of 12% and net profit margin of 10% and the dividend payout ratio is 70%. The dividend growth rate will be:

    A.   3.0%.

    B.   3.6%.

    C.   7.0%.

    D.   8.4%.

Correct Answer 2.   **B**
$$g = b \times ROE = 0.30 \times 12\% = 3.6\%$$

3.   The residual dividend model says that:
   A.   dividends paid should be earnings less capital expenditure.
   B.   dividends paid should be cash flow from operations less cash flow from investment.
   C.   dividends paid should be earnings less the amount needed to finance the optimal capital budget.
   D.   dividends paid should be cash flow from operations less the amount needed to finance the optimal capital budget.

Correct Answer 3.   C

---

4.   A stock is likely to rise following the announcement of a stock dividend since:
   A.   stock dividends will increase the liquidity of the shares.
   B.   stockholders will benefit since they receive additional stock without paying.
   C.   it is a signal from the management that they are positive about the firm's prospects.
   D.   investors prefer to receive cash today rather than wait for uncertain gains in the future.

Correct Answer 4.   C
A stock dividend is purely administrative and no cash changes hands, however it is generally viewed as a positive signal from the firm's management. Brokerage commissions are higher in percentage terms for low priced shares so A is often not true.

STUDY SESSION 12

Equity Investments: Securities Markets

Overview

We now move on to Asset Valuation which makes up a guideline weighting of 30% of the exam questions. In addition to this Study Session on securities markets, we look at equities, bonds, derivatives and alternative investments. We have built up knowledge of investment tools from the preceding Study Sessions and we are ready to examine the ways in which asset classes are analyzed and valued. This is a core part of the Level I material as reflected in the guideline weighting.

This is a short Study Session on security markets with a lot of descriptive, rather than analytical, material. We look at how markets function, then how stock and bond indexes are constructed and finally, we consider the efficiency of capital markets.

Reading Assignments

Investment Analysis and Portfolio Management, 7th edition, Frank K. Reilly and Keith C. Brown (South-Western, 2003)

52. "Organization and Functioning of Securities Markets," Ch. 4

53. "Security-Market Indicator Series," Ch. 5

54. "Efficient Capital Markets," Ch. 6

52 Organization and Functioning of Securities Markets

Learning Outcome Statements (LOS)

52-a	**Describe** the characteristics of a well-functioning securities market.
52-b	**Distinguish** between competitive bids, negotiated sales, and private placements for issuing bonds.
52-c	**Distinguish** between primary and secondary capital markets, and explain how secondary markets support primary markets.
52-d	**Distinguish** between call and continuous markets, compare and contrast the structural differences among national stock exchanges, regional stock exchanges, and the over-the-counter (OTC) markets, and compare and contrast major characteristics of exchange markets, including exchange membership, types of orders, and market makers.
52-e	**Describe** the process of selling a stock short and discuss an investor's likely motivation for selling short.
52-f	**Describe** the process of buying a stock on margin, compute the rate of return on a margin transaction, define maintenance margin and determine the stock price at which the investor would receive a margin call.
52-g	**Discuss** major effects of the institutionalization of securities markets.

Introduction

This Reading looks at the operation of primary and secondary bond and stock markets. Primary markets are for the issue of new securities to investors and secondary markets for trading between investors. We review the different dealing systems, role of participants in the markets, types of orders and the mechanics of margin transactions.

52   Concept Check Questions

1.   A call market is one in which:
    A.   short selling is not permitted.
    B.   dealers are making markets in stocks.
    C.   stock prices are determined by auction.
    D.   individual stocks are traded at specified times.

---

2.   The fourth market is:
    A.   the market where foreign shares are traded.
    B.   over-the-counter trading of shares which are listed on an exchange.
    C.   trading between two parties without a broker acting as intermediary.
    D.   over-the-counter trading of shares which are not listed on an exchange.

---

3.   The initial margin requirement is:
    A.   the market value of the stock less the amount borrowed.
    B.   the market value of the stock less the amount paid in cash.
    C.   the percentage of the transaction value that can be borrowed.
    D.   the percentage of the transaction value that must be paid for in cash.

4.   If an investor buys 1,000 shares at $50 and the initial margin is 60% and the maintenance margin is 30%, he will receive the first marginal call when the stock price falls below:

A. $14.00.

B. $21.00.

C. $28.57.

D. $49.99.

---

5.   A specialist is a:

A.   floor trader.

B.   market maker.

C.   commission broker.

D.   stock exchange employee who monitors prices for a specified sector in the market.

52   Concept Check Answers

1.   A call market is one in which:

   A.   short selling is not permitted.

   B.   dealers are making markets in stocks.

   C.   stock prices are determined by auction.

   D.   individual stocks are traded at specified times.

Correct Answer: 1.   D
B and C are types of continuous market.

---

2.   The fourth market is:

   A.   the market where foreign shares are traded.

   B.   over-the-counter trading of shares which are listed on an exchange.

   C.   trading between two parties without a broker acting as intermediary.

   D.   over-the-counter trading of shares which are not listed on an exchange.

Correct Answer: 2.   C
The fourth market refers to the market where shares are traded directly between investors. The investors are usually institutions which do not want to pay stock broker commissions for large orders.

---

3.   The initial margin requirement is:

   A.   the market value of the stock less the amount borrowed.

   B.   the market value of the stock less the amount paid in cash.

   C.   the percentage of the transaction value that can be borrowed.

   D.   the percentage of the transaction value that must be paid for in cash.

Correct Answer: 3.   D

4.   If an investor buys 1,000 shares at $50 and the initial margin is 60% and the maintenance margin is 30%, he will receive the first marginal call when the stock price falls below:

    A. $14.00.

    B. $21.00.

    C. $28.57.

    D. $49.99.

Correct Answer: 4.   C

The amount borrowed would be $20,000. We need to calculate when the value of the equity equals 30% of the total value of the stock. This is given by:

1,000P - $20,000 = 0.30(1,000P)

P = $28.57

5.   A specialist is a:

    A.   floor trader.

    B.   market maker.

    C.   commission broker.

    D.   stock exchange employee who monitors prices for a specified sector in the market.

Correct Answer: 5.   B

A specialist is a term in the U.S. for a market maker.

53 Security Market Indicator Series

Learning Outcome Statements (LOS)

53-a	**Distinguish** among the composition and characteristics of the three predominant weighting schemes used in constructing stock market series, **discuss** the source and direction of bias exhibited by each of the three predominant weighting schemes, and **compute** a price-weighted, a market-weighted, and an unweighted index series for three stocks.
53-b	**Compare** and **contrast** major structural features of domestic and global stock indexes, bond indexes, and composite stock-bond indexes.

Introduction

Security market indicator series, also called stock and bond market indexes, are widely used by market participants and investors in order to judge the strength or weakness of the market and measure portfolio performance. In order to use indexes it is important to understand how they are constructed and the implications of the different methods of weighting securities in an index.

Security market indexes

Security market indexes or series are used:

- To measure portfolio performance.
- For the construction of index funds.
- To examine factors that influence aggregate security price movements.
- By technical analysts.
- For beta calculation.

When constructing an index it is important to consider:

- The sample in the index must be representative of the population.
- The weighting given to the individual members in the sample (there are price-weighted, market-value-weighted and unweighted series).
- The mathematical method of calculating the index (arithmetic or geometric averaging or base period weighting).

53   Concept Check Questions

1.   If there are the same stocks included in a price-weighted index and a value-weighted index and the price-weighted index performs better than the value-weighted index it could be explained by:

    A.   there were a large number of stock splits.

    B.   there were a small number of stock splits.

    C.   high-priced stocks generally performed better than low-priced stocks.

    D.   low-priced stocks generally performed better than high-priced stocks.

---

2.   A value-weighted index is made up of two stocks, X and Y, and the following data is provided:

	December 31st 2004		December 31st 2005	
Stock	Price	Shares Outstanding	Price	Shares Outstanding
X	$25	10,000	$15	20,000*
Y	$50	6,000	$65	6,000

* after a 2 for 1 stock split

The base index is set at 100 on December 31st 2004. The index on December 31st 2005 is *closest* to:

    A.   98.18.

    B.   106.67.

    C.   125.45.

    D.   126.67.

3.   The Dow Jones Industrial Average has a downward bias due to the way that it adjusts for stock splits because:

A.   when a company has a stock split it is taken out of the index.

B.   a stock price will fall if there is a stock split leading to a decline in the index.

C.   the market capitalization of a company that has a stock split will fall, leading to a decline in the index.

D.   stocks of high growth and successful companies will have more stock splits which will reduce their weighting in the index.

53   Concept Check Answers

1.   If there are the same stocks included in a price-weighted index and a value-weighted index and the price-weighted index performs better than the value-weighted index it could be explained by:

    A.   there were a large number of stock splits.

    B.   there were a small number of stock splits.

    C.   high-priced stocks generally performed better than low-priced stocks.

    D.   low-priced stocks generally performed better than high-priced stocks.

Correct Answer: 1.   C

Stock splits, since they are more commonly done by successful companies, will tend to have a downward bias on the price-weighted index. High priced stocks are more heavily weighted in the price-weighted index so if they perform well it will lead to the price-weighted index outperforming the value-weighted index.

---

2.   A value-weighted index is made up of two stocks, X and Y, and the following data is provided:

Stock	December 31st 2004		December 31st 2005	
	Price	Shares Outstanding	Price	Shares Outstanding
X	$25	10,000	$15	20,000*
Y	$50	6,000	$65	6,000

* after a 2 for 1 stock split

The base index is set at 100 on December 31st 2004. The index on December 31st 2005 is *closest* to:

    A.   98.18.

    B.   106.67.

    C.   125.45.

    D.   126.67.

Correct Answer: 2.   C

Total market value on Dec. 31st 2004 is ($25 $\times$ 10,000) + ($50 $\times$ 6,000) = $550,000

Total market value on Dec. 31st 2005 is ($15 $\times$ 20,000) + ($65 $\times$ 6,000) = $690,000

The index = ($690,000/$550,000) $\times$ 100 = 125.45

3. The Dow Jones Industrial Average has a downward bias due to the way that it adjusts for stock splits because:

   A.   when a company has a stock split it is taken out of the index.

   B.   a stock price will fall if there is a stock split leading to a decline in the index.

   C.   the market capitalization of a company that has a stock split will fall, leading to a decline in the index.

   D.   stocks of high growth and successful companies will have more stock splits which will reduce their weighting in the index.

Correct Answer: 3.   D

54   Efficient Capital Markets

Learning Outcome Statements (LOS)

54-a	**Define** an efficient capital market, **discuss** arguments supporting the concept of efficient capital markets, **describe** and **contrast** the forms of the efficient market hypothesis (EMH): weak, semistrong, and strong, and **describe** the tests used to examine the weak form, the semistrong form, and the strong form of the EMH.
54-b	**Identify** six market anomalies and **explain** their implications for the semistrong form of the EMH, and **explain** the overall conclusions about each form of the EMH.
54-c	**Explain** the implications of stock market efficiency for technical analysis and fundamental analysis, **discuss** the implications of efficient markets for the portfolio management process and the role of the portfolio manager, and **explain** the rationale for investing in index funds.

Introduction

We now consider the efficiency of capital markets and whether all the information available about a security is already reflected in its price. Candidates need to examine the different forms of the Efficient Market Hypothesis (EMH) and the tests which support or disprove the hypothesis. Candidates also have to understand the implications of efficient markets for the portfolio manager and the rationale for the growth in index fund investing.

54   Concept Check Questions

1.   Which form of the Efficient Market Hypothesis (EMH) states that current security prices reflect all public information?

    A.   The weak-form EMH.

    B.   The strong-form EMH.

    C.   The semiweak-form EMH.

    D.   The semistrong-form EMH.

---

2.   The following are all anomalies that show that markets are not semistrong-form efficient *except*:

    A.   the size effect.

    B.   the January effect.

    C.   the neglected firm effect.

    D.   the accounting change effect.

---

3.   If a market is perfectly efficient then a portfolio manager should:

    A.   only hold cash.

    B.   select a portfolio of securities at random.

    C.   increase the systematic risk of the portfolio.

    D.   diversify away unsystematic risk and adjust the systematic risk of each portfolio to meet clients' objectives.

54   Concept Check Answers

1.   Which form of the Efficient Market Hypothesis (EMH) states that current security prices reflect all public information?
    A.   The weak-form EMH.
    B.   The strong-form EMH.
    C.   The semiweak-form EMH.
    D.   The semistrong-form EMH.

Correct Answer: 1.   D

---

2.   The following are all anomalies that show that markets are not semistrong-form efficient *except*:
    A.   the size effect.
    B.   the January effect.
    C.   the neglected firm effect.
    D.   the accounting change effect.

Correct Answer: 2.   D
Studies show that markets react rapidly to changes in accounting methods and this supports the semistrong form of the EMH.

3. If a market is perfectly efficient then a portfolio manager should:
    A. only hold cash.
    B. select a portfolio of securities at random.
    C. increase the systematic risk of the portfolio.
    D. diversify away unsystematic risk and adjust the systematic risk of each portfolio to meet clients' objectives.

Correct Answer: 3.   D

STUDY SESSION 13

Equity Investments: Industry and Company Analysis

Overview

This Study Session covers a diverse number of topics related to equity analysis and valuation. It works through stock market analysis, industry analysis and individual security analysis. The emphasis is on fundamental analysis and using discounted cash flows and relative approaches (for example price earnings ratios and price to book value multiples) to value equities. However a later Reading looks at technical analysis and the philosophy and the indicators used by analysts are examined. The Study Session consists of Readings taken from different source texts so the candidate is exposed to a number of different approaches to equity valuation.

Reading Assignments

55.   "An Introduction to Security Valuation," Ch. 11, *Investment Analysis and Portfolio Management*, 7th edition, Frank K. Reilly and Keith C. Brown (South-Western, 2003)

56.   "Stock-Market Analysis," Ch. 13, *Investment Analysis and Portfolio Management*, 7th edition, Frank K. Reilly and Keith C. Brown (South-Western, 2003)

57.   "Industry Analysis," Ch. 14, pp. 493-495, *Investment Analysis and Portfolio Management*, 7th edition, Frank K. Reilly and Keith C. Brown (South-Western, 2003)

58.   "Equity: Concepts and Techniques," Ch. 6, pp. 256-273, *International Investments*, 5th edition, Bruno Solnik and Dennis McLeavey (Addison Wesley, 2003)

59.   "Company Analysis and Stock Valuation," Ch. 15, pp. 540-544 and 559–577, *Investment Analysis and Portfolio Management*, 7th edition, Frank K. Reilly and Keith C. Brown (South-Western, 2003)

60.   "Technical Analysis," Ch. 16, *Investment Analysis and Portfolio Management*, 7th edition, Frank K. Reilly and Keith C. Brown (South-Western, 2003)

61.   "Introduction to Price Multiples," John D. Stowe, Thomas R. Robinson, Jerald E. Pinto, and Dennis W. McLeavey (AIMR, 2003)

55   An Introduction to Security Valuation

Learning Outcome Statements (LOS)

55-a	**Explain** the top-down approach, and its underlying logic, to the security valuation process.
55-b	**Explain** the various forms of investment returns.
55-c	**Calculate** and **interpret** the value of a preferred stock, or of a common stock, using the dividend discount model (DDM)
55-d	**Show** how to use the DDM to develop an earnings multiplier model, and **explain** the factors in the DDM that affect a stock's price-to-earnings (P/E) ratio.
55-e	**Explain** the components of an investor's required rate of return (i.e., the real risk-free rate, the expected rate of inflation, and a risk premium) and **discuss** the risk factors to be assessed in determining a country risk premium for use in estimating the required return for foreign securities.
55-f	**Estimate** the dividend growth rate, given the components of the required return on equity and incorporating the retention rate and current stock price.
55-g	**Describe** a process for developing estimated inputs to be used in the DDM, including the required rate of return and expected growth rate of dividends.

Introduction

In this Reading we focus on the application of discounted cash flow techniques in equity valuation. When valuing equities it is important to remember that the cash flows are not contractually agreed (as they usually are with a bond or money market instrument) so we need to adjust for the uncertainty of cash flows with a discount factor that includes an appropriate risk premium. Discounted cash flow concepts are core to this Reading but we also look at other issues including different valuation approaches and the drivers of a P/E multiple.

55   Concept Check Questions

1.   A firm is expected to pay a dividend of $3 next year and dividends are expected to grow at 5% per annum thereafter. If an investor in the company's stock has a required rate of return of 10% and the stock's current market price is $65 then the investor should:

   A.   sell his shares.

   B.   buy more shares.

   C.   do nothing since the stock is correctly priced.

---

2.   If a company has an earnings retention ratio of 60%, earnings are growing at 5% per annum and investors' required rate of return is 12%, the P/E of the stock is *closest* to:

   A.   3.33.

   B.   4.44.

   C.   5.71.

   D.   8.57.

3.   If the expected inflation rate in a country is 3% and the real risk-free rate is 6% then the required nominal risk-free rate is *closest* to:

    A.   2.9%.

    B.   9.0%.

    C.   9.2%.

    D.   18.0%.

---

4.   If a firm pays out 30% of its earnings as dividends, its return on equity is 12%, and its return on capital is 8%, then the long-term dividend growth rate is *closest* to:

    A.   2.4%.

    B.   3.6%.

    C.   5.6%.

    D.   8.4%.

55   Concept Check Answers

1.   A firm is expected to pay a dividend of $3 next year and dividends are expected to grow at 5% per annum thereafter. If an investor in the company's stock has a required rate of return of 10% and the stock's current market price is $65 then the investor should:

   A.   sell his shares.

   B.   buy more shares.

   C.   do nothing since the stock is correctly priced.

Correct Answer: 1.   A
Value = $3/(0.10 – 0.05) = $60

---

2.   If a company has an earnings retention ratio of 60%, earnings are growing at 5% per annum and investors' required rate of return is 12%, the P/E of the stock is *closest* to:

   A.   3.33.

   B.   4.44.

   C.   5.71.

   D.   8.57.

Correct Answer: 2.   C
P/E = $(D_1/E_1)/(k - g)$ = 0.40/(0.12 – 0.05) = 5.71

3.   If the expected inflation rate in a country is 3% and the real risk-free rate is 6% then the required nominal risk-free rate is *closest* to:

    A.   2.9%.

    B.   9.0%.

    C.   9.2%.

    D.   18.0%.

Correct Answer: 3.   C

NRFR = [1 +RRFR] [1 + E(I)] − 1 = (1.06)(1.03 − 1) = 9.18%

---

4.   If a firm pays out 30% of its earnings as dividends, its return on equity is 12%, and its return on capital is 8%, then the long-term dividend growth rate is *closest* to:

    A.   2.4%.

    B.   3.6%.

    C.   5.6%.

    D.   8.4%.

Correct Answer: 4.   D

g = Earnings Retention Rate x Return on Equity = 0.7 x 12% = 8.4%

56   Stock-Market Analysis

Learning Outcome Statements (LOS)

56-a	**Calculate** the earnings per share (EPS) of a stock market series and the expected P/E ratio (earnings multiplier) of a stock market series, using the series' expected dividend payout ratio, required rate of return, and expected growth rate of dividends.
56-b	**Estimate** and **interpret** the earnings multiplier of a stock market series, **explain** changes in it, and **calculate** the expected rate of return for a stock market series.
56-c	**Explain** how the top-down approach can be used to analyze the valuation of world stock markets.

Introduction

In this Reading we focus on estimating the future price level of a stock market index or series. The method used is to initially estimate the future P/E ratio based on the payout rate, investors' required return and the sustainable growth rate. The second step is to forecast earnings for the index based on sales, profit margins, tax and interest costs. Once these are combined we have an estimate for P, the index level. Again candidates will be expected to know which variables lead to a change in the P/E of an index.

57   Industry Analysis

Learning Outcome Statements (LOS)

57   **Describe** how structural economic changes (e.g., demographics, technology, politics, and regulation) may affect industries.

Introduction

In this short Reading we consider the effect of structural changes in the economy on industries, as opposed to cyclical changes which result from ups and downs in the business cycle. Structural changes occur when the economy is going through a major change in the way it functions.

LOS 57

Describe how structural economic changes (e.g., demographics, technology, politics, and regulation) may affect industries.

Structural economic changes

The following are all changes which are having a long-term effect on the U.S. economy.

Demographics

This includes changes in the size of the population, age distribution, geographical distribution, ethnic mix and income distribution. In the U.S. the aging of the population may lead to a shortage of entry level workers leading to higher labor costs. On the other hand, demand in industries which cater to older people, and the savings and financial services industry will benefit.

Lifestyles

In the U.S., fashions, as well as trends towards dual career families, higher divorce rates and so on, impact on many different industries.

Technology

Advances in technology affect both the producers and users of new technologies, as well as reducing demand for 'obsolete' products. Changes in technology drive increased capital expenditure as firms try to use technology to gain a competitive advantage. The retail industry is a particular example; advances in technology have led to major improvements in understanding customer preferences for products on a geographical basis, and also in inventory control.

Politics and regulations

Changes in regulations and tax reflect both economic and social government policies. Clearly changes in regulations can have a major impact on certain industries. The finance and banking industry is particularly subject to changing regulation. Most industries are affected by laws on minimum wages, and tariffs and quotas affect many industries involved in international trade.

56   Concept Check Questions

1.   A stock market series is expected to provide a return of 15%. If the beginning value is 200, the forecast dividend is 4, then the estimated end value of the index is:

    A.   222.

    B.   226.

    C.   230.

    D.   234.

---

2.   The calculation of EPS for a stock market series is *least likely* to involve forecasting:

    A.   interest expense.

    B.   the country's GDP.

    C.   operating profit margins.

    D.   investors' required rate of return.

---

57   Concept Check Questions

1.   Which of the following would be least likely to be a result of structural change in the U.S. economy?

    A.   Rising consumer confidence leading to a surge in auto sales.

    B.A rise in the minimum wage increasing costs for fast-food outlets.

    C.   Increasing demand for residential nursing care as the population ages.

    D.   The move in population away from cities leading to stronger demand for catalogue and online shopping.

56   Concept Check Answers

1.   A stock market series is expected to provide a return of 15%. If the beginning value is 200, the forecast dividend is 4, then the estimated end value of the index is:

    A.   222.

    B.   226.

    C.   230.

    D.   234.

Correct Answer: 1.   **B**

$0.15 = (EV - 200 + 4)/200$

$EV = 226$

---

2.   The calculation of EPS for a stock market series is *least likely* to involve forecasting:

    A.   interest expense.

    B.   the country's GDP.

    C.   operating profit margins.

    D.   investors' required rate of return.

Correct Answer: 2.   **D**

The investors' required rate of return is needed to calculate the earnings multiplier.

57   Concept Check Answers

1.   Which of the following would be least likely to be a result of structural change in the U.S. economy?

A.   Rising consumer confidence leading to a surge in auto sales.

B. A rise in the minimum wage increasing costs for fast-food outlets.

C.   Increasing demand for residential nursing care as the population ages.

D.   The move in population away from cities leading to stronger demand for catalogue and online shopping.

Correct Answer: 1.   A

Rising consumer confidence leading to a surge in auto sales would usually be the result of a cyclical move in the economy. The other choices reflect longer-term structural changes in the economy, so A is the best answer.

58   Equity: Concepts and Techniques

Learning Outcome Statements (LOS)

58-a	**Classify** business cycle stages and **identify**, for each stage, attractive investment opportunities.
58-b	**Discuss**, with respect to global industry analysis, the key elements related to return expectations.
58-c	**Describe** the industry life cycle and **identify** an industry's stage in its life cycle.
58-d	**Calculate** and **interpret** a concentration ratio and a Herfindahl index.
58-e	**Discuss**, with respect to global industry analysis, the elements related to risk, and **describe** the basic forces that determine industry competition.

Introduction

We now look at stocks in the context of their global industry. Whilst the country where a company is domiciled is clearly important, an investor will also need to analyse its competitors on a global basis. This Reading looks at the factors that need to be considered when evaluating a company in a global setting. It starts with an introduction to country analysis and the economic variables that analysts follow. When looking at economic growth it is important to differentiate between business cycles and long-term sustainable growth. Economic growth will feed thought to corporate profits and stock returns.

58   Concept Check Questions

1.   Which stage of the industry cycle is characterized by fast sales growth and high profit margins?

    A.   Mature growth.

    B.   Market maturity.

    C.   Pioneering development.

    D.   Rapid accelerating growth.

2.   An investor who follows an industry rotation strategy believes the economy has past its trough and there is confirmation of recovery. Which strategy would he/she be likely to follow?

    A.   Sell property.

    B.   Purchase stocks.

    C.   Purchase bonds

    D.   Sell commodities.

3.   An industry has a Herfindahl index of 0.05. Which statement might explain this?

    A.   The industry is an oligopoly.

    B.   The industry is dominated by one firm.

    C.   The industry has very few participants, each with an approximately equal market share.

    D.   The industry has a large number of participants with no single firm holding a large market share.

58   Concept Check Answers

1.   Which stage of the industry cycle is characterized by fast sales growth and high profit margins?

    A.   Mature growth.

    B.   Market maturity.

    C.   Pioneering development.

    D.   Rapid accelerating growth.

Correct Answer: 1.   **D**

---

2.   An investor who follows an industry rotation strategy believes the economy has past its trough and there is confirmation of recovery. Which strategy would he/she be likely to follow?

    A.   Sell property.

    B.   Purchase stocks.

    C.   Purchase bonds

    D.   Sell commodities.

Correct Answer: 2.   **B**
If the economy is in the recovery stage the best performance would be expected to come from
    cyclical stocks and commodities, and then property.

3.   An industry has a Herfindahl index of 0.05. Which statement might explain this?

    A.   The industry is an oligopoly.

    B.   The industry is dominated by one firm.

    C.   The industry has very few participants, each with an approximately equal market share.

    D.   The industry has a large number of participants with no single firm holding a large market share.

Correct Answer: 3.   **D**
A Hefindahl index of 0.05 indicates low concentration, equivalent to 20 firms with equal market shares of the market.

59 Company Analysis and Stock Selection

Learning Outcome Statements (LOS)

59-a	Differentiate between 1. a growth company and a growth stock, 2. a defensive company and a defensive stock, 3. a cyclical company and a cyclical stock, and 4. a speculative company and a speculative stock.
59-b	Describe and estimate the expected earnings per share (EPS) and earnings multiplier for a company.
59-c	Calculate and compare the expected rate of return based on the estimate of intrinsic value to the required rate of return.

Introduction

In this Reading we use the same methodology used in the valuation of a stock market index covered in Reading 56. To value individual stocks, we estimate the earnings multiplier (P/E) and earnings in order to arrive at an estimate for the future price of the stock. Candidates are also expected to be able to differentiate between the definitions for a growth, defensive, cyclical and speculative stock and company.

59   Concept Check Questions

1.   A growth stock

    A.   is an overvalued stock.

    B.   generates a return on capital above its cost of capital.

    C.   has a history of above average earnings and profits growth.

    D.   has above average stock price performance relative to companies of similar risk.

---

2.   An investment manager is anticipating a significant upward move in the market. He is most likely to consider buying

    A.   a value stock.

    B.   a cyclical stock.

    C.   a defensive stock.

---

3.   An investor requires a rate of return of 12% for investing in Company ABC's shares. He has calculated that their intrinsic value is $12.30 which he believes will be recognized by the market in one year's time. The shares are currently trading at $11.50 and the forecast annual dividend is $0.60. The investor should:

    A.   buy Company ABC's shares.

    B.   sell Company ABC's shares.

59   Concept Check Answers

1.   A growth stock
   A.   is an overvalued stock.
   B.   generates a return on capital above its cost of capital.
   C.   has a history of above average earnings and profits growth.
   D.   has above average stock price performance relative to companies of similar risk.

Correct Answer: 1.   D

---

2.   An investment manager is anticipating a significant upward move in the market. He is most likely to consider buying
   A.   a value stock.
   B.   a cyclical stock.
   C.   a defensive stock.

Correct Answer: 2.   B
A cyclical stock has a high beta so is expected to outperform in a rising market.

3.   An investor requires a rate of return of 12% for investing in Company ABC's shares. He has calculated that their intrinsic value is $12.30 which he believes will be recognized by the market in one year's time. The shares are currently trading at $11.50 and the forecast annual dividend is $0.60. The investor should:

A.   buy Company ABC's shares.

B.   sell Company ABC's shares.

Correct Answer: 3.   **A**

Expected return = (12.30 – 11.50 + 0.60)/11.50 = 12.17%.

This is above his required rate of return so he should buy the shares.

60   Technical Analysis

Learning Outcome Statements (LOS)

60-a	**Explain** the underlying assumptions of technical analysis and **explain** how technical analysis differs from fundamental analysis.
60-b	**Discuss** the advantages and challenges of technical analysis.
60-c	**Identify** examples of each of the major categories of technical indicators.

Introduction

This is a broad introduction to technical analysis, the philosophy or assumptions made by technical analysts, and the challenges to their work. Technical analysts differ from fundamental analysts in that they believe prices are driven by both rational and irrational factors. The Reading also looks at the signals technical analysts use to indicate that the market or an individual security price is moving into a new trend.

60   Concept Check Questions

1.   If the specialists' ratio of short sales to total sales is much lower then normal this would be seen as:

    A.   a sell signal by contrary-opinion technical analysts.

    B.   a buy signal by contrary-opinion technical analysts.

    C.   a sell signal by technical analysts who follow the smart money.

    D.   a buy signal by technical analysts who follow the smart money.

---

2.   If a contrary-opinion technical analyst saw that mutual fund cash balances were very low he would see this as a:

    A.   sell signal.

    B.   buy signal.

---

3.   Technical analysts are *least likely* to believe which of the following?

    A.   Security prices move in long-term trends.

    B.   Security prices can be driven by irrational behavior.

    C.   Security prices reflect all news released almost immediately.

60   Concept Check Answers

1.   If the specialists' ratio of short sales to total sales is much lower then normal this would be seen as:

A.   a sell signal by contrary-opinion technical analysts.

B.   a buy signal by contrary-opinion technical analysts.

C.   a sell signal by technical analysts who follow the smart money.

D.   a buy signal by technical analysts who follow the smart money.

Correct Answer: 1.   D

---

2.   If a contrary-opinion technical analyst saw that mutual fund cash balances were very low he would see this as a:

A.   sell signal.

B.   buy signal.

Correct Answer: 2.   A

3.   Technical analysts are *least likely* to believe which of the following?

    A.   Security prices move in long-term trends.

    B.   Security prices can be driven by irrational behavior.

    C.   Security prices reflect all news released almost immediately.

Correct Answer: 3.   C

61   Introduction to Price Multiples

Learning Outcome Statements (LOS)

61-a	Discuss the rationales for the use of price to earnings (P/E), price to book value (P/BV), price to sales (P/S), and price to cash flow (P/CF) in equity valuation and discuss the possible drawbacks to the use of each price multiple.
61-b	Calculate and interpret P/E, P/BV, P/S, and P/CF.

Introduction

This Reading discusses four of the most commonly used price multiples or ratios, price to earnings (P/E), price to book value (P/BV), price to sales (P/S), and price to cash flow (P/CF). The multiples are fairly simple to calculate, and readily accessed in newspapers etc. They can be used for comparing a stock to another stock, to an industry or a market. Ratios give a measure of the price of a stock relative to its earnings or assets, or other measure of value. If the characteristics of two companies are very similar the one trading on the lower multiple offers the better value.

We look at each of the four multiples in turn and consider the rationale for using the multiple and how it is defined and calculated.

61   Concept Check Questions

1.   A company is operating at the peak of the business cycle. Which of the following EPS calculations is likely to give the highest P/E ratio?

    A.   Leading P/E.

    B.   Trailing P/E

    C.   P/E using normalized earnings.

---

2.   One of the reasons price to book value is a useful valuation measure is because of the following:

    A.   it can be used to value loss-making companies.

    B.   it is useful for comparing the value of stocks across industries.

    C.   book value is not usually distorted by the accounting methods used.

    D.   book value has proved to be a good indicator of the market value of a company's assets.

61   Concept Check Answers

1.   A company is operating at the peak of the business cycle. Which of the following EPS calculations is likely to give the highest P/E ratio?

    A.   Leading P/E.

    B.   Trailing P/E

    C.   P/E using normalized earnings.

Correct Answer: 1.   C

Normalized earnings will calculate the earnings at the midpoint of the cycle so is likely to be lower than current or prospective earnings; hence the P/E will be higher on this basis.

---

2.   One of the reasons price to book value is a useful valuation measure is because of the following:

    A.   it can be used to value loss-making companies.

    B.   it is useful for comparing the value of stocks across industries.

    C.   book value is not usually distorted by the accounting methods used.

    D.   book value has proved to be a good indicator of the market value of a company's assets.

Correct Answer: 2.   A

STUDY SESSION 14

Fixed Income Investments: Basic Concepts

Overview

There are two Study Sessions covering fixed income investments. Study Session 14 provides definitions and descriptions of the main characteristics of different types of fixed income instruments, plus an introduction to the basic concepts behind bond valuation. Study Session 15 looks in greater detail at the methods of analyzing and measuring interest rate risk of fixed income instruments.

Study Session 14 starts with a description of the typical features that define fixed-income securities, i.e. the principal and coupon cash flows and the factors that may affect the regularity of such cash flows. In the second Reading the different types of risks related to investing in bonds are discussed. Interest rate risk is covered in greater detail as interest rates are the main determinant of the price movement of most high-grade bonds. The third Reading familiarises the candidates with the features of a variety of bond sectors, such as government and corporate bonds. The last Reading delves into the concept of yield spread, i.e. the additional yield on a bond relative to a given benchmark, as well as the external factors that may influence the level of yields expected by an investor.

Reading Assignments

Fixed Income Analysis for the Chartered Financial Analyst® Program, 2nd edition, Frank J. Fabozzi (Frank J. Fabozzi Associates, 2004)

62.   "Features of Debt Securities," Ch. 1

63.   "Risks Associated with Investing in Bonds," Ch. 2

64.   "Overview of Bond Sectors and Instruments," Ch. 3

65.   "Understanding Yield Spreads," Ch. 4

62   Features of Debt Securities

Learning Outcome Statements (LOS)

62-a	**Explain** the purposes of a bond's indenture, and **describe** affirmative and negative covenants.
62-b	**Describe** the basic features of a bond (e.g., maturity, par value, coupon rate, provisions for redeeming bonds, currency denomination, options granted to the issuer or investor), the various coupon rate structures (e.g., zero-coupon bonds, step-up notes, deferred coupon bonds, floating-rate securities), the structure of floating-rate securities (i.e., the coupon formula, caps and floors) and **define** accrued interest, full price, and clean price.
62-c	**Explain** the provisions for early retirement of debt, including call and refunding provisions, prepayment options, and sinking fund provisions, **differentiate** between a regular redemption price and a special redemption price, **explain** the importance of options embedded in a bond issue, and **indicate** whether such options benefit the issuer or the bondholder.
62-d	**Describe** methods used by institutional investors in the bond market to finance the purchase of a security (i.e., margin buying and repurchase agreements).

Introduction

This Reading looks at the main features and characteristics of different categories of bonds including the types of cash flows paid out by a bond issuer to an investor. We also examine the options given to investors or issuers resulting in the modification of the pattern of the principal and coupon cash flows and various provisions for the early retirement of debt. As with other Readings in this Study Session, many candidates who are not working in the U.S. debt markets will meet a lot of new terminology that they need to become familiar with.

62   Concept Check Questions

1.   Which of the following embedded options is increasingly valuable to an investor in a rising interest rate environment?

    A.   Put option.

    B.   Call option.

    C.   Interest rate cap.

    D.   Accelerated sinking fund provision.

---

2.   Which of the following has a variable quoted margin?

    A.   Inverse floater.

    B.   Dual index floater.

    C.   Deleveraged floater.

    D.   Extendible reset bond.

---

3.   Which of the following types of bonds are *most likely* to pay out interest periodically?

    A.   Accrual bonds.

    B.   Zero-coupon bonds.

    C.   Non-interest rate index floaters.

62   Concept Check Answers

1.   Which of the following embedded options is increasingly valuable to an investor in a rising interest rate environment?

    A.   Put option.

    B.   Call option.

    C.   Interest rate cap.

    D.   Accelerated sinking fund provision.

Correct Answer: 1.   A

---

2.   Which of the following has a variable quoted margin?

    A.   Inverse floater.

    B.   Dual index floater.

    C.   Deleveraged floater.

    D.   Extendible reset bond.

Correct Answer: 2.   D

---

3.   Which of the following types of bonds are *most likely* to pay out interest periodically?

    A.   Accrual bonds.

    B.   Zero-coupon bonds.

    C.   Non-interest rate index floaters.

Correct Answer: 3.   C

Accrual bonds and zero coupon bonds pay interest only at maturity. Non-interest rate index floaters use reference rates other than interest rates but they pay out periodic coupons.

63   Risks Associated with Investing in Bonds

Learning Outcome Statements (LOS)

63-a	**Explain** the risks associated with investing in bonds (e.g., interest rate risk, call and prepayment risk, yield curve risk, reinvestment risk, credit risk, liquidity risk, exchange rate risk, volatility risk, inflation risk, and event risk).
63-b	**Identify** the relationship among a bond's coupon rate, the yield required by the market, and the bond's price relative to par value (i.e., discount, premium, or equal to par).
63-c	**Explain** how features of a bond (e.g., maturity, coupon, and embedded options) affect the bond's interest rate risk.
63-d	**Identify** the relationship among the price of a callable bond, the price of an option-free bond, and the price of the embedded call option.
63-e	**Explain** the interest rate risk of a floating-rate security and why such a security's price may differ from par value.
63-f	**Compute** and **interpret** the duration of a bond, given the bond's change in price when interest rates change, the approximate percentage price change of a bond, given the bond's duration, and the approximate new price of a bond, given the bond's duration and new yield level, **explain** why duration does not account for yield curve risk for a portfolio of bonds, **explain** how the yield level impacts the interest rate risk of a bond.
63-g	**Explain** the disadvantages of a callable or prepayable security to an investor.
63-h	**Identify** the factors that affect the reinvestment risk of a security and **explain** why prepayable amortizing securities expose investors to greater reinvestment risk than nonamortizing securities.
63-i	**Describe** the various forms of credit risk (i.e., default risk, credit spread risk, downgrade risk) and **describe** the meaning and role of credit ratings.
63-j	**Explain** why liquidity risk is important to investors even if they expect to hold a security to the maturity date.
63-k	**Describe** the exchange rate risk an investor faces when a bond makes payments in a foreign currency.
63-l	**Describe** inflation risk and **explain** why it exists.

| 63-m | **Explain** how yield volatility affects the price of a bond with an embedded option and how changes in volatility affect the value of a callable bond and a putable bond. |
| 63-n | **Describe** the various forms of event risk (e.g., natural catastrophe, corporate takeover/restructuring, and regulatory risk) and the components of sovereign risk. |

Introduction

Investors in bonds face a number of risks when buying bonds. Numerous different risks are listed in this Reading, but the main risks to focus on are interest rate risk, credit risk, reinvestment and prepayment risk. Candidates are introduced to the concept of duration: duration measures the interest rate risk of a bond or portfolio of bonds. Duration will be covered in more detail in the next Study Session.

63   Concept Check Questions

1.   Which of the following is *least likely* to be classified as event risk?

    A.   Yield curve risk.

    B.   Political change risk.

    C.   Regulatory change risk.

    D.   Natural catastrophe risk.

---

2.   A bond is initially priced at 97.99. If the yield declines by 50 basis points, the price increases to 99.99. If the yield rises by 50 basis points, the price decreases to 94.89. The duration of the bond is:

    A.   0.50.

    B.   1.00.

    C.   5.25.

    D.   0.50.

---

3.   From question 2 above, if the par value of the bond is $100,000 then the dollar duration is:

    A. $500.

    B. $1,000.

    C. $5,250.

    D. $10,500.

63   Concept Check Answers

1.   Which of the following is *least likely* to be classified as event risk?

    A.   Yield curve risk.

    B.   Political change risk.

    C.   Regulatory change risk.

    D.   Natural catastrophe risk.

Correct Answer: 1.   A

---

2.   A bond is initially priced at 97.99. If the yield declines by 50 basis points, the price increases to 99.99. If the yield rises by 50 basis points, the price decreases to 94.89. The duration of the bond is:

    A.   0.50.

    B.   1.00.

    C.   5.25.

    D.   0.50.

Correct Answer: 2.   C

The duration = $(99.99 - 94.89)/(2 \times 97.99 \times 0.005) = 5.25$

3.   From question 2 above, if the par value of the bond is $100,000 then the dollar duration is:

    A. $500.

    B. $1,000.

    C. $5,250.

    D. $10,500.

Correct Answer: 3.   C

The dollar duration will be 5.25% x $100,000 = $5,250

64   Overview of Bond Sectors and Instruments

Learning Outcome Statements (LOS)

64-a	**Describe** the different types of international bonds (e.g., Eurobonds, global bonds, sovereign debt).
64-b	**Describe** the types of securities issued by the U.S. Department of the Treasury (e.g. bills, notes, bonds, and inflation protection securities), **differentiate** between on-the-run and off-the-run Treasury securities, **discuss** how stripped Treasury securities are created, and **distinguish** between coupon strips and principal strips.
64-c	**Describe** a mortgage-backed security, and **explain** the cash flows for a mortgage-backed security, **define** prepayments and **explain** prepayment risk.
64-d	**Describe** the types and characteristics of securities issued by federal agencies (including mortgage passthroughs and collateralized mortgage obligations).
64-e	**State** the motivation for creating a collateralized mortgage obligation, **describe** the types of securities issued by municipalities in the United States, and **distinguish** between tax-backed debt and revenue bonds.
64-f	**Describe** insured bonds and prerefunded bonds.
64-g	**Summarize** the bankruptcy process and bondholder rights, **explain** the factors considered by rating agencies in assigning a credit rating to a corporate debt instrument, and **describe** secured debt, unsecured debt, and credit enhancements for corporate bonds.
64-h	**Distinguish** between a corporate bond and a medium-term note.
64-i	**Describe** a structured note, **explain** the motivation of their issuance by corporations, **describe** commercial paper, and **distinguish** between directly-placed paper and dealer-placed paper and **describe** the salient features, uses and limitations of bank obligations (negotiable CDs and bankers acceptances).
64-j	**Define** an asset-backed security, **describe** the role of a special purpose vehicle in an asset-backed securities transaction, **state** the motivation for a corporation to issue an asset-backed security, and **describe** the types of external credit enhancements for asset-backed securities.
64-k	**Describe** collateralized debt obligations.
64-l	**Contrast** the structures of the primary and secondary markets in bonds.

Introduction

This Reading starts with a description of the different types of international bonds and then moves on to look at the U.S. bonds that are available in the market. It describes the characteristics of different categories of Treasury securities and corporate bonds including bankruptcy issues and credit ratings. We also look at the differences between corporate bonds, MTNs and commercial paper. The structure of asset-backed securitisation is described in this Study Session as well as of collateralized debts. Again this Reading contains a lot of detail and new terms; candidates will have to make the required effort to remember the key expressions.

64   Concept Check Questions

1.   The legal entity that is used in asset securitization for bankruptcy remoteness is:
    A.   a rating agency.
    B.   an indenture trustee.
    C.   an investment bank.
    D.   a special purpose vehicle.

2.   The motivation for a corporation to issue an asset-backed security is:
    A.   to dispose of unproductive assets.
    B.   to strengthen the affirmative covenants of all the issued debt securities.
    C.   to obtain funding which is lower in cost than the corporation's rating allows.
    D.   to take advantage of the legal loophole in the jurisdiction of a different country.

3.   Which of the following is *least likely* to relate to primary market activities?
    A.   Underwriting.
    B.   Over-the-counter.
    C.   Firm commitment.
    D.   Best efforts arrangement.

4.   Bankers acceptances are:

   A.   negotiable certificates of deposit.

   B.   guarantees issued by a bank on a municipal bond.

   C.   nonnegotiable longer-term (over 1 year) certificates of deposit.

   D.   short-term IOUs created by a non-financial firm and guaranteed by a bank.

---

5.   Which of the following have the features of being underwritten by international syndicates, offered simultaneously to investors in a number of countries, are outside the jurisdiction of any single country and are issued in unregistered form?

   A.   Eurobonds.

   B.   Yankee bonds.

   C.   Samurai bonds.

   D.   Treasury bonds.

64   Concept Check Answers

1.   The legal entity that is used in asset securitization for bankruptcy remoteness is:
    A.   a rating agency.
    B.   an indenture trustee.
    C.   an investment bank.
    D.   a special purpose vehicle.

Correct Answer: 1.   D

---

2.   The motivation for a corporation to issue an asset-backed security is:
    A.   to dispose of unproductive assets.
    B.   to strengthen the affirmative covenants of all the issued debt securities.
    C.   to obtain funding which is lower in cost than the corporation's rating allows.
    D.   to take advantage of the legal loophole in the jurisdiction of a different country.

Correct Answer: 2.   C

3.   Which of the following is *least likely* to relate to primary market activities?
    A.   Underwriting.
    B.   Over-the-counter.
    C.   Firm commitment.
    D.   Best efforts arrangement.

Correct Answer: 3.   **B**

4.   Bankers acceptances are:
    A.   negotiable certificates of deposit.
    B.   guarantees issued by a bank on a municipal bond.
    C.   nonnegotiable longer-term (over 1 year) certificates of deposit.
    D.   short-term IOUs created by a non-financial firm and guaranteed by a bank.

Correct Answer: 4.   **D**

5.   Which of the following have the features of being underwritten by international syndicates, offered simultaneously to investors in a number of countries, are outside the jurisdiction of any single country and are issued in unregistered form?
    A.   Eurobonds.
    B.   Yankee bonds.
    C.   Samurai bonds.
    D.   Treasury bonds.

Correct Answer: 5.   **A**

65   Understanding Yield Spreads

Learning Outcome Statements (LOS)

65-a	**Identify** the interest rate policy tools available to a central bank (such as the U.S. Federal Reserve or the European Central Bank).
65-b	**Describe** a yield curve and the different yield curve shapes observed, **explain** the basic theories of the term structure of interest rates (i.e., pure expectations theory, liquidity preference theory, and market segmentation theory) and **describe** the implications of each theory for the shape of the yield curve; **explain** the different types of yield spread measures (e.g., absolute yield spread, relative yield spread, yield ratio), and **compute** yield spread measures given the yields for two securities.
65-c	**Explain** why investors may find a relative yield spread to be a better measure of yield spread than the absolute yield spread, **distinguish** between an intermarket and intramarket sector spread, and **describe** a credit spread and **discuss** the suggested relationship between credit spreads and the economic well being of the economy.
65-d	**Identify** how embedded options affect yield spreads.
65-e	**Explain** how the liquidity of an issue affects its yield spread relative to Treasury securities and relative to other issues that are comparable in all other ways except for liquidity and **describe** the relationships that are argued to exist among the size of an issue, liquidity, and yield spread.
65-f	**Compute** the after-tax yield of a taxable security and the tax-equivalent yield of a tax-exempt security.
65-g	**Define** LIBOR and why it is an important measure to funded investors who borrow short term.

Introduction

The Reading starts with looking at how interest rates are determined and the tools that are available to central banks to set the level of interest rates. Theories concerning the shape of the yield curve are also explained.

A yield spread is the additional yield over and above that offered by the risk-free benchmark security, to compensate investors for taking additional risk. The Reading investigates the different kind of risks associated with the different kinds of yield spreads and the factors that may affect the behavior of the yield spread such as the presence of embedded options, the liquidity of an issue or even the size of an issue.

65   Concept Check Questions

The following information is given:

Issue	Yield
10-year on-the-run Treasury 6% coupon	6.15%
10-year ABG Corporation Series J 5% coupon	7.85%
10-year IBN Limited 8.0% coupon	8.00%

1.   From the table above, what is the absolute yield spread between IBN Limited and ABG Corporation bonds?

    A.   0.015%.

    B.   3.000%.

    C.   3 basis points.

    D.   15 basis points.

2.   Using the data above, the yield ratio between the 10-year ABG Corp and the 10-year Treasury is *closest* to:

    A.   0.78.

    B.   0.83.

    C.   1.20.

    D.   1.28.

3.   An investor paying a marginal 32% tax rate is offered a tax-exempt bond yielding 4.20%. What should a taxable bond, with similar maturity, yield in order to be a taxable-equivalent offer to the investor?

    A.   1.01%.

    B.   5.54%.

    C.   6.18%.

    D.   13.13%.

65   Concept Check Answers

The following information is given:

Issue	Yield
10-year on-the-run Treasury 6% coupon	6.15%
10-year ABG Corporation Series J 5% coupon	7.85%
10-year IBN Limited 8.0% coupon	8.00%

1.   From the table above, what is the absolute yield spread between IBN Limited and ABG Corporation bonds?

    A.   0.015%.

    B.   3.000%.

    C.   3 basis points.

    D.   15 basis points.

Correct Answer: 1.   **D**
The absolute yield spread = 8.0% - 7.85% = 0.15% or 15 basis points.
Do not use the coupon rates.

---

2.   Using the data above, the yield ratio between the 10-year ABG Corp and the 10-year Treasury is *closest* to:

    A.   0.78.

    B.   0.83.

    C.   1.20.

    D.   1.28.

Correct Answer: 2.   **D**
The yield ratio 7.85%/6.15% = 1.28.
Again do not use the coupon rates.

3.   An investor paying a marginal 32% tax rate is offered a tax-exempt bond yielding 4.20%. What should a taxable bond, with similar maturity, yield in order to be a taxable-equivalent offer to the investor?

    A.   1.01%.

    B.   5.54%.

    C.   6.18%.

    D.   13.13%.

Correct Answer: 3.   C

The taxable equivalent yield is $0.042\% / (1 - 0.32) = 6.18\%$

STUDY SESSION 15

Fixed Income Investments: Analysis and Valuation

Overview

This Study Session moves on to more interesting material and some key topics are covered; not only are they important for the Level I exam, but they provide a foundation for Level II and Level III fixed income topics.

We start to analyse and value bonds. In the first Reading, we look at different valuation methods, including the arbitrage-free valuation free approach. In the second Reading, we examine different ways of measuring yield and candidates need to be comfortable switching between spot and forward rates. The next concept that is looked at in more depth than in the previous Study Session is duration, which measures a bond's interest rate sensitivity. Candidates need to understand the differences between alternative definitions of duration, be able to calculate effective duration for option-free bonds, and work out the movement in price of a bond due to a specified change in interest rates. Convexity is also covered; it is used to obtain a closer approximation of the interest rate sensitivity of a bond.

Reading Assignments

Fixed Income Analysis for the Chartered Financial Analyst® Program, 2nd edition, Frank J. Fabozzi (Frank J. Fabozzi Associates, 2004)

66.   "Introduction to the Valuation of Debt Securities," Ch. 5

67.   "Yield Measures, Spot Rates, and Forward Rates," Ch. 6

68.   "Introduction to the Measurement of Interest Rate Risk," Ch. 7

66   Introduction to the Valuation of Debt Securities

Learning Outcome Statements (LOS)

66-a	**Describe** the fundamental principles of bond valuation.
66-b	**Identify** the types of bonds for which estimating the expected cash flows is difficult and **explain** the problems encountered when estimating the cash flows for these bonds.
66-c	**Determine** the appropriate interest rates for valuing a bond's cash flows, **compute** the value of a bond, given the expected annual or semi-annual cash flows and the appropriate single (constant) or multiple (arbitrage-free rate curve) discount rates, **explain** how the value of a bond changes if the discount rate increases or decreases and **compute** the change in value that is attributable to the rate change, and **explain** how the price of a bond changes as the bond approaches its maturity date and **compute** the change in value that is attributable to the passage of time.
66-d	**Compute** the value of a zero-coupon bond, **explain** the arbitrage-free valuation approach and the market process that forces the price of a bond toward its arbitrage-free value, **determine** whether a bond is undervalued or overvalued, given the bond's cash flows, appropriate spot rates or yield to maturity, and current market price, **explain** how a dealer can generate an arbitrage profit.

Introduction

The Reading covers the fundamentals of valuing a bond. It starts with the general principle of valuation, that the value of a financial asset is the present value of its expected future cash flows. The steps in the valuation process are examined, starting with estimating the cash flows, determining the appropriate discount rates and discounting the expected cash flows. The difficulties often come with correctly estimating the cash flows and with selecting the appropriate discount rates. Candidates are expected to be able to compute the value of a bond using a discounted cash flow approach.

The Reading also investigates the price volatility of bonds (interest rate sensitivity) and the factors that affect volatility. Bonds, like any other assets can be mispriced. We learn how to calculate the intrinsic value of bonds and how dealers can take advantage of any mispricing.

66   Concept Check Questions

1.   A 5-year zero-coupon bond with a maturity value of $5,000 is valued using a 10% discount rate. The value is *closest* to:

    A. $1,000.00.

    B. $3,069.57.

    C. $3,104.61.

    D. $5,000.00.

---

2.   The behavior of the price of a bond changes as it approaches its maturity date. This is known as:

    A.   stripping.

    B.   reconstitution.

    C.   pull to par value.

    D.   arbitrage-free valuation approach.

66   Concept Check Answers

1.   A 5-year zero-coupon bond with a maturity value of $5,000 is valued using a 10% discount rate. The value is *closest* to:

    A. $1,000.00.

    B. $3,069.57.

    C. $3,104.61.

    D. $5,000.00.

Correct Answer: 1.   **B**

$\$5,000/(1 + 0.10/2)^{5 \times 2} = \$3,069.57$

2.   The behavior of the price of a bond changes as it approaches its maturity date. This is known as:

    A.   stripping.

    B.   reconstitution.

    C.   pull to par value.

    D.   arbitrage-free valuation approach.

Correct Answer: 2.   **C**

'Pull to par value' is the tendency of a bond to be closer to par value as it approaches maturity.

67   Yield Measures, Spot Rates and Forward Rates

Learning Outcome Statements (LOS)

67-a	**Explain** the sources of return from investing in a bond (i.e., coupon interest payments, capital gain/loss, reinvestment income).
67-b	**Compute** the traditional yield measures for fixed-rate bonds (e.g., current yield, yield to maturity, yield to first call, yield to first par call date, yield to refunding, yield to put, yield to worst, cash flow yield), **explain** the assumptions underlying traditional yield measures and the limitations of the traditional yield measures.
67-c	**Explain** the importance of reinvestment income in generating the yield computed at the time of purchase, and **calculate** the amount of income required to generate that yield and **discuss** the factors that affect reinvestment risk.
67-d	**Compute** the bond equivalent yield of an annual-pay bond, and **compute** the annual-pay yield of a semiannual-pay bond.
67-e	**Compute** the theoretical Treasury spot rate curve, using the method of bootstrapping and given the Treasury par yield curve and **compute** the value of a bond using spot rates.
67-f	**Explain** the limitations of the nominal spread and **differentiate** among the nominal spread, the zero-volatility spread, and the option-adjusted spread for a bond with an embedded option, and **explain** the option cost.
67-g	**Explain** a forward rate, and **compute** the value of a bond using forward rates **and explain** and **illustrate** the relationship between short-term forward rates and spot rates and **compute** spot rates given forward rates, and forward rates given spot rates.

Introduction

Yields are the main measure of investment performance of bonds. Here we look into a variety of yield measures and in what circumstances they are used. We also investigate the reinvestment risk, i.e. the risk that might prevent an investment from generating its expected yield or yield to maturity. We then explore what spot and forward rates are, how they are derived and why they are important. Candidates are expected to be able to value bonds using these different discount rates.

67 Concept Check Questions

1.   Which of the following is the *least accurate* statement regarding reinvestment risk?

A.   For zero-coupon bonds, the reinvestment income is important to produce the yield promised at purchase date.

B.   For bonds bought at a premium, rather than at a discount, the reinvestment income is more important to produce the yield promised at the purchase date.

C.   The longer the time to maturity the more the bond is dependent on the reinvestment income to produce the yield promised at the purchase date.

D.   The higher the coupon rate the more the bond is dependent on the reinvestment income to produce the yield promised at the purchase date.

2. Given:

Period	Years	Annual yield to maturity (BEY)	Price	Spot rate (BEY)
1	0.5	4.00		4.0000
2	1.0	4.30		4.3000
3	1.5	4.65	100	4.6606

The 6-month forward rate, one year from now is *closest* to:

A.   4.3000%.

B.   4.4803%.

C.   5.3535%.

D.   5.3837%.

67   Concept Check Answers

1.   Which of the following is the *least accurate* statement regarding reinvestment risk?

A.   For zero-coupon bonds, the reinvestment income is important to produce the yield promised at purchase date.

B.   For bonds bought at a premium, rather than at a discount, the reinvestment income is more important to produce the yield promised at the purchase date.

C.   The longer the time to maturity the more the bond is dependent on the reinvestment income to produce the yield promised at the purchase date.

D.   The higher the coupon rate the more the bond is dependent on the reinvestment income to produce the yield promised at the purchase date.

Correct Answer: 1.   A

Zero-coupon bonds have no reinvestment risk since they have no interim income from coupons to be reinvested.

---

2.   Given:

Period	Years	Annual yield to maturity (BEY)	Price	Spot rate (BEY)
1	0.5	4.00		4.0000
2	1.0	4.30		4.3000
3	1.5	4.65	100	4.6606

The 6-month forward rate, one year from now is *closest* to:

A.   4.3000%.

B.   4.4803%.

C.   5.3535%.

D.   5.3837%.

Correct Answer: 2.   D

$_1f_2 = (1 + z_3)^3/(1 + z_2)^2 -1 = (1.023303)^3/(1.02150)^2 -1 = 1.0269 - 1 = 2.6919\%$
The 6-month forward rate, one year from now, is $2 \times 2.6919\% = 5.3837\%$

68 Introduction to the Measurement of Interest Rate Risk

Learning Outcome Statements (LOS)

68-a	**Distinguish** between the full valuation approach (the scenario analysis approach) and the duration/convexity approach for measuring interest rate risk, and **explain** the advantage of using the full valuation approach.
68-b	**Compute** the interest rate risk exposure of a bond position or of a bond portfolio, given a change in interest rates.
68-c	**Demonstrate** the price volatility characteristics for option-free bonds when interest rates change (including the concept of "positive convexity"), **demonstrate** the price volatility characteristics of callable bonds and prepayable securities when interest rates change (including the concept of "negative convexity"), **describe** the price volatility characteristics of putable bonds.
68-d	**Compute** the effective duration of a bond, given information about how the bond's price will increase and decrease for given changes in interest rates and **compute** the approximate percentage price change for a bond, given the bond's effective duration and a specified change in yield.
68-e	**Distinguish** among the alternative definitions of duration (modified, effective or option-adjusted, and Macaulay), **explain** why effective duration, rather than modified duration or Macaulay duration, should be used to measure the interest rate risk for bonds with embedded options, **describe** why duration is best interpreted as a measure of a bond's or portfolio's sensitivity to changes in interest rates, **compute** the duration of a portfolio, given the duration of the bonds comprising the portfolio and **discuss** the limitations of the portfolio duration measure.
68-f	**Discuss** the convexity measure of a bond and **estimate** a bond's percentage price change, given the bond's duration and convexity measure and a specified change in interest rates.
68-g	**Differentiate** between modified convexity and effective convexity.
68-h	**Compute** the price value of a basis point (PVBP), and **explain** its relationship to duration.

Introduction

This is perhaps the most important topic in bond risk analysis: interest rate sensitivity which is also known as price volatility. As the name suggests, it revolves around the relationship between price and yield of a bond.

Firstly we look at the different approaches of measuring the interest rate sensitivity, either using a full valuation approach or using duration/ convexity measures. Then we explore the behaviour of the price volatility of a bond either with or without the presence of embedded options. Candidates are expected to be able to calculate the price change of a bond when the duration is known. We also look at different types of duration and their limitations, and the convexity of a bond and its importance.

68 Concept Check Questions

1. Given the following information on a bond

    Duration   =   7.5670

    Convexity =   41.0935

    Yields fall by: 250 basis points

The total estimated price change in percentage terms is *closest* to:

    A.   2.57%.

    B.   7.57%.

    C.   18.92%.

    D.   21.49%.

---

2. Which of the following is *least likely* to be a characteristic of bonds with positive convexity?

    A.   The percentage price change for a given yield change is not the same for all bonds.

    B.   For a large change in yields, the percentage price decrease is greater than the percentage price increase.

    C.   For small change in yields, the percentage changes are roughly the same, whether the yield increases or decreases.

    D.   For a large change in yields, the percentage price change is not the same for an increase in yields as it is for a decrease in yields.

68   Concept Check Answers

1.   Given the following information on a bond

    Duration   =   7.5670

    Convexity   =   41.0935

    Yields fall by: 250 basis points

The total estimated price change in percentage terms is *closest* to:

    A.   2.57%.

    B.   7.57%.

    C.   18.92%.

    D.   21.49%.

Correct Answer: 1.   **D**

Estimated change using duration	7.5670% x 0.025 x 100	=	18.9175
Convexity adjustment:	41.0935 x (0.025)² x 100	=	2.5684
Total estimated percentage price change		=	21.4858

---

2.   Which of the following is *least likely* to be a characteristic of bonds with positive convexity?

    A.   The percentage price change for a given yield change is not the same for all bonds.

    B.   For a large change in yields, the percentage price decrease is greater than the percentage price increase.

    C.   For small change in yields, the percentage changes are roughly the same, whether the yield increases or decreases.

    D.   For a large change in yields, the percentage price change is not the same for an increase in yields as it is for a decrease in yields.

Correct Answer: 2.   **B**

On the contrary, for a large change in yields, the percentage price increase is greater than the percentage price decrease.

STUDY SESSION 16

Derivative Investments

Overview

This is a long STUDY SESSION and provides an introduction to the characteristics and pricing of the different types of derivatives – forwards, futures, options and swaps. Some of the calculations are reasonably demanding but candidates should make every attempt to comprehend the material and make the necessary calculations. Derivatives are a key topic and will be important at Level II and III when you will explore further how they are used by managers to hedge risk or alter risk–return characteristics of portfolios to meet client objectives.

The first Reading is a general overview of derivatives; all the concepts are revisited in later Readings. The next four Readings examine the characteristics of forwards, futures, options and swaps in more detail and candidates will become familiar with the main contracts based on different underlying assets. The final Reading looks at how options can be used to manage risk.

Reading Assignments

Analysis of Derivatives for the CFA® Program, Don Chance (AIMR, 2003)
69. "Derivative Markets and Instruments," Ch. 1
70. "Forward Markets and Contracts," Ch. 2, pp. 25-37
71. "Futures Markets and Contracts," Ch. 3, pp. 81-103
72. "Option Markets and Contracts," Ch. 4, pp. 159-194
73. "Swap Markets and Contracts," Ch. 5, pp. 269-285
74. "Risk Management Applications of Option Strategies," Ch. 7, pp. 411-429

69   Derivative Markets and Instruments

Learning Outcome Statements (LOS)

69-a	**Define** a derivative and **differentiate** between exchange-traded and over-the-counter derivatives.
69-b	**Define** a forward commitment, **identify** the types of forward commitments and **describe** the basic characteristics of forward contracts, futures contracts, and swaps.
69-c	**Define** a contingent claim and **identify** the types of contingent claims.
69-d	**Describe** the basic characteristics of options and **distinguish** between an option to buy (call) and an option to sell (put).
69-e	**Discuss** the purposes and criticisms of derivative markets.
69-f	**Explain** the concept of arbitrage and the role it plays in determining prices and in promoting market efficiency.

Introduction

This is an introductory reading which looks briefly at the two categories of derivatives, forward contracts and contingent claims, and how they are traded: OTC or on an exchange. It gives an introduction to the terminology used in forwards, futures, swaps and options markets and outlines the main concepts. All of the terms are covered in more detail later in the Study Session.

69 Concept Check Questions

1.   The seller of a put option:

    A.   pays a fee for the right to sell the underlying asset at a future date.

    B.   pays a fee for the right to buy the underlying asset at a future date.

    C.   receives a fee and may be obliged to sell the underlying asset at a future date.

    D.   receives a fee and may be obliged to buy the underlying asset at a future date.

---

2.   Which of the following statements concerning futures and forward contracts is *most accurate?*

    A.   Only forward contracts are guaranteed by a clearinghouse.

    B.   Forward contracts tend to be more heavily regulated than futures contracts.

    C.   A futures contract is a type of forward contract that has standardized contract terms.

    D.   A forward contract is a type of futures contract that is traded on a recognized exchange.

69   Concept Check Answers

1.   The seller of a put option:

    A.   pays a fee for the right to sell the underlying asset at a future date.

    B.   pays a fee for the right to buy the underlying asset at a future date.

    C.   receives a fee and may be obliged to sell the underlying asset at a future date.

    D.   receives a fee and may be obliged to buy the underlying asset at a future date.

Correct Answer: 1.   D

---

2.   Which of the following statements concerning futures and forward contracts is *most accurate?*

    A.   Only forward contracts are guaranteed by a clearinghouse.

    B.   Forward contracts tend to be more heavily regulated than futures contracts.

    C.   A futures contract is a type of forward contract that has standardized contract terms.

    D.   A forward contract is a type of futures contract that is traded on a recognized exchange.

Correct Answer: 2.   C

A futures contract is a type of forward contract that has standardized contract terms and is traded on a regulated exchange.

70   Forward Markets and Contracts

Learning Outcome Statements (LOS)

70-a	**Discuss** the differences between the positions held by the long and short parties to a forward contract in terms of delivery/settlement and default risk.
70-b	**Describe** the procedures for settling a forward contract at expiration, and **discuss** how a party to a forward contract can terminate a position prior to expiration and how credit risk is affected by the way in which a position is terminated.
70-c	**Differentiate** between a dealer and an end user of a forward contract.
70-d	**Describe** the characteristics of equity forward contracts.
70-e	**Describe** the characteristics of forward contracts on zero-coupon and coupon bonds.
70-f	**Explain** the characteristics of the Eurodollar time deposit market, **define** LIBOR and Euribor, and **describe** the characteristics of forward rate agreements (FRAs).
70-g	**Calculate** and **interpret** the payment at expiration of an FRA, **explain** each of the component terms, and **describe** the characteristics of currency forward contracts.

Introduction

We now look one-by-one at the different types of derivatives. We start with forwards. A forward contract is a commitment between two parties to do a transaction at a later date with the price and terms set in advance. It is assumed that no money changes hands at the beginning of the contract. In addition to describing the characteristics of forward contracts and how they are settled, candidates need to be familiar with the payments made at expiration on contracts where the underlying is a bond, equity or equity index, interest rate or currency rate.

70   Concept Check Questions

1.   A corporate treasurer knows that they will receive a large cash inflow in 180 days' time. He is concerned that interest rates, are going to fall and he wishes to put the money on 90-day LIBOR on receipt. He should consider taking a:

   A.   long position in a 6 x 3 FRA.

   B.   short position in a 6 x 3 FRA.

   C.   long position in a 6 x 9 FRA.

   D.   short position in a 6 x 9 FRA.

2.   An investor enters into a forward contract to purchase 100,000 shares in a security in 90 days' time. The contract is priced at $25. At the expiry of the contract the share price is $28. If it is cash settlement the investor:

   A.   makes a payment of $300,000.

   B.   receives a payment of $300,000.

   C.   makes a payment of $28,000,000.

   D.   receives a payment of $28,000,000.

3.   If an investor has taken a long position in a forward contract but then wishes to terminate the contract prior to expiry he can:

   A.   do nothing, it is impossible to terminate contracts.

   B.   go to the exchange and request an immediate cash settlement of the contract.

   C.   take a short position in a new contract with same expiry and underlying asset as the original contract.

   D.   go back to the counterparty and take a long position in another contract with the same expiry and underlying asset as the original contract.

70   Concept Check Answers

1.   A corporate treasurer knows that they will receive a large cash inflow in 180 days' time. He is concerned that interest rates, are going to fall and he wishes to put the money on 90-day LIBOR on receipt. He should consider taking a:

  A.   long position in a 6 x 3 FRA.

  B.   short position in a 6 x 3 FRA.

  C.   long position in a 6 x 9 FRA.

  D.   short position in a 6 x 9 FRA.

Correct Answer: 1.   D

A short position will generate a profit if interest rates fall which will offset the loss from placing the cash inflow on deposit at a lower rate. A 6 x 9 FRA is required, that is a 180-day forward contract based on deposits that mature in 270 days.

---

2.   An investor enters into a forward contract to purchase 100,000 shares in a security in 90 days' time. The contract is priced at $25. At the expiry of the contract the share price is $28. If it is cash settlement the investor:

  A.   makes a payment of $300,000.

  B.   receives a payment of $300,000.

  C.   makes a payment of $28,000,000.

  D.   receives a payment of $28,000,000.

Correct Answer: 2.   B

Since it is cash settlement, rather than delivery, then only the net payment changes hands. In this case the investor has made a profit since he had a long position and the share price has risen.

3.   If an investor has taken a long position in a forward contract but then wishes to terminate the contract prior to expiry he can:

   A.   do nothing, it is impossible to terminate contracts.

   B.   go to the exchange and request an immediate cash settlement of the contract.

   C.   take a short position in a new contract with same expiry and underlying asset as the original contract.

   D.   go back to the counterparty and take a long position in another contract with the same expiry and underlying asset as the original contract.

Correct Answer: 3.   C

   Taking a short position will mean that they no longer have any net exposure to price movements in the underlying asset.

71   Futures Markets and Contracts

Learning Outcome Statements (LOS)

71-a	**Identify** the institutional features that distinguish futures contracts from forward contracts and **describe** the characteristics of futures contracts.
71-b	**Differentiate** between margin in the securities markets and margin in the futures markets.
71-c	**Describe** how a futures trade takes place.
71-d	**Describe** how a futures position may be closed out (i.e., offset) prior to expiration.
71-e	**Define** initial margin, maintenance margin, variation margin, and settlement price.
71-f	**Describe** the process of marking to market and **compute** the margin balance, given the previous day's balance and the new futures price.
71-g	**Explain** price limits, limit move, limit up, limit down, and locked limit.
71-h	**Describe** how a futures contract can be terminated by a close-out (i.e., offset) at expiration, delivery, an equivalent cash settlement, or an exchange-for-physicals.
71-i	**Explain** delivery options in futures contracts.
71-j	**Distinguish** among scalpers, day traders, and position traders.
71-k	**Describe** the characteristics of the following types of futures contracts: Treasury bill, Eurodollar, Treasury bond, stock index, and currency.

Introduction

We next turn to futures contracts which are in many ways similar to forward contracts except that they are exchange traded and have standardized contracts. This has some important implications including the requirement for an investor using futures to deposit margin. Candidates will be expected to know the characteristics of futures contracts and be able to compute margin payments and the pricing of different types of contract.

71   Concept Check Questions

1.   A trader sells one wheat futures contract, which is for 5,000 bushels of wheat, at $4 per bushel. The trader posts an initial margin of $1,500. If the required maintenance margin is $1,100 the trader would first receive a maintenance margin call at a wheat price *closest* to:

 A. $2.93 per bushel.

 B. $3.92 per bushel.

 C. $4.08 per bushel.

 D. $5.45 per bushel.

2.   A scalper is:

 A.   executing transactions for investment managers.

 B.   employed by the exchange to stabilize futures prices.

 C.   making heavy bets on the direction of the futures market.

 D.   avoiding taking any long-term position in the futures market.

3.   The additional funds that a futures trader must deposit when she receives a margin call are the:
    A.   initial margin.
    B.   variation margin.
    C.   maintenance margin.

---

4.   A major function of a clearinghouse in the futures market is to:
    A.   act as a counterparty to each trade.
    B.   buy and sell seats on the exchange.
    C.   regulate the operations of the exchange.
    D.   take positions in the market to reduce price volatility.

71   Concept Check Answers

1.   A trader sells one wheat futures contract, which is for 5,000 bushels of wheat, at $4 per bushel. The trader posts an initial margin of $1,500. If the required maintenance margin is $1,100 the trader would first receive a maintenance margin call at a wheat price *closest* to:
  A. $2.93 per bushel.

  B. $3.92 per bushel.

  C. $4.08 per bushel.

  D. $5.45 per bushel.

Correct Answer: 1.   C
When he has made a loss of $400 he would receive a margin call, this is equivalent to a price rise of 8 cents, since he sold the contract.

2.   A scalper is:
  A.   executing transactions for investment managers.

  B.   employed by the exchange to stabilize futures prices.

  C.   making heavy bets on the direction of the futures market.

  D.   avoiding taking any long-term position in the futures market.

Correct Answer: 2.   D
  Scalpers are members of the exchange who are aiming to profit from the differences between bid and ask prices without taking exposure to the direction of futures price moves.

3.   The additional funds that a futures trader must deposit when she receives a margin call are the:

    A.   initial margin.

    B.   variation margin.

    C.   maintenance margin.

Correct Answer: 3.   **B**

---

4.   A major function of a clearinghouse in the futures market is to:

    A.   act as a counterparty to each trade.

    B.   buy and sell seats on the exchange.

    C.   regulate the operations of the exchange.

    D.   take positions in the market to reduce price volatility.

Correct Answer: 4.   **A**

72   Option Markets and Contracts

Learning Outcome Statements (LOS)

72-a	**Identify** the basic elements and **describe** the characteristics of option contracts.
72-b	**Define** European option, American option, moneyness, payoff, intrinsic value, and time value and **differentiate** between exchange-traded options and over-the-counter options.
72-c	**Identify** the different types of options in terms of the underlying instruments.
72-d	**Compare** and **contrast** interest rate options to forward rate agreements (FRAs).
72-e	**Explain** how option payoffs are determined, and **show** how interest rate option payoffs differ from the payoffs of other types of options.
72-f	**Define** interest rate caps and floors.
72-g	**Identify** the minimum and maximum values of European options and American options.
72-h	**Explain** how the lower bounds of European calls and puts are determined by constructing portfolio combinations that prevent arbitrage, and **calculate** an option's lower bound.
72-i	**Determine** the lowest prices of European and American calls and puts based on the rules for minimum values and lower bounds.
72-j	**Describe** how a portfolio (combination) of options establishes the relationship between options that differ only by exercise price.
72-k	**Explain** how option prices are affected by the time to expiration of the option.
72-l	**Explain** put-call parity for European options, given the payoffs on a fiduciary call and a protective put.
72-m	**Explain** the relationship between American options and European options in terms of the lower bounds on option prices and the possibility of early exercise.
72-n	**Explain** how cash flows on the underlying asset affect put-call parity and the lower bounds of option prices.
72-o	**Identify** the directional effect of an interest rate change on an option's price.
72-p	**Describe** the impact of a change in volatility on an option's price.

Introduction

This Reading examines options. Options are quite different from forwards and futures since the holder of an option has the right, but not the obligation, to buy or sell an underlying asset. Also the option buyer must pay the option seller for this right or option at the beginning of the contract. In addition to covering definitions and characteristics of options, candidates have to be able to calculate option payoffs, understand lower bounds for option prices and put-call parity. Some of the formulas and calculations look somewhat intimidating but the concepts behind the formulae are not difficult and the candidate should attempt to master the concepts to help them memorize the formulae.

72   Concept Check Questions

1.   A European option can be exercised at

    A.   the expiration date only.

    B.   any time up to or at expiration.

---

2.   If a put option has an exercise price of $30 and the underlying stock is trading in the market at $20 then the put option is:

    A. $20 in-the-money.

    B. $10 in-the-money.

    C. $10 out-of-the-money.

    D. $20 out-of-the-money.

3.   An investor buys a call option at a premium of $10 on a stock which has a market price of $60. If the exercise price is $62 the investor will:

A.   make a loss if the stock price rises above the breakeven point of $70.

B.   make a loss if the stock price rises above the breakeven point of $72.

C.   make a profit if the stock price rises above the breakeven point of $70.

D.   make a profit if the stock price rises above the breakeven point of $72.

---

4.   If the stock price is lower than the strike price then a put option is:

A.   is in-the-money and has no intrinsic value.

B.   is out-of-the-money and has no intrinsic value.

C.   is in-the-money and has a positive intrinsic value.

D.   is out-of-the-money and has a positive intrinsic value.

72   Concept Check Answers

1.   A European option can be exercised at

    A.   the expiration date only.

    B.   any time up to or at expiration.

Correct Answer: 1.   A
B. is an American option.

---

2.   If a put option has an exercise price of $30 and the underlying stock is trading in the market at $20 then the put option is:

    A. $20 in-the-money.

    B. $10 in-the-money.

    C. $10 out-of-the-money.

    D. $20 out-of-the-money.

Correct Answer: 2.   B
The exercise price is $10 above the market price so if the option was exercised today the shares could be sold at $30 and bought back at $20 in the market, generating a gain of $10.

3.   An investor buys a call option at a premium of $10 on a stock which has a market price of $60. If the exercise price is $62 the investor will:

    A.   make a loss if the stock price rises above the breakeven point of $70.

    B.   make a loss if the stock price rises above the breakeven point of $72.

    C.   make a profit if the stock price rises above the breakeven point of $70.

    D.   make a profit if the stock price rises above the breakeven point of $72.

Correct Answer: 3.   **D**

    Breakeven is when $0 = $ maximum $[\,0, (S - X)] -$ premium, when $S = \$72$

---

4.   If the stock price is lower than the strike price then a put option is:

    A.   is in-the-money and has no intrinsic value.

    B.   is out-of-the-money and has no intrinsic value.

    C.   is in-the-money and has a positive intrinsic value.

    D.   is out-of-the-money and has a positive intrinsic value.

Correct Answer: 4.   **C**

73   Swap Markets and Contracts

Learning Outcome Statements (LOS)

73-a	**Describe** the characteristics of swap contracts and **explain** how swaps are terminated.
73-b	**Define** and **give** examples of currency swaps and **calculate** and **interpret** the payments on a currency swap.
73-c	**Define** and **give** an example of a plain vanilla interest rate swap and **calculate** the payments on an interest rate swap.
73-d	**Define** and **give** examples of equity swaps and **calculate** and **interpret** the payments on an equity swap.

Introduction

This is the last Reading which examines the characteristics of a specific type of derivative. We look at swaps which are essentially a series of forward rate agreements. The two parties agree to exchange payments; usually at least one party will make a payment which is dependent on a variable such as an interest rate or equity index level. Candidates should be able to calculate the payments for currency, interest rate and equity swaps.

73   Concept Check Questions

1.   Two parties enter into a plain vanilla 10-year interest rate swap agreement. The party which pays a fixed rate agrees to pay 6% and the other party to pay LIBOR, on a notional principal of $10 million. Payments are in arrears and LIBOR is 5% when the agreement is signed, 5½% at the end of the first year and 6½ % at the end of the second year. The party who is paying a fixed rate will, at the end of the first year:

   A.   make a net payment of $50,000.

   B.   make a net payment of $100,000.

   C.   receive a net payment of $50,000.

   D.   the pay-fixed party will receive a net payment of $100,000.

---

2.   Two parties X and Y enter into a ten-year fixed-for-fixed currency swap. Party X holds US dollars and wishes to exchange these for Yen, Party Y holds Yen and wishes to exchange these for US dollars. The principal is $100 million. The US dollar = Yen 110 when the agreement is signed and the fixed rate on US dollars is set at 6% and Yen at 1%. At the end of the first year:

   A.   Party X pays Yen 110 million, and Party Y pays US dollars 6 million.

   B.   Party Y pays Yen 110 million, and Party X pays US dollars 6 million.

   C.   Party X pays Yen 11,110 million, and Party Y pays US dollars 106 million.

   D.   Party Y pays Yen 11,110 million, and Party X pays US dollars 106 million.

3.   In which of the following types of derivative transaction is the exchange clearinghouse the counterparty for each trade?

  A.   Swaps.

  B.   Futures.

  C.   Forwards.

73   Concept Check Answers

1.   Two parties enter into a plain vanilla 10-year interest rate swap agreement. The party which pays a fixed rate agrees to pay 6% and the other party to pay LIBOR, on a notional principal of $10 million. Payments are in arrears and LIBOR is 5% when the agreement is signed, 5½% at the end of the first year and 6½ % at the end of the second year. The party who is paying a fixed rate will, at the end of the first year:

    A.   make a net payment of $50,000.

    B.   make a net payment of $100,000.

    C.   receive a net payment of $50,000.

    D.   the pay-fixed party will receive a net payment of $100,000.

Correct Answer: 1.   **B**
The payment at the end of the first year is based on LIBOR when the agreement is signed which is 5%. The fixed-rate payment will be $600,000; the floating-rate payment will be $500,000.

2.   Two parties X and Y enter into a ten-year fixed-for-fixed currency swap. Party X holds US dollars and wishes to exchange these for Yen, Party Y holds Yen and wishes to exchange these for US dollars. The principal is $100 million. The US dollar = Yen 110 when the agreement is signed and the fixed rate on US dollars is set at 6% and Yen at 1%. At the end of the first year:

    A.   Party X pays Yen 110 million, and Party Y pays US dollars 6 million.

    B.   Party Y pays Yen 110 million, and Party X pays US dollars 6 million.

    C.   Party X pays Yen 11,110 million, and Party Y pays US dollars 106 million.

    D.   Party Y pays Yen 11,110 million, and Party X pays US dollars 106 million.

Correct Answer: 2.   **A**
Party X pays interest on the Yen borrowed which is:
Yen11,000 million x 1% = Yen 110 million.
Party Y pays interest on the US dollars borrowed which is:
US dollars 100 million x 6% = US dollars 6 million.
The principals would be exchanged at the beginning of the agreement.

3.   In which of the following types of derivative transaction is the exchange clearinghouse the counterparty for each trade?

   A.   Swaps.

   B.   Futures.

   C.   Forwards.

Correct Answer: 3.   B
Forwards and swaps are not traded on an exchange and there is counterparty risk.

74   Risk Management Applications of Option Strategies

Learning Outcome Statements (LOS)

74-a	**Determine** the value at expiration, profit, maximum profit, maximum loss, breakeven underlying price at expiration, and general shape of the graph of the strategies of buying and selling calls and buying and selling puts, and **explain** each strategy's characteristics.
74-b	**Determine** the value at expiration, profit, maximum profit, maximum loss, breakeven underlying price at expiration, and general shape of the graph of the covered call strategy and the protective put strategy, and **explain** each strategy's characteristics.

Introduction

This is a brief introduction to how derivatives, in particular options, can be used to manage risk. Options allow the holder to capture much of the upside if prices move in one direction and limit their losses if prices move in the other direction making them attractive for portfolio managers meeting specific client risk-return objectives. In this Reading we look at strategies that are frequently used by equity managers and candidates need to be able to interpret the relevant payoff diagrams as well as calculate profits, losses and breakeven prices.

74   Concept Check Questions

1.   A portfolio insurance strategy for a diversified stock portfolio can be implemented by:

   A.   buying a put option on the stock index representing the underlying stock portfolio.

   B.   writing a put option on the stock index representing the underlying stock portfolio.

   C.   buying a call option on the stock index representing the underlying stock portfolio.

   D.   writing a covered call option on the stock index representing the underlying stock portfolio.

---

2.   An investor writes a put option at a premium of $6 on a stock with an exercise price of $62. If the stock price is $70 at expiration the investor will make a profit of:

   A. $2.

   B. $6.

   C. $8.

   D. $14.

74   Concept Check Answers

1.   A portfolio insurance strategy for a diversified stock portfolio can be implemented by:

    A.   buying a put option on the stock index representing the underlying stock portfolio.

    B.   writing a put option on the stock index representing the underlying stock portfolio.

    C.   buying a call option on the stock index representing the underlying stock portfolio.

    D.   writing a covered call option on the stock index representing the underlying stock portfolio.

Correct Answer: 1.   **A**
In the situation that the stock market index falls, the losses on the underlying portfolio will be offset by the profits on the put option.

---

2.   An investor writes a put option at a premium of $6 on a stock with an exercise price of $62. If the stock price is $70 at expiration the investor will make a profit of:

    A. $2.

    B. $6.

    C. $8.

    D. $14.

Correct Answer: 2.   **B**
The put option will lapse worthless since the exercise price is lower than the market price, so the investor makes a profit of the premium that he collected.

STUDY SESSION 17

Alternative Investments

Overview

This is a short Study Session that gives a brief introduction to alternative investments. 'Alternative investments' refer to a variety of investments, including real estate and venture capital, that complement the 'traditional' asset classes such as stocks, bonds and other instruments traded in the financial markets. It is also often used to refer to alternative strategies which may use traditional assets but have different objectives such as targeting absolute returns. Hedge funds, for example, use alternative strategies.

The Study Session looks at the characteristics of alternative investments including risk and return and how investments are valued. The Study Session is based on just one Reading and it works through a range of different investments: open and closed-end funds, exchange traded funds, real estate, venture capital, hedge funds, closely-held companies and finally commodities.

Reading Assignments

International Investments, 5th edition, Bruno Solnik and Dennis McLeavey (Addison Wesley, 2004)

75.   "Alternative Investments," Ch. 8

75   Alternative Investments

Learning Outcome Statements (LOS)

75-a	**Distinguish** between an open-end and a closed-end fund.
75-b	**Explain** how the net asset value of a fund is calculated.
75-c	**Explain** the nature of various fees charged by investment companies.
75-d	**Distinguish** among style, sector, index, global, and stable value strategies in equity investment.
75-e	**Distinguish** among exchange traded funds (ETFs), traditional mutual funds, and closed-end funds.
75-f	**Explain** the advantages and risks of ETFs.
75-g	**Describe** the forms of real estate investment.
75-h	**Explain** the characteristics of real estate as an investable asset class.
75-i	**Describe** the various approaches to the valuation of real estate.
75-j	**Calculate** the net operating income (NOI) from a real estate investment.
75-k	**Calculate** the value of a property using the sales comparison and income approaches.
75-l	**Calculate** the after-tax cash flows, net present value, and yield of a real estate investment.
75-m	**Explain** the various stages in venture capital investing.
75-n	**Discuss** venture capital investment characteristics and the challenges to venture capital valuation and performance measurement.
75-o	**Calculate** the net present value (NPV) of a venture capital project, given the project's possible payoff and conditional failure probabilities.
75-p	**Discuss** the descriptive accuracy of the term "hedge fund" and **define** hedge fund in terms of objectives, legal structure, and fee structure, and **describe** the various classifications of hedge funds.
75-q	**Discuss** the benefits and drawbacks to fund of funds investing.
75-r	**Discuss** the leverage and unique risks of hedge funds.
75-s	**Discuss** the performance of hedge funds, the biases present in hedge fund performance measurement, and **explain** the effect of survivorship bias on the reported return and risk measures for a hedge fund data base.

75-t	**Explain** how the legal environment affects the valuation of closely held companies.
75-u	**Describe** alternative valuation methods for closely held companies and **distinguish** among the bases for the discounts and premiums for these companies.
75-v	**Discuss** distressed securities investing and the similarities between venture capital investing and distressed securities investing.
75-w	**Discuss** the role of commodities as a vehicle for investing in production and consumption.
75-x	**Discuss** the motivation for investing in commodities, commodities derivatives, and commodity-linked securities.
75-y	**Discuss** the sources of return on a collateralized commodity futures position.

Introduction

Alternative investments differ from traditional investments; they tend to be less liquid, to be in inefficient markets and require longer holding periods. Often investing in them involves particular legal or tax considerations. The main features of alternative investments are:

- Illiquidity.
- Difficulty in determining current market values.
- Limited historical risk and return data.
- Extensive investment analysis required.

The main attraction of alternative investments is the potential for earning a higher alpha than is available in more efficient markets. Recall that alpha is the excess risk-adjusted return.

Candidates will be expected to be familiar with the unique characteristics and advantages and disadvantages of investing in each asset. They will also need to be able to apply appropriate methods to value real estate and venture capital investments.

Investment companies

An investment company is a financial intermediary that pools investors' funds and invests them on their behalf giving a proportional share of the pooled fund performance to each investor. The investments can be in any specified asset class or combination of asset classes. An investment management company is appointed by the directors of the investment company to do the actual management of the investments.

Investment (Fund) Companies

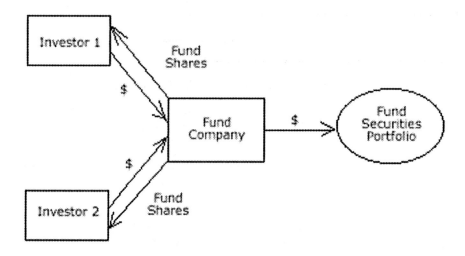

Open-end investment companies offer a redemption feature. However closed-end funds issue shares that are traded in the secondary market.

75   Concept Check Questions

1.   Investors in a load open-end fund:
   A.   purchase shares at the net asset value.

   B.   purchase shares at a discount to the net asset value.

   C.   pay an annual management charge which is called a load.

   D.   purchase shares at the net asset value plus an initial charge.

---

2.   Which of the following is the *least appropriate* method of valuing real estate?
   A.   Cost approach.

   B.   Income approach.

   C.   Leveraged approach.

   D.   Comparative sales approach.

---

3.   A property which is considered a lower risk investment than another property investment will have a:
   A.   lower market capitalization rate.

   B.   higher market capitalization rate.

4.   The after-tax cash flow from a real estate investment adjusts the net operating income for all of the following *except*:

   A.   Cost of debt.

   B.   Depreciation costs less tax savings.

   C.   Taxation on capital gains when the property is sold.

---

5.   Investing in a hedge fund is *least likely* to be attractive because:

   A.   The returns are higher than those available on equity funds.

   B.   The volatility of returns is lower than that of a fund investing in equities.

   C.   The fund will provide greater transparency than a traditional mutual fund.

   D.   The return from the fund is likely to have a low correlation with listed stocks and bonds.

---

6.   Capital for product development and research is:

   A.   seed financing.

   B.   start-up financing.

   C.   first-stage financing.

   D.   second-stage financing.

7.   Which of the following is *least likely* to be a characteristic of hedge funds?
   A.   They usually attempt to hedge out all market risk.
   B.   The managers are often compensated by incentive fees.
   C.   They have the flexibility to use derivatives and leverage.
   D.   They aim to generate positive returns regardless of whether markets are rising or falling.

8.   Investors in commodity funds often use futures since they:
   A.   are cheap to use.
   B.   provide an income.
   C.   provide access to professional management.
   D.   are less volatile than the underlying commodity prices.

75   Concept Check Answers

1.   Investors in a load open-end fund:
    A.   purchase shares at the net asset value.
    B.   purchase shares at a discount to the net asset value.
    C.   pay an annual management charge which is called a load.
    D.   purchase shares at the net asset value plus an initial charge.

Correct Answer: 1.   D

---

2.   Which of the following is the *least appropriate* method of valuing real estate?
    A.   Cost approach.
    B.   Income approach.
    C.   Leveraged approach.
    D.   Comparative sales approach.

Correct Answer: 2.   C

---

3.   A property which is considered a lower risk investment than another property investment will have a:
    A.   lower market capitalization rate.
    B.   higher market capitalization rate.

Correct Answer: 3.   A
    The market capitalization rate reflects the investors' required rate of return from the property, a low risk project will tend to have a low capitalization rate and therefore, for equal net operating income, a higher value.

4.   The after-tax cash flow from a real estate investment adjusts the net operating income for all of the following *except*:

   A.   Cost of debt.

   B.   Depreciation costs less tax savings.

   C.   Taxation on capital gains when the property is sold.

Correct Answer: 4.   B

   NOI is before depreciation, and depreciation is a non-cash item, so no adjustment is made for the depreciation, although the tax saving is included in the calculation.

5.   Investing in a hedge fund is *least likely* to be attractive because:

   A.   The returns are higher than those available on equity funds.

   B.   The volatility of returns is lower than that of a fund investing in equities.

   C.   The fund will provide greater transparency than a traditional mutual fund.

   D.   The return from the fund is likely to have a low correlation with listed stocks and bonds.

Correct Answer: 5.   C

6.   Capital for product development and research is:

   A.   seed financing.

   B.   start-up financing.

   C.   first-stage financing.

   D.   second-stage financing.

Correct Answer: 6.   A

7.   Which of the following is *least likely* to be a characteristic of hedge funds?
   A.   They usually attempt to hedge out all market risk.
   B.   The managers are often compensated by incentive fees.
   C.   They have the flexibility to use derivatives and leverage.
   D.   They aim to generate positive returns regardless of whether markets are rising or falling.

Correct Answer: 7.   A
Many funds (e.g. global macro funds) deliberately take on market risk.

---

8.   Investors in commodity funds often use futures since they:
   A.   are cheap to use.
   B.   provide an income.
   C.   provide access to professional management.
   D.   are less volatile than the underlying commodity prices.

Correct Answer: 8.   A

STUDY SESSION 18

Portfolio Management

Overview

At Level I, portfolio management only accounts for one Study Session and a guideline weighting of 5% of the examination questions. However the concepts covered here are an important foundation for both Level II and especially Level III when the syllabus centres on portfolio management.

This Study Session starts with a review of the relationship between risk and return and the components of risk and return. The next section moves on to client policy statements and setting risk and return objectives. These topics are revisited many times in Level III. In the last two Reading Assignments, candidates are introduced to modern portfolio theory including how to structure portfolios to obtain the optimal risk and return trade-off. This is followed by an introduction to capital market theory and the Capital Asset Pricing Model (CAPM) which formally links the return of a security or portfolio to its systematic or beta risk.

Reading Assignments

Investment Analysis and Portfolio Management, 7th edition, Frank K. Reilly and Keith C. Brown (South-Western, 2003)

76.   "The Investment Setting," Ch. 1, pp. 16–29

77.   "The Asset Allocation Decision," Ch. 2

78.   "An Introduction to Portfolio Management," Ch. 7

79.   "An Introduction to Asset Pricing Models," Ch. 8, pp. 237–256

76   The Investment Setting

Learning Outcome Statements (LOS)

76-a	**Explain** the concept of required rate of return and **discuss** the components of an investor's required rate of return.
76-b	**Differentiate** between the real risk-free rate of return and the nominal risk-free rate of return and compute both return measures.
76-c	**Explain** the risk premium and the associated fundamental sources of risk, and why these sources are complementary to systematic risk.
76-d	**Define** the security market line and **discuss** the factors that cause movements along, changes in the slope of, and shifts of the security market line.

Introduction

This Reading Assignment looks at basic concepts and how risk and return are related in investment. Investors' required returns are derived from the real risk-free rate, plus an inflation premium and a premium for taking on risk. We also consider the difference between risks that can be diversified away in a portfolio and systematic risk which cannot be diversified. The security market line (SML) graphically links the required return to the systematic risk and candidates need to know which factors will lead to a move in the SML.

76   Concept Check Questions

1.   The sources of risk of an investment include all of the following *except:*

    A.   country risk.

    B.   liquidity risk.

    C.   variance risk.

    D.   financial risk.

---

2.   If the government adopts an unanticipated tighter monetary policy this is likely to:

    A.   lead to a flatter security market line.

    B.   lead to a steeper security market line.

    C.   lead to an upward shift in the security market line.

    D.   lead to a downward shift in the security market line.

---

3.   If an investor selects an investment with a high level of systematic risk relative to the market, and the market is expected to rise sharply, then the expected return

    A.   is lower than the market.

    B.   is higher than the market.

    C.   is independent of the market.

76   Concept Check Answers

1.   The sources of risk of an investment include all of the following *except:*

   A.   country risk.

   B.   liquidity risk.

   C.   variance risk.

   D.   financial risk.

Correct Answer: 1.   C

Variance of rates of return is a measure of risk.

---

2.   If the government adopts an unanticipated tighter monetary policy this is likely to:

   A.   lead to a flatter security market line.

   B.   lead to a steeper security market line.

   C.   lead to an upward shift in the security market line.

   D.   lead to a downward shift in the security market line.

Correct Answer: 2.   C

Monetary tightening will be likely to lead to a higher NRFR and higher required rates of returns for all investments.

---

3.   If an investor selects an investment with a high level of systematic risk relative to the market, and the market is expected to rise sharply, then the expected return

   A.   is lower than the market.

   B.   is higher than the market.

   C.   is independent of the market.

Correct Answer: 3.   B

Higher systematic risk leads to higher expected return, if the market return is above the risk-free rate.

77   The Asset Allocation Decision

Learning Outcome Statements (LOS)

77-a	**Describe** the steps in the portfolio management process and **explain** the need for a policy statement.
77-b	**Explain** why investment objectives should be expressed in terms of risk and return and **list** the factors that may affect an investor's risk tolerance.
77-c	**Describe** the return objectives of capital preservation, capital appreciation, current income, and total return and **describe** the investment constraints of liquidity, time horizon, tax concerns, legal and regulatory factors, and unique needs and preferences.
77-d	**Describe** the importance of asset allocation, in terms of the percentage of a portfolio's return that can be explained by the target asset allocation and list reasons for the differences in the average asset allocation among citizens of different countries.

Introduction

Asset allocation is the process of deciding how to divide an investor's assets between different countries and asset classes. The asset allocation decision is extremely important since it, rather than stock selection, is the key factor in determining the performance of a portfolio. Studies show that the asset allocation policy accounts for about 90% of funds' performance. Candidates need to understand how determining a client's objectives and constraints and the subsequent asset allocation decision fit in to the overall investment process.

77   Concept Check Questions

1.   An investor looking for capital appreciation over the long term would be likely to invest mainly in:

    A.   Treasury bills.

    B.   common stocks.

    C.   long-term corporate bonds.

    D.   long-term government bonds.

2.   Which of the following is the most important factor in determining the return generated by an investment portfolio?

    A.   Asset allocation.

    B.   Industry selection.

    C.   Individual security selection.

3.   The policy statement is important because it:

A.   is used to set the benchmark for the client's portfolio.

B.   provides information on the products that are managed by the portfolio manager.

C.   provides information on the portfolio manager's style of management and past performance record.

77   Concept Check Answers

1.   An investor looking for capital appreciation over the long term would be likely to invest mainly in:

    A.   Treasury bills.

    B.   common stocks.

    C.   long-term corporate bonds.

    D.   long-term government bonds.

Correct Answer: 1.   **B**

Common stocks provide superior returns over the long term and offer the potential for positive real investment returns.

---

2.   Which of the following is the most important factor in determining the return generated by an investment portfolio?

    A.   Asset allocation.

    B.   Industry selection.

    C.   Individual security selection.

Correct Answer: 2.   **A**

---

3.   The policy statement is important because it:

    A.   is used to set the benchmark for the client's portfolio.

    B.   provides information on the products that are managed by the portfolio manager.

    C.   provides information on the portfolio manager's style of management and past performance record.

Correct Answer: 3.   **A**

The policy statement is important because it allows the clients to set out their own requirements, rather than providing information on the portfolio manager's products and performance.

78   An Introduction to Portfolio Management

Learning Outcome Statements (LOS)

78-a	**Define** risk aversion and **cite** evidence that suggests that individuals are generally risk averse.
78-b	**List** the assumptions about individuals' investment behaviour of the Markowitz Portfolio Theory.
78-c	**Compute** expected return for an individual investment and for a portfolio.
78-d	**Compute** the variance and standard deviation for an individual investment.
78-e	**Compute** the covariance of rates of return, and **show** how it is related to the correlation coefficient.
78-f	**List** the components of the portfolio standard deviation formula, and **explain** which component is most important to consider when adding an investment to a portfolio.
78-g	**Describe** the efficient frontier and **explain** its implications for an investor willing to assume more risk.
78-h	**Define** optimal portfolio and **show** how each investor may have a different optimal portfolio.

Introduction

Now we move on to analyzing risk and return in more detail, not just for individual securities but also for portfolios. Candidates should be comfortable using the equations for computing portfolio return and risk (variance or standard deviation), covariance and correlation. This leads on to studying the Markowitz efficient frontier which determines which portfolios offer an investor the best trade-off between risk and return. This in turn paves the way for the capital market theory covered in the next Reading Assignment.

78   Concept Check Questions

1.   The correlation coefficient between the returns of two assets is 0.6 and the standard deviations of returns of the two assets are 7% and 12%. The covariance of returns is *closest* to:

    A.   14.0.

    B.   50.4.

    C.   71.4.

    D.   140.0.

---

2.   If the returns from two assets have a correlation coefficient of 0 it means that:

    A.   the returns are not correlated.

    B.   there is perfect positive correlation between the returns.

    C.   there is perfect negative correlation between the returns.

    D.   there is an error, a correlation coefficient of 0 is not possible.

3.   The efficient frontier represents portfolios that:

   A.   offer the highest return for a given level of total risk.

   B.   offer the highest return for a given level of systematic risk.

   C.   are equally attractive to an investor with a specified level of total risk tolerance.

   D.   are equally attractive to an investor with a specified level of systematic risk tolerance.

78   Concept Check Answers

1.   The correlation coefficient between the returns of two assets is 0.6 and the standard deviations of returns of the two assets are 7% and 12%. The covariance of returns is *closest* to:

  A.   14.0.

  B.   50.4.

  C.   71.4.

  D.   140.0.

Correct Answer: 1.   B

$$r_{xy} = \frac{\text{cov ariance}_{xy}}{\sigma_x \sigma_y}$$

$$\text{cov ariance} = 0.6 \times 7 \times 12 = 50.4$$

---

2.   If the returns from two assets have a correlation coefficient of 0 it means that:

  A.   the returns are not correlated.

  B.   there is perfect positive correlation between the returns.

  C.   there is perfect negative correlation between the returns.

  D.   there is an error, a correlation coefficient of 0 is not possible.

Correct Answer: 2.   A

3.   The efficient frontier represents portfolios that:

    A.   offer the highest return for a given level of total risk.

    B.   offer the highest return for a given level of systematic risk.

    C.   are equally attractive to an investor with a specified level of total risk tolerance.

    D.   are equally attractive to an investor with a specified level of systematic risk tolerance.

Correct Answer: 3.   **A**

79   An Introduction to Asset Pricing Models

Learning Outcome Statements (LOS)

79-a	**List** the assumptions of the capital market theory.
79-b	**Explain** what happens to the expected return, the standard deviation of returns, and possible risk-return combinations when a risk-free asset is combined with a portfolio of risky assets.
79-c	**Identify** the market portfolio and **describe** the role of the market portfolio in the formation of the capital market line (CML).
79-d	**Define** systematic and unsystematic risk and **explain** why an investor should not expect to receive additional return for assuming unsystematic risk.
79-e	**Describe** the capital asset pricing model, **diagram** the security market line (SML), and **define** beta.
79-f	**Calculate** and **interpret** using the SML, the expected return on a security and **evaluate** whether the security is undervalued, overvalued, or properly valued.
79-g	**Explain** how the systematic risk of an asset is estimated using the characteristic line.

Introduction

This Reading Assignment focuses on the Capital Asset Pricing Model (CAPM). This is a model for pricing risky assets and links the required return to the systematic risk of the asset. Candidates should know the assumptions made by capital market theory, and understand the concepts of a risk-free asset and market portfolio representing a portfolio of risky assets. They should also be prepared to calculate required rates of return using CAPM which can be compared to expected rates of return to decide whether an asset is over or undervalued.

79   Concept Check Questions

1.   The characteristic line:

    A.   is a regression line used to estimate a stock's systematic risk.

    B.   is a regression line used to estimate a stock's standard deviation.

    C.   indicates the required rate of return of a stock given its systematic risk.

    D.   indicates the required rate of return of a stock given its standard deviation.

---

2.   The expected return from a market is 12% and the risk free rate is 5% and a stock has a beta of 0.5. The required rate of return from the stock is:

    A.   6.0%.

    B.   8.5%.

    C.   11.0%.

    D.   14.5%.

3.   If a stock lies below the security market line it is:
   A.   overvalued.
   B.   undervalued.

---

4.   In a rapidly rising market, a stock with a beta of less than 1 is expected to:
   A.   outperform the market.
   B.   underperform the market.

79 Concept Check Answers

1. The characteristic line:

   A. is a regression line used to estimate a stock's systematic risk.

   B. is a regression line used to estimate a stock's standard deviation.

   C. indicates the required rate of return of a stock given its systematic risk.

   D. indicates the required rate of return of a stock given its standard deviation.

Correct Answer: 1. A

---

2. The expected return from a market is 12% and the risk free rate is 5% and a stock has a beta of 0.5. The required rate of return from the stock is:

   A. 6.0%.

   B. 8.5%.

   C. 11.0%.

   D. 14.5%.

Correct Answer: 2. B

$$R_x = R_f + \beta[E(R_m) - R_f] = 5\% + 0.5(12\% - 5\%) = 8.5\%$$

3.   If a stock lies below the security market line it is:
   A.   overvalued.
   B.   undervalued.

Correct Answer: 3.   A
The return is less than the required return using CAPM.

---

4.   In a rapidly rising market, a stock with a beta of less than 1 is expected to:
   A.   outperform the market.
   B.   underperform the market.

Correct Answer: 4.   B
The stock is expected to rise by less than the market.

Terminology

Appraisal – for real estate, the process of estimating the current market value of a property.

Comparative sales approach – the value of a real estate is , at the most, the cost of the land and constructing the building at current prices.

Income approach – the value of real estate is the present value of it future income.

Market capitalization rate – divide a property's net operating income by the appropriate market capitalization rate to arrive at an estimate for its current market value. It reflects the rate of return required by investors in such a property.

Positive leverage – the return from a real estate investment is higher than the cost of debt, an investor will achieve a higher rate of return if he/she uses leverage to purchase the property.

Real Estate Investment Trust (REIT) – a closed-end investment company that invests in real estate and mortgages on real estate.

Real Estate Limited Partnership (RELP) – a real estate syndicate that invests in different types of real estate.

Seed financing – venture capital provided for product development and market research, the product is still at the 'idea' stage.

Start-up financing – venture capital provided for early stage product development and initial marketing.

First-stage financing – venture capital provided for initial commercial manufacture and sales.

Mezzanine (or bridge) financing – venture capital provided for a company that expects to go public in the near future.

Turnarounds – capital provided to restructure a company that has problems.

Leveraged buyouts (LBOs) – capital to fund a management group (a management buyout) or other investors who wish to purchase a business or company.

Investment company – a company that sell its own shares and uses the proceeds to buy stocks, bonds or other financial instruments.

Closed-end investment company – an investment company that issues a fixed number of shares, the shares are then traded in the secondary market.

Open-end investment company – a company that offers new shares to investors and redeems shares continuously.

Mutual fund – an open-end investment company.

No-load fund – shares are sold at net asset value, with no sales charge added.

Load fund – a fund that makes an initial sales charge, so the offering price is the net asset value plus a load.

Thank you for reading our book

Appendix A:

Exhibits

Exhibit 1: Accounting Statements

Exhibit 2: Puts and Calls

Exhibit 3: PE Breakdown

Exhibit 4: Ratios

Exhibit 1: Accounting Statements

Income Stmt: Particular moment in the life of an asset

Convert assets into profit to return to Inv or Stkhldrs Equity

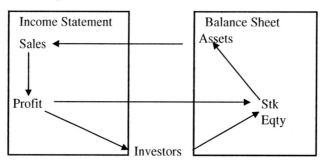

Income Statement
Sales

Profit

Investors

Balance Sheet
Assets

Stk
Eqty

Assets come into Balance Sheet in SE to get to Assets

Statement of Cash Flows

Decisions
Income Statement

Balance Sheet

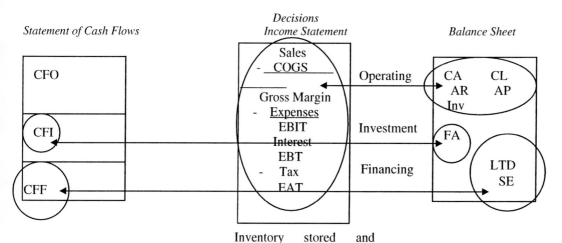

CFO

CFI

CFF

Sales
- COGS

Gross Margin
- Expenses
EBIT
Interest
EBT
- Tax
EAT

Operating

Investment

Financing

CA   CL
AR   AP
Inv

FA

LTD
SE

Inventory stored and converted to product

CEOs look at things from viewpoint of Cash Flow ... to pay bills, liquidity

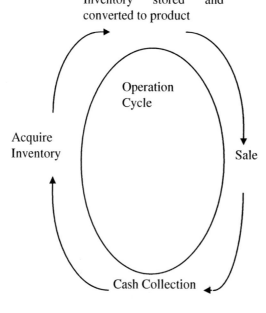

Operation Cycle

Acquire Inventory

Sale

Cash Collection

A growing company never has enough cash collection to grow the inventory.

CEO is always looking for something which will grow cash.

Newspaper cycles daily,
Boeing could take years

Notes:

Exhibit 2: Puts and Calls

Interpret the diagrams that depict the expiration-day values of the long call, short call, long put and short put strategies;
(X = strike price, S = Stock price, C = cost of Call, P = cost of Put)

Long Call

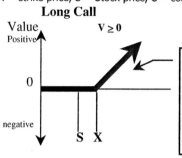

Value of the long call will be the amount over strike the stock is trading. **Long call will never have a value less than zero.**

Long Put

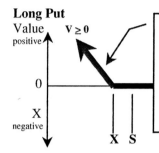

Value of the long put will be the amount less than the strike that the stock is trading. **Long put will never have a value less than zero.**

Short Call

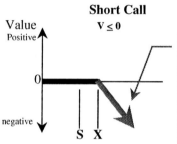

Value of the short call will be the amount over the strike the stock is trading. **Short call will never have a value greater than zero.**

Short Put

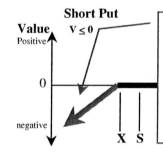

Value of the short put will be the amount less than the strike the stock is trading. **Short put will never have a value greater than zero.**

Interpret the **profit/loss** diagrams for the long call, short call, long put, and short put strategies;

Long Call

Loss ≤ C, Profit > X+C

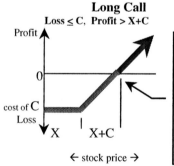

Profit of the long call is the amount over the strike + cost of the call (X+C). Loss on the call is the amount the stock is under the call + strike, not to exceed the cost of the call.

Long Put

Loss ≤ X+P, Profit < X

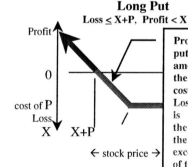

Profit the long put is the amount under the strike and cost of the put. Loss on the put is the amount the stock is over the strike, not to exceed the cost of the put.

Short Call

Loss ≥ X+C, Profit < X+C

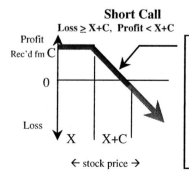

Profit of the short call is the amount under the strike + cost of the call (X+C), not to exceed the proceeds received from the call. Loss on the call is the amount the stock is over the call + strike.

Short Put

Loss ≥ X, Profit > X

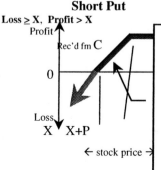

Profit the short put is the amount more than the strike of the put, not to exceed the proceeds received from the put. Loss on the put is the amount the stock is less than the strike.

Notes:

Exhibit 3: PE Breakdown

Note: 3 Stage ROE   Profit Margin * Total Asset Turnover * Financial Leverage

	NI	*	Sales	*	Total Assets
	Sales		Total Assets		Equity

Editor's Review:

Income Statement	
Sales	
- COGS	
Gross Margin	
- Expenses	(mgmt hides it's perks if EAT is OK)
EBIT	
- Interest	Bank happy
EBT	What mgmt earns for shareholders
- Taxes	Gov't happy
EAT	Stockholders happy

EAT = EBT - EBT(t)
EAT = EBT(1-t)

Expected EPS = Expected Sales/share   *   Expected Net profit Margin

Income Stmt: Next year's projected

We know last year's P & P/E
Can calc next year's earnings
then Proportion via P/E to get $P_{proj\,EOY}$

[(S)   (EBDIT) - D - I] (1-t)
pending   ratio   Depr Inter tax
sales   per shr Exp adj

$$P_{proj\,EOY} = (E_{Proj\,EOY})(P/E)$$

Earnings, DDM & ROE Calc

$$\frac{P}{E} = \frac{Div/Earn}{k-g}$$

Dividend pay-out
k - g

(Retention) (ROE)

k = Real Rate + Interest Prem + Risk Prem
Nominal rate should really multiply

Tax * Interest * Oper'g * Asset * Financial
Reten   Burden   Profit   Turnover   Leverage
Rate   Margin

$k = R_f + \beta(R_m - R_f)$ β is # units of risk in the stock
Stockholders want and pay for k, k determines the P

$\dfrac{NI}{EBT}$ * $\dfrac{EBT}{EBIT}$ * $\dfrac{EBIT}{Sls}$ * $\dfrac{Sls}{Assets}$ * $\dfrac{Assets}{Equity}$

$$P_0 = \frac{D_1}{k-g}$$

$$WACC = (w_e k_e) + (w_d k_d)$$

$$P_0 = \frac{D_1}{k-g}$$

⎡ Oper   Total   -Interest ⎤ Financial * Tax
⎢ Profit * Asset   Expense   ⎥ * Leverage   Retention
⎣ Margin   Turnover   Rate   ⎦ *Multiplier* *Rate**

⎡ $\dfrac{EBIT}{Sls}$ * $\dfrac{Sls}{Assets}$ - $\dfrac{Int}{Assets}$ ⎤ * $\dfrac{Assets}{Equity}$ * (1 - T)

Note: tax ret (1-t)

$$Return_{Estimated} = \frac{Cash\ Div + Price_{End} - Price_{Now}}{Price_{Now}}$$

Bad side

Good side

$$P_0 = \frac{D_1}{k-g}$$ restate: $k = \dfrac{D}{P} + g$ = $k = R_f + \beta(R_m - R_f)$ also $k = (1+RR)(1+IP)(1+RP)$

real   infl   risk
should be in equilibrium

Exhibit 4: Ratios

calculate the financial ratios in each major category of analysis and discuss the uses of those ratios;
Common Size Statements: B/S in percent of Total Assets, I/S in percent of Sales
Quickly compare two different size firms, same firm trends over time, structure of firm's financial
   statements
Internal Liquidity (Solvency): ability of firm to meet future short term obligations, compare near term
   obligations with current assets or cash flows

$$\text{Current Ratio:}\quad \frac{\text{Current Assets}}{\text{Current Liabilities}}\qquad\qquad \text{Working Capital} = CA - CL$$

$$\text{Quick ratio}\qquad \frac{\text{Cash} + \text{mkt sec} + AR}{CL}\qquad \text{not include. inventory}$$

$$\text{Acid Test}\qquad \frac{CA - Inv}{CL}\qquad\qquad \text{a.k.a. Quick Ratio}$$

$$\text{Cash ratio}\qquad \frac{\text{Cash} + \text{mkt sec}}{CL}\qquad \text{even more conservative}$$

$$\text{Receivables Turnover}\quad \frac{\text{Net Annual Sales}}{\text{Avg Receivables}}\quad \text{Avg collection:}\quad \frac{365}{\text{Annual Turnover}}$$

$$\text{Days Receivable}\quad \frac{365}{\text{Avg Receivables}}\qquad \text{Avg \# of days to get paid}$$

$$\text{Working Cap / Sales}\quad \frac{CA - CL}{\text{Net Sales}}\quad \text{higher \% indicates more liquidity}$$

$$\text{Payables Turnover}\quad \frac{COGS}{@ AP}\quad @ \text{ payable period:}\quad \frac{365}{\text{Annual Turnover}}$$
   (do they pay their bills)

Operating Performance: How well management is operating the business

Operating Efficiency Ratios: How management uses its assets and capital

Activity ratios: sales per something
   Inventory Turnover $\dfrac{COGS}{@ \text{ Inventory}}$ @ Inventory period $\dfrac{365}{\text{Inventory}}$
   Turnover

$$\text{Total Asset Turnover}\quad \frac{\text{Net Sales}}{@ \text{ Tot Net Assets}}\qquad \text{high or low relative to industry?}$$
   low: tie up too much assets

$$\text{Fixed Asset Turnover}\qquad \frac{\text{Net Sales}}{@ \text{ Net Fixed Assets}}\qquad \text{utilization of fixed assets}$$
   hi: old depr equipment

Equity Turnover $\qquad$ Net Sales $\qquad$ excludes CL & LT Debt

Average Equity

Receivables Turnover $\underline{\text{Net Annual Sales}}$ Avg collection period: $\underline{\qquad 365 \qquad}$

Avg Receivables Annual Turnover

Operating Profitability: rate of profit on sales, % return on capital

(How good is mgmt turning profits into sales)

Note: Run down Income Statement and ratio to Sales (GP, EBIT, EBT, EAT)

EBIT: Mgmt earns

Tax: Government earns

Interest: Banker's earn

EBT: Stockholder's earn

Gross Profit Margin $\underline{\text{Gross Profit}}$ (GP = Sls - COGS)

Net Sales relative cost price position in industry?

Operating Profit Margin $\underline{\text{Operating Profit}}$ (EBIT)

Net Sales variability is business risk indicator

Net Profit Margin $\underline{\text{Net Income}}$ NI = EAT

Net Sales

EBT Margin $\underline{\qquad \text{EBT} \qquad}$ before tax profit margin

Net Sales

Common Size Income Statement

lists all expense and income items as a % of sales

(Inc Stmt: / Sls) (Bal: / Sls or Tot Assets)

Return on Total Capital $\underline{\text{Net Income + Interest Expense}}$ Debt, Pref. Stock, C Stock

Average Total Capital return on all capital

employed

Return on Total Equity $\underline{\text{Net Income}}$ ROE

@ Total Equity

Return on Owners Equity $\underline{\text{Net Income – Preferred Dividend}}$

@ Common Equity

Return on Equity (ROE): DuPont System duPont formulation

ROE = NI / Equity or EAT/Equity

3 Step ROE = $\underline{NI}$ = Net   *   Asset   *   Financial   a.k.a.Equity Multiplier
               Equity   Profit   Turnover   Leverage
                      Margin

$$\frac{NI}{Sls} \;*\; \frac{Sls}{Assets} \;*\; \frac{Assets}{Equity} \qquad Note: \frac{(Sls)(Assets)}{(Sls)(Assets)}$$

4 Step ROE = $\underline{NI}$ = Tax   *   Interest   *   Oper'g   *   Asset   *   Financial
               Equity   Reten   Burden   Profit   Turnover   Leverage

$$\frac{NI}{EBT} \;*\; \frac{EBT}{EBIT} \;*\; \frac{EBIT}{Sls} \;*\; \frac{Sls}{Assets} \;*\; \frac{Assets}{Equity}$$

5 Step Equation = $\left[\begin{array}{c} \text{Oper} \;*\; \text{Total} \;-\; \text{Interest} \\ \text{Profit} \quad \text{Asset} \\ \text{Margin} \quad \text{Turnover} \end{array}\right.$ Financial   *   Tax
                                        Expense   *   Leverage   Retention
                                         Rate   Multiplier   Rate

$$\left[\frac{EBIT}{Sls} \;*\; \frac{Sls}{Assets} \;-\; \frac{Int}{Assets}\right] \;*\; \frac{Assets}{Equity} \;*\; (1-T)$$

Financial Risk: Uncertainty of returns to equity holders due to a firm's use of fixed   obligation debt securities

Debt / Equity   remember firm value is Db + Eq
                                 Db=1, Eq=2, firm value = 3, D/E = ½
                                 (not D/E=1/3, easy mistake in a hurry)

LTD / LT Cap   LTD = Long Term Debt   LT Cap = Long Term Capital

Total Debt / Total Capital

Interest Coverage $\dfrac{EBIT}{Interest\ Expense}$ $\dfrac{NI + Tax + Int\ Exp}{Int\ Exp}$

(Note: Look for this on the exam

Cash Flow / LTD

Cash Flow / Total Debt

Growth Analysis

Retention rate   earnings retained / total earnings
      (remember: growth = retention rate * ROE)

ROE   see above, profitability

Total Asset Turnover   see above, operational performance

Total Assets / Equity   note component of ROE

Net Profit Margin   see above, profitability

Sustainable growth rate   g = retention * ROE

    retention rate = 1 – (Oper Inc after taxes)

Risk Analysis: uncertainty of income flows for the total firm and for sources of capital

    Business Risk: Uncertainty of income caused by a firm's industry
        Variability of sales due to products, customers, production methods

    Business Risk   Coefficient of variation of operating income   CV = σ/mean

    $$\frac{\text{Standard Deviation of Operating Earnings (OE)}}{\text{Mean Operating Earnings}} \qquad \begin{array}{l}\text{need 5<Thru> 10 yrs}\\ \text{to compute coef of variation}\end{array}$$

    Sales Volatility   Coefficient of Variation of Sales   CV = σ/mean

    $$\frac{\text{sd of sales}}{\text{mean sales}} \qquad \text{prime determinant of earnings variability}$$

Operating Leverage   %ΔOE / %ΔSls   or   Σ | [%ΔOE] / [%ΔSls] | / N   employment of fixed production
    costs direction of change not important, but relative size of the change is relevant

    OL = % change in operating earnings / % change in   sales , calc from #'s not %

FinancialExam Features

Using FinancialExams Quizzer

In Brief

The FinancialExams Quizzer exam software is designed to identify your personal areas of weakness relative to passing specific exam objectives. Once this software determines just what those weaknesses are, it will force you to continually face them until you can demonstrate mastery over them. Then it will find something else to haunt you with.

To use this software successfully, follow these simple steps.

1) Spend some time getting familiar with the program. When you're ready to settle down to work, clear the history (the button is on the main screen). Do not clear the history again until all of the following steps have been completed.

2) Take four (4) Adaptive Exams. During this process, you have no choices. The software is in control. It is using its internal logic to determine your strengths and weaknesses on a topic-by-topic basis. (Note: You don't have to take all four at one sitting.)

3) After the four Adaptive Exams, look at your Historical Analysis (the button is on the main screen). This will give you a graphical presentation of how you have done cumulatively in each category. Let this be your guide as to which subcategories to begin studying. Start with your weakest and work your way up.

4) Begin taking Study Sessions on selected topics. Select the Category and Subcategories that you will be focusing on. You have two primary goals in Study Session mode.

a) See and answer every question on that topic at least once. Keep in mind that any question answered incorrectly will be in the very next Study Session you take on that topic. Once you are able to answer it correctly, it will get shuffled to the bottom of the deck. When you have cycled through available questions, correctly answered questions will begin to reappear.

b) Achieve a minimum score of at least 85% on each and every subcategory topic before moving on to the Simulated Exam. If you want to bounce around a little between subcategories a little, that's okay. The program will remember where you left off. However, it's important that you don't cheat yourself on this step.

5) Take the Simulated Exam. Don't be too disappointed if you don't pass the first time. The software has been gaining knowledge about your weaknesses and has just done everything in its power to make you fail this exam. Aren't you glad that wasn't the real thing?

6) Clear your history and repeat the above steps two more times. That's right... two more times. But now, achieve a minimum of 90% and 95% respectfully on each pass through before taking the Simulated Exam.

You will find that the number of Study Sessions and the amount of time necessary to achieve these scores will get smaller. The better you know the material, the quicker the whole process becomes.

The rest of this document goes into more detail on using specific features of the FinancialExams Quizzer software. Spend some time getting to know this program. It has helped thousands of people achieve their certification goals. It can do the same for you.

Study Session

FinancialExams Quizzer tests your knowledge as you learn about new subjects through interactive quiz sessions. Study Session questions are selected from a single database for each session, dependent on the subcategory selected and the number of times each question has been previously answered correctly. In this way, questions you have answered correctly are not repeated until you have answered all the new questions. Questions that you have missed previously will reappear in later sessions and keep coming back to haunt you until you get the question correct. In addition, you can track your progress by displaying the number of questions you have answered with the Historical Analysis option. You can reset the progress tracking by clicking on the Clear History button. Each time a question is presented the answers are randomized so you will not memorize a pattern or letter that goes with the question. You will start to memorize the correct answer that goes with the question concept.

Practice Exams

FinancialExams Quizzer also provides Adaptive and Simulated certification exams. Questions are chosen at random from the database. The Simulated Exam is a timed test that presents a similar number of questions as the real exam. A break from testing occurs at the mid-point of the exam. The Adaptive Exam presents a fixed number questions with a maximum time allotment. The Adaptive Exam is most helpful in identifying areas of weakness in the candidate's knowledge of the exam objectives.

After you finish an exam, FinancialExams Quizzer displays your score and the passing score required for the FinancialExams Quizzer test. You may display the exam results of this specific exam from this menu. You may review each question, display the correct answer, identify a resource, link to an available electronic book and view an explanation for the answer.

FinancialExams Quizzer Features

1.	Each database contains 200 to 1200+ questions	2.	Easy to install
3.	Easy to upgrade	4.	Multiple choice Style questions
5.	Essay style questions	6.	Fill-in-the-blank Style questions
7.	Performance based questions	8.	Flash Card Style questions
9.	Questions randomized	10.	Hot Spot Style questions
11.	Print a category of questions	12.	Drag/Drop/Mix/Match questions
13.	☐Single module studies	14.	Answers randomized
15.	Simulation exam studies	16.	Print one question
17.	Instant exam feedback	18.	Cheat key or Flash Card option
19.	Statistical analysis	20.	Instant question feedback
21.	Individual exam analysis	22.	Adaptive exam studies
23.	Font selection	24.	Skills assessment
25.	Graphics	26.	Historical analysis
27.	User Notes creation	28.	Resizable screen
29.	Some Links to Electronic Book content	30.	Most have Explanations
31.	Free version updates via e-mail	32.	References

Online Help

This manual installs on your PC along with the FinancialExams Quizzer. To access it, select Contents from the Help pull-down menu. Additional help can be obtained via:

Email:

> Support@BFQPress.com
> AskTheExpert@BFQPress.com
> CustomerService@BFQPress.com

Telephone:

> Toll Free: (888) 992-3131
> International: (281) 992-3131
> Fax: (281) 482-5390

Changing subjects

FinancialExams Quizzer provides several practice exams to test your knowledge. To change exams:

1.   Click the Change Exam button in the Main window.
2.   Select the exam for the test you want to run from the Select Exam window.
3.   Click OK to change to the selected exam, or the Cancel to keep the current exam.

Changing the number of questions

You can choose the number of questions presented in each quiz session. To change the number of questions:

1.   Click on the box to the right of the Number of Questions field in the Main window.
2.   Type a number of questions, between 1 and 250, in the Number of Questions field.
3.   If the number of questions selected exceeds the number available in the chosen subcategory, all that are available will be displayed.

Changing the subcategories

Each FinancialExams Quizzer subject has a number of categories and subcategories. You can take a test on any one or any combination of the subcategories.

1.   From the Subcategories frame, select the desired general category from the Categories drop down list.
2.   Select the desired subcategory from the list box. To select multiple subcategories, hold down the CTRL key while clicking items in the list box.

Setting up your printer

FinancialExams Quizzer allows you to customize your print jobs.

1.   Select Options from the View pull-down menu.
2.   Select the Printing Options radial button. The Printing Options window appears.
3.   Select the options for your printer.
4.   Click OK to exit and save changes.

Printing questions

FinancialExams Quizzer allows you to print questions from your tests, with or without the correct answer(s) marked. To print the question(s), select the desired print option from the File pull-down menu in the Question window.

Using FinancialExams Quizzer options

FinancialExams Quizzer provides a number of additional options to customize your test. The following options are available:

1 Stop On Wrong Answers
2 Enable Cheat Key
3 Resizable Screen
4 Font Setting

To select an advanced option, select Options from the View pull-down menu. The Exam Preferences window appears.

Adaptive Exam

Adaptive testing is a time saving option used to identify the candidate's strengths and weaknesses. Before using Adaptive testing, clear historical Analysis. Before you learn about your subject using the Quizzer Study Sessions, you should take the Adaptive exams. This exam style does not simulate all of the exam environments that are found on certification exams. You cannot choose specific subcategories for the Adaptive exam and once a question has been answered you cannot go back to a previous question. You have a time limit in which to complete the adaptive exam. This time varies from subject to subject, although it is usually 15 to 25 questions in 30 minutes. When the time limit has been reached, your exam automatically ends.

How to take advantage of Adaptive testing:

1. Clear the Historical Analysis
2. Take four (4) adaptive exams in a row. Study the contents after each adaptive exam.
3. View the historical analysis to identify your strength and weakness at the end of the four (4) adaptive exams.
4. Go back to reviewing using the Study Sessions by Sub Category
5. Repeat process until you are ready to pass the real exam.

Take the Adaptive Exam

1. Click the Adaptive Exam radial button from the Main window.
2. Click the Start button. The Adaptive Exam window appears.
3. Click the circle to the left of the correct answer. There may be more than one correct answer. Text in the bottom left corner of the window instructs you to Choose the Best Answer (if there is only one answer) or Mark All Correct Answers (if there is more than one correct answer).
4. Click the Next button to continue.

After the allotted time has elapsed, the exam exits to review mode. To quit the test at any time, click the Finish button. After you have completed the Adaptive exam, FinancialExams Quizzer displays your score and the passing score required for the test. Display your exam results by selecting Details You may review each question, display the correct answer, and view an explanation for the answer (if available).

Reviewing an Adaptive Exam

After you have taken an Adaptive exam, you can review the questions, your answers, and the correct answers. You may only review your questions immediately after completing an Adaptive exam. To review your questions:

1.   Click the Correct Answer button.
2.   To see your answer, click the Your Answer button.

Starting a Study Session

After you choose a subcategory to test yourself on, start the Study Session.

To start a study session:

1.   Select the Study Session radial button.
2.   Click the Start button. The Question window appears. Optionally, you can select Study Session from the Start pull-down menu. Click the checkbox to the left of the correct answer. There may be more than one correct answer. Text in the bottom left corner of the window instructs you to Choose the Best Answer (if there is only one answer) or Mark All Correct Answers (if there is more than one correct answer).
3.   Click the Next button to continue. FinancialExams Quizzer provides immediate feedback on your answer at the bottom of the window.

If you answered the question correctly, a new question appears. If you did not answer the question correctly, you may try to guess again or move to the next question. If you have selected the Prompt on Wrong Answers option, you have the following choices:

1.   To try again, click the Try Again button.
2.   To move to the next question after an incorrect guess, click the Next Question button.
3.   View the correct answer
4.   View the Explanation option

To quit the test at any time, click the Finish button.

Checking your score during a test

The X% button displays the current percentage of questions that have been answered correctly.

1. Click the X% button. A window appears displaying the number of questions that have been asked and the number of questions that have been answered correctly.
2. Click OK to return to the test.

Checking your performance

Click the QID button. A window appears, displaying the number of times you have been asked this question and the number of times you have answered this question correctly.

Checking your overall progress

1. Click the Historical Analysis button from the Main window. The Historical Analysis window appears.
2. FinancialExams Quizzer displays your progress in each test using a graphical progress bar. Hold the cursor over the progress bar and a dialog box will open. The number of times you have answered questions in that category correctly as a percentage of the total number of questions is displayed.
3. To get detailed information on your performance on any subject, click and hold the progress bar for that subject. FinancialExams Quizzer displays the performance details in the bottom left hand corner of the screen.

Simulated Exam

After you have learned about your subject using the Study Sessions, you can take a simulated exam. This exam simulates the exam environment that might be found on a certification exam. You cannot choose subcategories for a Simulated Exam. You have a fixed limit equal to that of the real exam to complete the Simulated Exam. When this time limit has been reached, your exam automatically ends.

Take the Simulated Exam

1. Click the Simulated Exam radial button from the Main window.
2. Click the Start button. The Simulated Exam window appears.
3. Click the circle to the left of the correct answer.

There may be more than one correct answer. Text in the bottom left corner of the window instructs you to Choose the Best Answer (if there is only one answer) or Mark All Correct Answers (if there is more than one correct answer).

4.   If you are unsure of the answer and wish to mark the question so you can return to it later, check the Mark box in the upper left hand corner. To review which questions you have marked, which you have answered, and which you have not answered, click the Review button.

5.   Click the Next button to continue.

After the allotted time for testing, the exam exits to review mode. To quit the test at any time, click the Finish button. After you have completed the Simulated Exam, FinancialExams Quizzer displays your score and the passing score required for the test. Display your exam results by selecting Details. You may review each question, display the correct answer, and view an explanation for the answer (if available).

Reviewing a Simulated Exam

After you have taken a simulated exam, you can review the questions, your answers, and the correct answers. You may only review your questions immediately after a Simulated Exam.

To review your questions:

1.   Click the Correct Answer button.
2.   To see your answer, click the Your Answer button.

FlashCard Option

After you have learned about your subject using the Study Sessions, Adaptive, and Simulated exam go to the Thinking Option. The FlashCard environment is very different and will help you more that you might believe on a certification exam. **The Flash Card Option is very effect when used with Terminology or Glossary "Fill-in-the-Blank" style questions.**

Read the displayed question, Think of the answer, Hit the F4 Function key to display the correct answer, Read the Answer, Go to the next question.

1.   You should not view the answer until you have thought about the answer.
2.   You have an unlimited time limit to think about each question.
3.   Use this option a few days before the real exam to go through a lot of questions in a short period of time.
4.   The FlashCard option can be used as a review of all questions in the database.
5.   Use the FlashCard option to provide Positive Feed Back with Correct Answers.

Starting a FlashCard Session

After you choose a subcategory to test yourself on, start FlashCards.

1. Select the FlashCards Session radial button.
2. Click the Start button. The Question window appears. Optionally, you can select FlashCards Session from the Start pull-down menu. You will find no answers to check or any visible area to type your answer into.
3. This is the time to THINK of the answer. Pause a moment than hit the F4 function on your keyboard. (CheatKey)
4. Review the displayed answer. Did you get it correct?
5. When you are ready to proceed Click the Next button to continue.

How to use a FlashCards

1. Read the displayed question
2. Think of the answer
3. Hit the F4 Function key to display the correct answer
4. Read the Answer
5. Go to the next question.

To quit the test at any time, click the Finish button.

Note: Some questions may ask for more than one answer: Bypass questions that state "Which of the Following" and "Select all that apply" etc.

Taking Notes

While you are taking your exam, you may wish to write down notes about a particular question that you can use in later Study Sessions. FinancialExams Quizzer allows you to enter notes about each question. The notes will be permanently stored in the database for the subject you are studying. You can also use this feature to record any comments you have about a particular question and send it in for review. If you would like to print or view your notes, you can export your notes to a standard text editor.

Take notes from a study session

Create your own information or reference.

1. Click the Notes button from the Question window.
2. Type your note.
3. Click OK to keep the note, or Cancel to delete the note.

Note: You cannot take notes during a Simulated or Adaptive session until you have finished the exam and have entered the Review mode.

Export your notes

Click the Notes button from the Main window and export to Note Pad or any text editor you wish to use.

Now that you have purchased this product you have access to the Instructors/Authors that authored this book. Send you questions to us and we will answer them for you.

This is a free Feature of Http://www.financialexams.com

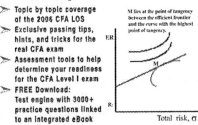
Receive your ExamWise purchase price back when you upgrade to TotalRecall Publication's complete series: *InsidersChoice For CFA 2006 Level I Certification: The Candidates Guide to Chartered Financial Analyst 2006 Level-I Learning Outcome Statements (With Download Exam of 3000+ Practice Questions)*

Our InsidersChoice series teaches the entire CFA Level I curriculum, eliminating the impossible task of predicting what will be covered on the actual examination. Its purpose is to help you master the Learning Outcome Statements as quickly and as effectively as possible so you can pass the CFA Level I exam your first time. This one compact study guide and accompanying test engine will give you with all the information, practice exams, and test-taking tips that you need to reach a passing level and feel confident that you are ready for the real exam.

ExamInsight
For CFA 2006 Level I Certification:

The Candidates Guide To (CFA)
Chartered Financial Analyst 2006 Level I
Learning Outcome Statements
ISBN 1-59095-922-1

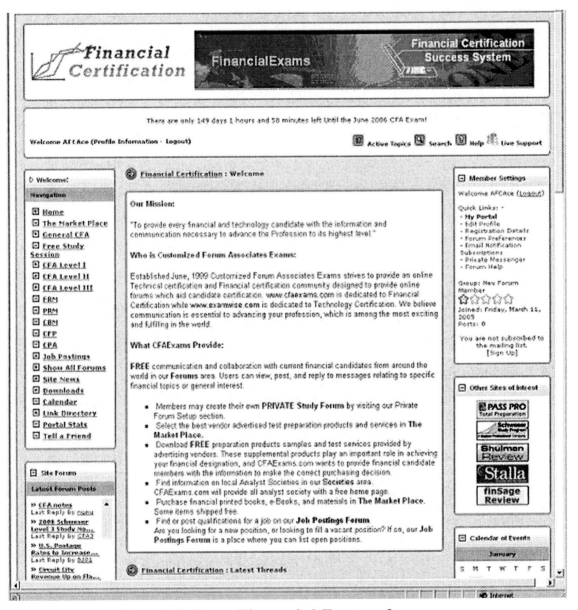

Special: Free Financial Forum Access:
Visit http://www.cfaexams.com

FREE Demo at www.cfaexams.com/cfademo

ebooster limited is the authorized distributor for TotalRecall Publications materials in Europe, the Middle East and Africa. We stock the full range of TRP products and charge at competitive prices, especially for volume orders. Come to us direct or order from your favorite distributors and retailers including Amazon.co.uk, Waterstones, Borders, Books Etc., Gardners and Bertram Books.

e/booster limited **FAO: Chris MacNeil** **502, trottenham** **Court Rd** **London, England** **W1T 1JY**	**Office** **+44 (0) 207 993 2253** **Fax** **+44 (0) 207 993 2253**	**email:** office@ebooster.co.uk **Web Site** www.ebooster.co.uk

Download Instructions

The Financial Certification Center (TFCC) version 4.0
Chartered Financial Analyst (CFA) Level 1 Exam

System Requirements: Windows 95 & 98, Windows NT, Windows 2000/XP, and Windows Server 2003 with a minimum of 40 MB hard disk space and 64 MB RAM

The Center For Financial Certification, Inc. will help you accomplish your CFA Certifications. This state of art software program is designed to cut your study time in half, and get you to a passing knowledge level in the easiest and shortest amount of time possible. The program will adapt to you personally, and then lay out a prioritized study plan that will visually show you your progress on a day to day basis. When the software has recognized that you are at a passing level in each objective category, you're ready to sit for the exam. It's really that easy!

Installation: To obtain the FE practice exam simply visit the engine download link. **http://snipurl.com/CFA2006L1**Download the winzip file and Install the latest version of the Financial Exams Engine . Execute File Name FEQuizL1.exe.

License Key

License keys: CFA Level I

1. FE-JV 2006 CFA Level-I Concept Check = 276271646771

2. Financial Terminology Evaluation = 322478807587

Download Supplemental Information:

To obtain additional printable content visit these download links locations for free downloads.
   Preliminary Reading Assignments and Concept Question Workbook
   Candidate's CFA Level I 2006 Updates

Visit:

http://www.financialexams.com/member_signup.php
http://www.cfaexams.com/forum/registration_rules.asp
or contact sales@totalrecallpress.com for Download and Installation Instructions:
   Please use InsidersChoice Workbook as the Subject.

Starting FinancialExams To start the program the next time (if it doesn't start automatically), select FinancialExams from the Program's menu. Assistance with running and using FE is available under the Help menu.

FREE Content Downloads and Financial Forums
Call 281-992-3398   888-992-3398

www.financialexams.com
www.cfaexams.com

Good Luck with your certification!
Your Book Registration Number is IC-94501-3000

Printed in the United States
57199LVS00004B/69